T0330305

Climate Change, Radical Uncertainty and Hope

Climate Change, Radical Uncertainty and Hope

Theology and Economics in Conversation

Jan Jorrit Hasselaar

Amsterdam University Press

Cover illustration: Lot Bakker

Cover design: Coördesign, Leiden
Lay-out: Crius Group, Hulshout

ISBN	978 90 4855 847 6
e-ISBN	978 90 4855 848 3
DOI	10.5117/9789048558476
NUR	700

Printed and bound by CPI Group (UK) Ltd, Croydon, CR0 4YY

Table of Contents

Preface

In the last decade radical uncertainty has made itself felt in new and powerful ways. The financial crisis of 2007-09 blew away the illusion of certainty among decision-makers. The COVID-19 pandemic and the war in Ukraine have made us all aware that our world is deeply interconnected and vulnerable, and that the future is radically uncertain. The focus of this study is on radical uncertainty in the context of climate change.

In this publication I combine theology and economics, disciplines often considered as incompatible as cat and dog. This incompatibility has intuitively always dissatisfied me, because what both disciplines have at least in common is the same reality or the same 'oikos', to use the Greek word for household, that can also be found in the word 'eco-nomics'. Climate change should challenge us to come out of our comfort zone, because addressing such a multifaceted and global issue can never be the task of one discipline alone. In this study I go on a journey to discipline my intuition, investigating whether and how the two disciplines can strengthen each other in developing a social response to radical uncertainty in the context of climate change. My point of departure is theology.

Anthropogenic climate change, distinguished from climate change caused by natural factors, can be easily described as an economic problem, because it is the result of many economic exchanges between consumers and producers. However, Amartya Sen (Nobel Prize Winner in Economic Sciences 1998) has argued that non-economic factors like political, sociological and philosophical ones are often at the heart of economic problems:

> Taking an interest in them [non-economic factors] is part of our own heritage. After all, the subject of modern economics was in a sense founded by Adam Smith, who had an enormously broad view of economics… An economic analyst ultimately has to juggle many balls, even if a little clumsily, rather than giving a superb display of virtuosity with one little ball. (Klamer, 1989, p. 141)

This study considers climate change not just as an economic problem, but as a shared problem in both theology and economics. I have therefore taken up the challenge to juggle the balls of theology and economics in order to contribute to a fuller and wiser understanding of our response to radical uncertainty in the context of climate change.

The title of this study is '*Climate Change, Radical Uncertainty and Hope: Theology and Economics in Conversation*'. Radical uncertainty in the context of climate change is often surrounded by a widespread atmosphere of fear and apocalypse, but I argue here that radical uncertainty does not carry with it its own interpretation. There is more than one way of interpreting radical uncertainty in climate change. In this research I investigate an interpretation of hope. In everyday language hope is often used glibly, for example in the remark: I hope that tomorrow the sun will shine. The focus here is on a neglected understanding of hope based on the work of Jonathan Sacks, leading British intellectual and former Chief Rabbi of the United Hebrew Congregations of the Commonwealth. Sacks' understanding of hope, derived from the ancient narrative of the Exodus, orients us to the possibility of gradually starting together something new and liberating in the midst of radical uncertainty. This research is in the field of theology. However, I will argue that the theological approach employed is not contrary to economics insights, but emerges out of economic debate, and is remarkably compatible with certain lines of economic thought. What is more, I show that theology and economics can learn from each other in the conversation developed in this research. Jonathan Sacks passed away during this study. May his memory be a blessing to us all.

In this research I do not use the Christian designation Old Testament, because this can be seen as implying that the Old is completed in the New. This would be a wrong and outdated implication. The real challenge is to consider both Testaments as old-new sources of inspiration in every time and context. Instead of using the term Old Testament I will refer to the Hebrew Bible. In quoting the biblical text I use the version commonly quoted in scholarship, namely the New Revised Standard Version (NRSV), except in the chapters dealing with the work of Jonathan Sacks. If required by the context, I use his translation

The chapters 1 and 3 through 8 of this study draw upon previous work of mine published in *The International Journal of Public Theology* (2020a), *Fullness of Life and Justice for All* (2020b), *Water in Times of Climate Change* (2021), *De moderne theologen* (2022a) and *The Calling of the Church in Times of Polarization* (2022b).

This interdisciplinary research has been a thoroughly enriching journey. It has been a project I could not have done on my own. I am very grateful for the people who have supported me directly and indirectly. Many people I would like to thank, but I cannot list them all here. There are some, however,

I don't want to pass over, since without their commitment, support and friendship I do not think this work could have been done. A special thanks to Professor Azza Karam, Professor Erik Borgman, Professor Arjo Klamer, Dr. Roel Jongeneel and Professor Toine van den Hoogen. It has been a joy and a privilege to work with you on this publication. With gratitude I thank the sisters of the Priorij Emmaus monastery in Maarssen for their hospitality, daily structure and prayers I experienced several times during this project. Unfortunately, your doors are closed now. I pray that the spirit in your monastery of seeking a balance between *vita activa* (active life) and *vita contemplativa* (contemplative life) may find other ways to serve our reality. I am grateful to Myra Scholz for editing this book. Any errors remain my own doing, of course. Lot, thank you for designing together the front page of this publication.

Finally, I'd like to thank my parents Jan Hasselaar and Hannie Hasselaar-Kelderman. Ma, you have shown how we can embrace radical uncertainty in times of corona. In the first lockdown (2020), when nursing homes were closed for visitors, you put your trust in love by bringing Pa home when his condition worsened and he entered his last phase on earth. At home, meaning and perspective were created in a situation that could have been very different in the nursing home. From one moment to the next, Pa and all of us were surrounded by love and attention. Heaven became a place on earth. Last, but surely not least, 'thanx' to my beautiful and beloved nieces and nephews for who you are, and the joy, play and pizzas that you bring.

Bibliography

Hasselaar, J.J. (2020a). Hope in the Context of Climate Change: Jonathan Sacks' Interpretation of the Exodus and Radical Uncertainty. *International Journal of Public Theology* 14, pp. 224–240.

Hasselaar, J.J. (2020b). Hope to Embrace Radical Uncertainty in Climate Change. In E. Van Stichel, T. Eggensperger, M. Kalsky, & U. Engel (eds.), *Fullness of Life and Justice for All* (pp. 51-68). Adelaide, Australia: ATF Theology. https://dx.doi.org/10.2307/j.ctv16t6ms2.8

Hasselaar, J.J., & IJmker, E.C. (eds.). (2021). *Water in Times of Climate Change: A Values-driven Dialogue.* Amsterdam, The Netherlands: Amsterdam University Press.

Hasselaar, J.J. (2022a). Jonathan Sacks. In M. Poorthuis, & W. Veen (eds.), *De moderne theologen: Perspectieven op de 21ste eeuw* (pp. 290-297). Amsterdam, The Netherlands: Boom uitgevers.

Hasselaar, J.J., Pattberg, P. & Smit, P.B. (2022b). Sowing Hope in a Polarized Agri-
    cultural Debate. In H. Zorgdrager & P. Vos (Eds.), *The Calling of the Church in
    Times of Polarization. Volume 46: Studies in Reformed Theology* (pp. 155-176).
    Leiden, The Netherlands: Brill.
Klamer, A. (1989). A Conversation with Amartya Sen. *Journal of Economic Perspec-
    tives, 3*(1), 135-150. http://dx.doi.org/10.1257/jep.3.1.135

1. Introduction

Abstract

This chapter introduces hope, based on the work of Jonathan Sacks, as a possible alternative to pessimism and optimism in dealing with radical uncertainty in climate change. Sacks' understanding of hope can be seen as an account of the good life, a renewed way of doing theology. Understood in this way, hope highlights key assumptions for addressing radical uncertainty: (1) *emunah* (a type of trust), (2) *chessed* (a type of love, including the covenant), and (3) change of identity (including the Sabbath). The chapter brings in Wentzel van Huyssteen's postfoundational approach to explore the relevance of an interdisciplinary conversation between theology and economics for a social response to radical uncertainty in the context of climate change.

Keywords: hope, Jonathan Sacks, Miroslav Volf, social response to climate change, radical uncertainty, Wentzel van Huyssteen, postfoundational approach

1.1 The neglected notion of hope

'Should we respond with optimism to climate change, Tata', asks Irene. The Dutch newspaper *Trouw* recounts a conversation between the sociologist Zygmunt Bauman and his daughter, the architect Irena Bauman. Tata (Polish for father) answers his daughter by stating that it is wrong to divide the world into optimists and pessimists. He says that there is a third possibility: a hopeful response to climate change. (Van Rootselaar, 2014) This remark by Zygmunt Bauman merits closer attention. In the view of the cultural critic Terry Eagleton hope "… has been a curiously neglected notion in an age which, in Raymond Williams's words, confronts us with "the felt loss of a future"" (Eagleton, 2015, p. xi). Optimism and pessimism, in their 'pure' form, can be seen as views of history and human society. A pessimistic view can be described as considering change as evil because it is a deviation

Hasselaar, J.J., *Climate Change, Radical Uncertainty and Hope: Theology and Economics in Conversation*. Amsterdam: Amsterdam University Press, 2023

DOI 10.5117/9789048558476_CH01

from a certain good period in the past. In stark contrast, an optimistic view conceives of progress ultimately as good. (Schillebeeckx, 1983, pp. 97-98) But what is the meaning of hope, especially in the context of climate change, which is considered one of the most urgent questions that confronts us with a loss of a future. A reason why hope is a neglected notion might be that in today's language hope is likely to lapse into delusion and suggests (half-fearful) expectations like 'I hope that tomorrow the sun will shine' or 'I hope my train is on time'. This study takes a rather different approach regarding hope. It explores a profound and articulated understanding of hope in the context of climate change by using the work of Jonathan Sacks.

1.2   Jonathan Sacks

Jonathan Sacks (1948-2020) was a prominent author on hope in the first two decades of the twenty-first century. A British public intellectual and Chief Rabbi of the United Hebrew Congregations of the Commonwealth (1991–2013), Sacks held professorships at several academic institutions including Yeshiva University, King's College London and New York University. Standing in a long tradition, Sacks argues that hope is neither about (half-fearful) expectations, nor the same as optimism that rejects the complexity of reality. Hope, for Sacks, is a dimension in reality that was first discovered by patriarchs and matriarchs like Abraham, Sarah, Isaac, Rebekah, Leah, Rachel and Jacob. They discovered that they were not alone in this world and that this is good news. Hope does not reject the complexity of reality with its fear and despair, but does not surrender to either. (Sacks, 2009b, pp. 2-10) In Sacks' understanding of hope, hope is already there, but to claim its potential, people are invited to learn gradually that something new and liberating is possible (Sacks, 2011, pp. 206-207).

1.3   Theology as the good life

This research stands in a tradition of theology as a perspective of the good life. In their 2019 manifesto 'For the Life of the World', Volf and Croasmun plea for a renewal of (Christian) theology in Western societies along this line of the good life. In their view, academic theology is in a state of external and internal crisis. The external crisis is visible in a lack of employment opportunities for academic theologians. These theologians are also losing their traditional audience in Christian communities and are not able to acquire a new one. And there is a loss of intellectual reputation of academic theology within the academy and beyond its walls. (Volf and Croasmun, 2019, pp. 36-45) This external crisis stems, at least in part, from an internal crisis. Volf and Croasmun consider the most important crisis of theology to be an internal one in which theology has forgotten its own purpose, namely to employ theology in order to discern, articulate and pursue accounts of a flourishing or good life. In their view, this internal crisis has led to two coping strategies: (1) embracing the research ideal of natural sciences and their methodologies, and (2) clutching nostalgically to past convictions and ways of life. Volf and Croasmun plea for theology as a perspective of the good life. They argue that theology defined as the good life is not an innovation. There is a broad legacy for articulating visions of the good life within theology. It is possible to read, explicitly or implicitly, all great theologians as different versions of an account of the good life. Volf and Croasmun name only a few theologians like Augustine, Maximus the Confessor, Thomas of Aquinas, Bonaventura, Luther, Calvin, C.S. Lewis, Jürgen Moltmann and Gustavo Gutiérrez. (Volf and Croasmun, 2019, p. 62 and p. 112) In one way or another, all of these theologians advocate a vision of the flourishing life rooted in modes of thinking or being oriented towards God.

In the Dutch 2020 theological book of the year, *Alle dingen nieuw*, Erik Borgman argues in the same direction with his plea for a theology in the 21st century based on two basic themes: (1) God's presence in our finite reality, and (2) that this presence is good news, because it fundamentally transforms our reality (Borgman, 2020, p. 319). Borgman also highlights here a perspective on reality of the good life, rooted in our orientation towards God. Let me be clear, other forms of theology are important too. By analogy with my understanding of economics as a collection of models to study reality (section 2.2), I view diverse forms of theology as models to study different aspects of reality. In this study I employ theology as a perspective of the good life, based on the work of Jonathan Sacks, to explore the question that lies ahead of us, namely how to deal with radical uncertainty in the context of climate change. I will come back to this question in section 1.4.

In this study I will argue that Sacks' understanding of hope, based on the awareness that we are not alone in this world and that this is good news, is also an account of the good life. Key assumptions of his account of the good life are: (1) *emunah*, a particular kind of trust (2) *chessed*, a particular kind of love with linkage to the covenant, and (3) change of identity with linkage to the Sabbath. Sacks' view of the good life is thematized in the particularity of Judaism which is nevertheless able to engage the world around it, without any recourse to reductionism. The special contribution made by the thought of Jonathan Sacks is that it not only continues

> ... the venerable Jewish philosophical tradition of maintaining traditional faith in the face of external intellectual challenges, but also moves beyond this tradition by showing how core Jewish teachings can address the dilemmas of the secular world itself. What makes Lord Sacks's approach so effective is that he is able to do this without any expectation of the wider world taking on Judaism's theological beliefs... His work challenges religious thinkers to chart a new direction for religious thought that works towards a form of universalism in which they can simultaneously remain proud of their particularity. (Harris, Rynhold & Wright, 2012, pp. xvi/xvii)

In line with this quotation, in this study I will not only investigate Sacks' understanding of hope in relation to climate change. I will also bring it in conversation with the wider world, in particular the academic discipline of economics. At first sight, it may be seem surprising that I, a Christian theologian, turn to Sacks, who is neither a Christian nor a theologian in the strict sense of the word. However, I will argue that economics brings me to theological questions. And answering these questions leads me to the work of Jonathan Sacks. In section 2.8 I will give a clear argument for choosing Sacks. This argument will be further developed in section 3.6.

1.4 Conversation with economics on radical uncertainty in climate change

Climate change can be seen as one of the key and most urgent contemporary challenges. This becomes clear from the fact that on 25 September 2015 the General Assembly of the United Nations adopted climate change as Sustainable Development Goal (SDG) 13. This response to climate change (SDG 13) is part of the larger agenda Transforming Our World: The 2030 Agenda for Sustainable Development (United Nations, 2015). What is more, in December 2015, 195 countries adopted the Paris Agreement during the 21st session of the Conference of the Parties (COP21) of the United Nations Framework Convention on Climate Change (UNFCCC). One of the key achievements of the Paris Agreement was the goal of limiting global temperature increase to well below 2 degrees Celsius, while urging efforts to limit the increase to 1.5 degrees. In article 4 of the agreement, this goal is further defined as reaching greenhouse gases (GHGs)[1] emissions neutrality in the second half of the century. (United Nations, 2016)

Nevertheless, during the period 2010-2019 CO_2 rose, although the rate of emissions growth slowed. In 2020, CO_2 emissions dropped temporarily due to responses to the COVID-19 pandemic. Since then, however, CO_2 emissions have exceeded pre-pandemic levels recorded in early 2019. (IPCC, 2022b, p. 2-19-21) Increasingly since the Fifth Assessment Report of Inter-governmental Panel on Climate Change (IPCC) in 2013-2014, widespread, pervasive impacts to ecosystems, people, settlements, and infrastructure have been attributed to human-induced climate change. It has caused, for example, widespread deterioration of ecosystem resilience, reduction in water and food security, especially in vulnerable regions, shifts in seasonal timing, local loss of species, hydrological changes and retreat of glaciers. (IPCC, 2022a, p. 9) Near-term actions that limit global warming to close to 1.5°C would substantially reduce projected losses and damages related to climate change in human systems and ecosystems, compared to higher warming levels. (IPCC, 2022a, p. 13)

In 2010 a special issue of the International Journal of Public Theology was dedicated to climate change and the common good. The contributions came from different theological and ecclesial traditions and addressed several levels of climate change. However, the contributions rarely interacted with a broader audience. (Pearson, 2010, p. 270) This was a missed opportunity, because–as Conradie argues–theology needs to collaborate with other sciences to address the challenges associated with climate change. Addressing such a multifaceted and global issue can never be done by one discipline alone. (Conradie & Koster, 2020, p. 13) What is more, there is even one SDG, number 17, entirely dedicated to stimulating cooperation in order to achieve the other SDGs, including a response to climate change.

In the view of David Tracy there are several 'publics' theology can engage with. He distinguishes three 'publics': academy, church (in my view better described in today's interreligious world as 'religious institutions') and society. (Tracy, 1981, p. 5) Stackhouse considers Tracy's distinction of three 'publics' insufficient at the present time. "With the rise of publicly held, high-tech, multi-national and trans-national corporations and of largely corporate-regulated, global market-system of exchange, the economy has

---

1   GHGs are a diverse group that includes carbon dioxide (CO_2), nitrous oxide (N_2O), and halocarbons (a group of gases including CFC (chlorofluorocarbon)). In this study I will use CO_2 as shorthand for GHGs generally.

become an increasingly independent public realm..." (Stackhouse, 2007, p. 110). Stackhouse adds a fourth dimension to the three publics of Tracy, the economic public. The distinction between several publics or audiences is useful for reasons of focus, clarity and language. Although it is impossible to keep these publics distinct from one another.

This research focuses on a conversation between theology and economics. Economics is related to Tracy's public of the academy and not directly to the economic public of Stackhouse. In short, economics refers to an academic discipline, while economy refers to the domain of economic actors and activities. As a consequence, this research does not include for example a topic like (reflection on) Islamic banking and finance.

In contrast to theological contributions, the significance of economics in developing a response to climate change is widely recognized (IPCC, 2014, p. 213). Nevertheless there is at least one topic economists struggle to address in their response to climate change. In the next chapter I will argue that this topic emerges out of a debate within economics on risk and uncertainty in the context of climate change. In line with an increasing number of economists like John Kay and Mervin King, I argue that mainstream economics runs into serious limitations when it comes to decision-making under conditions of radical uncertainty. This has not only become clear in climate change, but also in the financial crisis of 2007-09 and in the COVID-19 pandemic starting in 2020. All these are manifestations of an increasingly interconnected world in which radical uncertainty becomes more visible. I will argue that the limitations of economics in addressing radical uncertainty invite a conversation with theology about hope.

The economist John Maynard Keynes ranked hope among animal spirits like spontaneous optimism, nerves, hysteria, whim and sentiment (Keynes 2008, p. 105). During the last century, Keynes' animal spirits were largely absent from economics. But times are changing. In the wake of the global financial crisis, George A. Akerlof (Nobel Prize Winner in Economic Sciences 2001) and Robert J. Shiller (Nobel Prize Winner in Economic Sciences 2013) stressed in their book *Animal Spirits* the necessity of a return of animal spirits in economics in order to arrive at a more realistic picture of the economy (Akerlof and Shiller, 2009, p. 168).

Here I take a rather different understanding of hope in order to address radical uncertainty in climate change. This study brings the work of Rabbi Jonathan Sacks on hope in conversation with economics. There are at least three reasons for doing so. First, radical uncertainty as uncertainty inherent in the human condition is of central concern in Sacks' work. Second, standing in a long and nuanced tradition going back to Maimonides, Sacks shows that hope, in Hebrew *Tikvah*, is neither a subjective whim, nor a wish list. In Sacks' understanding, hope is best expressed in a narrative about a learning process to embrace radical uncertainty. Third, Sacks' approach of *Torah veḥokmah*, which means the relation between Torah and secular wisdom (including natural and social sciences), might be useful to stimulate a conversation between theology and the public of economics.

Nevertheless, a conversation between theology and economics has hardly been attempted in recent times. Therefore, I develop van Huyssteen's postfoundational approach to rationality, originally created to facilitate the interaction between theology and natural sciences, into a methodology that seems promising for enabling a conversation between theology and economics. A postfoundational approach to rationality, as I will show in chapter 3, assumes neither a universal form of rationality nor an extreme relativism of rationality. A postfoundational approach rather recognizes the embeddedness of all human reflection in human culture, including specific research and confessional traditions. It recognizes that everybody comes to interdisciplinary interactions with questions, assumptions and arguments shaped by a certain culture. As a consequence, participants can pose different questions, perceive various facts differently, and favour different explanations. Working together on a shared problem then does not lead to extreme relativism of each contribution. In working together participants might provide a fuller understanding of the problem and a better practical response. (van Huyssteen, 1999, pp. 7-9)

For van Huyssteen, a critical reflection of one's own embeddedness is a precondition for an interdisciplinary interaction. Therefore, in chapter 5 and 6 I assess whether the candidates selected for a postfoundational interaction in this study have critically reflected on their own embeddedness. Such an assessment raises questions about my own embeddedness, so let me be very clear about that. I was raised in an Orthodox Protestant middle-class family in Veenendaal, a mainly white and Christian village in the Netherlands, North-Western Europe. I am the second of four children. My father worked as an insurance agent. My mother was a nurse, before she stayed at home to take care of the children. I was raised in a safe and secure context, which has contributed to a sense of self-confidence. In my youth I spent long periods of time in hospital due to an illness which had a significant impact on me. My elder brother and I were the first ones in the family who went to university. I studied (social and institutional) economics and theology at the University of Utrecht. As part of my Masters in development economics I did research in the batik industry in Java (Indonesia) and spent a month with indigenous people in the Eastern part of the country, both enriching experiences. To complete my study in theology, I went to Geneva, the ecumenical institute of Bossey. Bossey is an international centre that brings together students from diverse churches, cultures and backgrounds for ecumenical learning, academic study and personal exchange. My PhD was earned at the Vrije Universiteit Amsterdam. Given this background, in the present study I will refer mostly to theological sources from (Western) Christianity and (Western) Judaism instead of sources from other religions (e.g. Islam or Buddhism). When it comes to economics, I will position myself in a debate that is taking place predominantly at Western universities. I will also limit my sources to English and Dutch literature. As stated above, a postfoundational approach to rationality states that each participant of an interdisciplinary study brings something to the table, informed by her or his history, experience and background. Here I have shown some of my background. That is part of what I will bring to the table in this study.

A final remark regarding van Huyssteen's postfoundational approach, to avoid misunderstanding: this approach, and therefore this study, seeks a conversation between practitioners of different disciplines in order to create a fuller understanding of, and formulate better (practical) responses to radical uncertainty in the context of climate change. What is required now is a conversation and not a fusion. As a consequence, this approach does not aim for a new economic model, but to stimulate a conversation between theology and economics on a shared problem.

1.5   A reader's guide: Outline of the study

Above I have argued that a proper response to climate change demands collaboration between theology and other sciences. Conradie, however, rightly notes that this is easier said than done (Conradie & Koster, 2020, p. 14). It appears to be challenging to work across different fields of study. What is more, a conversation between theology and economics has rarely been undertaken in recent times. This research is an exploratory study in the field of theology. At the same time, it brings together experts who normally do not meet, let alone interact. Therefore, in this study we are going on a challenging journey to bridge the disciplines of theology and economics on the shared problem of radical uncertainty in the context of climate change.

In order to stimulate a constructive journey, let me be very clear about my argument in this research. After this first chapter, the study is structured as follows. Chapter 2 states the problem of this research. It subsequently defines economics, using the work of Dan Rodrik. Then I give a review of economic research on climate change in order to state the problem of this study in detail. The problem statement emerges out of long-standing controversies between economists about the question of how to guide collective decision-making in the context of climate change. In this chapter the controversies are illustrated by one notable controversy, namely between the prominent economists William Nordhaus and Nicolas Stern based on the social cost-benefit analysis. I maintain that radical uncertainty attached to the future is considered a risk, and as a result is actually ignored, which leads to strong disagreement among economists. This chapter makes a clear distinction between risk and uncertainty, relying on the arguments of several economists, and puts decision-making under conditions of radical uncertainty at centre stage. It is here, I argue that a way opens for an interaction between theology and economics.

The aim of chapter 3 is to develop a methodology that allows an interaction between theology and economics. A short review shows that there has hardly been any equal conversation between theology and economics in recent times. Therefore, the chapter explores van Huyssteen's postfoundational approach as a methodology that seems promising for enabling a conversation between theology and economics. The key to a postfoundational interdisciplinary interaction is expressed in the notion of transversal reasoning (TR). TR facilitates a performative, dynamic and multi-levelled conversation between theology and science. It is stated that this postfoundational approach refers especially to the interaction between theology and natural sciences. Nevertheless, the point made here is that this approach is appropriate for any interdisciplinary conversation as long as the three guidelines for TR are mutually honoured: (1) there is a focus on specific theologians and scientists instead of the rather a-contextual terms 'theology and science'; (2) these theologians and scientists engage in specific kinds of theologies and sciences with postfoundational characteristics; (3) the interaction has to be on a clearly defined and shared problem. The chapter continues then with the last of these and defines radical uncertainty in climate change in depth, using work of Hannah Arendt. Drawing on insights obtained from studying 'theologian' Jonathan Sacks, I propose to use his work, especially his understanding of hope, in order to study radical uncertainty in the context of climate change, and to do so in interaction with economics. The chapter then proposes TR between Jonathan Sacks and the economists Bart Nooteboom, Samuel Bowles,

Dan Ariely[2] and John Kay & Mervyn King. This results in the following research question:

> *What is the relevance of a conversation between the theologian Jonathan Sacks and the economists Bart Nooteboom, Samuel Bowles, Dan Ariely and John Kay & Mervin King for a social response to radical uncertainty in the context of climate change?*

The aim of chapter 4 is to answer the twofold question: What is the meaning and possible societal impact of Jonathan Sacks' understanding of hope? In order to achieve this aim, I develop a systematic overview of Sacks' approach of *Torah vehokmah*. Sacks' *Torah vehokmah* refers to an ongoing conversation between Torah (theology and philosophy) and *hokmah* (secular wisdom, including natural and social sciences). Here particular attention is given to Sacks' interpretation of the narrative of the Exodus, because Sacks' understanding of hope is derived from this narrative. In elucidating the concept of hope, Sacks provides a particular account of how the good life addresses radical uncertainty. This account is based on the assumptions of *emunah* (a form of trust), *chessed* (a form of love, including the institution of the covenant) and change of identity (including the institution of a public Sabbath). The chapter highlights examples of earlier societal impacts of this account of the good life and contemporary debates in climate change that directly or indirectly argue for such an account in climate change.

The aim of the chapters 5 through 8 is to develop a pilot study of TR. The focus is on a reasoning between Jonathan Sacks and the economists Bart Nooteboom, Samuel Bowles, Dan Ariely and John Kay & Mervyn King. These economists are selected for two reasons. First, I will argue that their work can be construed as a postfoundational approach to economics. Second, concepts in their work relate to the critical assumptions underlying Sacks' understanding of hope. The point of departure in this TR is Sacks' understanding of hope and its narrative mode as presented in chapter 4 with the following critical assumptions: *emunah*, *chessed* (including the institution of the covenant) and change of identity (including the institution of a public Sabbath). In chapter 5 TR between Sacks and Nooteboom is on *emunah*. In

---

2 In a post of the research blog Data Colada (17 August 2021) concerns were raised of possible fraud in a 2012 paper of Dan Ariely that he co-wrote. Ariely acknowledges that he undoubtedly made a mistake, but insists his actions were innocent. At this moment of writing (19 November 2022) the paper has been retracted, but Ariely has not been condemned. Therefore, it is still justified to use his work. For the research blog of Data Colada see: http://datacolada.org/98.

chapter 6 it is between Sacks and Bowles on *chessed* and between Sacks and Nooteboom on the governance of *chessed*. In chapter 7 TR between Sacks and Bowles is on change of identity, and between Sacks and Ariely on the governance of change of identity. The last TR, in chapter 8, is between Sacks and John Kay & Mervyn King on the narrative. Each turn of TR consists of two parts. The first part deals with the question whether the critical assumptions or the narrative mode of Sacks' understanding of hope and the concept of the economist concerned can interact. If so, to what extent can similarities and differences be found? Do the concepts supplement, deepen or exclude one another? The second part of TR concerns the relevance of the conversation in part 1 for a social response to radical uncertainty in the context of climate change.

The last chapter answers the central question by giving a summary of the main conclusions and provides an evaluation.

1.6   Conclusion

In this introductory chapter hope emerged as an alternative to pessimism and optimism in climate change. It stated that this study explores an understanding of hope in the context of climate change by using the work of Jonathan Sacks. Sacks' understanding of hope fits in a tradition of theology as a perspective of the good life. Key assumptions of this account of the good life are: (1) *emunah*, (2) *chessed*, including the covenant, and (3) change of identity, including the Sabbath. Following David Tracy, there are several publics theology can engage with. This study limits itself to the academic public and focuses on a conversation between theology and economics. The reason for this is that conventional economics runs into serious limitations in addressing radical uncertainty regarding climate change. A conversation between theology and economics has hardly been attempted in recent times. The study uses van Huyssteen's postfoundational approach to develop a conversation. Finally, in order to stimulate a fruitful interaction between theology and economics, a reader's guide is given.

Bibliography

Akerlof, G.A., & Shiller, R.J. (2009). *Animal Spirits: How Human Psychology Drives the Economy, and Why It Matters for Global Capitalism*. Princeton, NJ: Princeton University Press.

Borgman, E. (2020). *Alle dingen nieuw: Een theologische visie voor de 21ste eeuw: Inleiding en Invocatio*. Utrecht, The Netherlands: KokBoekencentrum Uitgevers.

Conradie, E.M., & Koster, H.P. (Eds.). (2020). *T&T Clark Handbook of Christian Theology and Climate Change*. London, United Kingdom: T&T Clark.

Eagleton, T. (2015). *Hope without Optimism*. Charlottesville: University of Virginia Press.

Harris, M.J., Rynhold, D., & Wright, T. (Eds.). (2013). *Radical Responsibility: Celebrating the Thought of Chief Rabbi Lord Jonathan Sacks*. New Milford, CT: Maggid Books.

IPCC. (2014). *Climate change 2014: Mitigation of Climate Change. Contribution of Working Group III to the Fifth Assessment Report of the Intergovernmental Panel on Climate Change*. Cambridge, United Kingdom and New York, NY: Cambridge University Press.

IPCC. (2022a). *Climate Change 2022: Impacts, Adaptation and Vulnerability. Contribution of Working Group II to the Sixth Assessment Report of the Intergovernmental Panel on Climate Change*. United Kingdom and New York, NY: Cambridge University Press.

IPCC. (2022b). *Climate Change 2022: Mitigation of Climate Change. Contribution of Working Group III to the Sixth Assessment Report of the Intergovernmental Panel on Climate Change*. United Kingdom and New York, NY: Cambridge University Press.[3]

Keynes, J.M. (2008). *The General Theory of Employment, Interest and Money* (later edition). Middletown, RI: BN Publishing.

Pearson, C. (2010). Editorial: Special Issue–Climate Change and the Common Good. *International Journal of Public Theology, 4*. Leiden, The Netherlands: Brill, 269-270. Retrieved from http://www.brill.com/international-journal-public-theology

Rootselaar, F. van. (2014, 15 February). De mens kan niet wereldwijd denken. *Trouw*. Retrieved from https://www.trouw.nl/nieuws/de-mens-kan-niet-wereldwijd-denken~b1d47b61/

Sacks, J. (2009b). *Future Tense: Jews, Judaism, and Israel in the Twenty-First Century*. New York, NY: Schocken Books.

Sacks, J. (2011). *The Dignity of Difference: How to Avoid the Clash of Civilizations* (Rev. ed.). London, United Kingdom: Continuum.

Schillebeeckx, E. (1983). *God among Us: The Gospel Proclaimed*. New York, NY: Crossroad.

Stackhouse, M. L. (2007). *Globalization and Grace: Volume 4: Globalization and Grace (Theology for the 21st Century)*. New York, NY: Continuum.

---

3   These three IPCC-references differ in style from that proposed by the IPCC. This is due to the APA citation style guidelines used here.

Tracy, D. (1981). *The Analogical Imagination: Christian Theology and the Culture of Pluralism*. New York, NY: Crossroads.

United Nations, General Assembly. (2015, 25 September). *Transforming Our World: The 2030 Agenda for Sustainable Development*. Retrieved from https://sdgs. un.org/2030agenda

United Nations, Framework Convention on Climate Change. (2016, 29 January). *Report of the Conference of the Parties on Its Twenty-First Session, held in Paris from 30 November to 13 December 2015*. Retrieved from https://unfccc.int/resource/ docs/2015/cop21/eng/10a01.pdf

van Huyssteen, J.W. (1999). *The Shaping of Rationality: Toward Interdisciplinarity in Theology and Science*. Grand Rapids, MI: Wm. B. Eerdmans Publishing.

Volf, M. & Croasmun, M. (2019). *For the Life of the World: Theology That Makes a Difference*. Grand Rapids, MI: Brazos Press.

2. Stating the Problem: Radical Uncertainty

Abstract

The aim here is to state the problem of this research. Based on a review of economic research on climate change, it is argued that radical uncertainty, the uncertainty inherent in the human condition, is not adequately addressed by the critical assumptions underlying conventional economic modelling, in particular the social cost-benefit analysis (SCBA). This is supported by an illustration of a controversy between leading economists William Nordhaus and Nicolas Stern. Following Dan Rodrik's approach to economics, the critical assumptions underlying SCBA are questioned, resulting in the necessity for alternative assumptions to address more properly radical uncertainty. After an overview of economic literature on radical uncertainty, the study chooses a theological track to investigate alternative critical assumptions. There follows a review of eco-theology, which leads to the work of Jonathan Sacks.

Keywords: Dan Rodrik, William Nordhaus, Nicolas Stern, social cost-benefit analysis, decision-making under radical uncertainty, eco-theology, Jonathan Sacks

2.1 Introduction

In this chapter I state the problem of this study. I start by defining economics. Then, I give a review of the economic research on climate change, which leads to discussion of the SCBA as an important tool to support decision-making in the context of climate change. In section 3 the role of the Ramsey rule within SCBA is discussed. Section 4 presents the Stern/Nordhaus-controversy in order to illustrate difficulties with the Ramsey rule. In section 5 it is argued that these difficulties have to do with the uncertainty involved. Section 6 presents several faces of uncertainty in climate change and introduces the

Hasselaar, J.J., *Climate Change, Radical Uncertainty and Hope: Theology and Economics in Conversation*. Amsterdam: Amsterdam University Press, 2023
DOI 10.5117/9789048558476_CH02

concept of radical uncertainty. Section 7 discusses radical uncertainty in economic research, which invites a section on theology, climate change and radical uncertainty (section 8). Section 9 concludes this chapter.

2.2   Economics

Let me introduce my formulation of the problem statement by explaining what I mean by economics. In this study I employ an approach to economics as expressed in Dan Rodrik's *Economics Rules* (2015). In his view, economics is not primarily a social science devoted to understanding how the economy works, but a way of doing social science. Rodrik describes economics as a collection of models to study social life. (2015, p. 7) By doing so, he criticizes the tendency among economists to consider economics the province of universal laws like natural sciences. Rodrik states that economists, generally speaking, "… are prone to mistake a model for *the* model, relevant and applicable under all conditions" (Rodrik, 2015, p. 6). In his view, "we cannot look to economics for universal explanations or prescriptions that apply regardless of context. The possibilities of social life are too diverse to be squeezed into unique frameworks" (Rodrik, 2015, p. 8). Rodrik views an economic model as a partial map that illuminates a fragment of social life in order to enhance our understanding of how the world works and how it can be improved (2015, p. 83). For him:

> What makes a model useful is that it captures an aspect of reality. What makes it indispensable, when used well, is that it captures *the most relevant aspect of reality in a given context*. Different contexts -different markets, social settings, countries, time periods, and so on – require different models. (Rodrik, 2015, p. 11)

In this quotation, Rodrik states that an economic model is useful when it directs attention to only the aspects of reality that really matter. For Rodrik, the strength of an economic model is that it simplifies the world by highlighting only the most relevant aspect in a certain context. "We can understand the world only by simplifying it" (Rodrik, 2015, p. 44). The most relevant aspect of context has to be sufficiently represented by what Rodrik calls the 'critical assumptions' of a model. "We can say an assumption is critical if its modification in an arguably more realistic direction would produce a substantive difference in the conclusion produced by the model" (Rodrik, 2015, p. 27). The key skill of an economist, for Rodrik, is to wisely pick from the menu of available alternative models in each setting. The applicability of a model in a setting depends then on how closely its critical assumptions approximate reality. Rodrik argues that it is not only perfectly legitimate, but also necessary, to question a model's efficacy when its critical assumptions do not sufficiently approximate the given setting. In such a case, the appropriate response is "... to construct alternative models with more fitting assumptions—not to abandon models per se" (Rodrik, 2015, p. 29). Economics, as defined here, is not limited to any single economic school of thought that makes a priori assertions of a general kind about the world, for example only neoclassical or behavioural thinking. Economics is defined as drawing on any or all schools of thought—neoclassical, social, neo-Keynesian, Austrian, behavioural, institutional, ecological, etc.—as long as they offer relevant insight in the context of a particular problem.

For Rodrik the focus of economics is on problem solving. "Economics provides many of the stepping-stones and analytic tools to address the big public issues of our time" (Rodrik, 2015, p. 211). In section 1.4 we have seen that climate change is one of the big contemporary public issues. Economics has an extensive toolbox of models that have been applied to climate change. In the following I give a review of the economic research on climate change in order to state the problem of this study.

2.3   Economics on climate change

Within economics the global climate can be described as a public good. The climate meets the two characteristics of a public good. First, those who fail to pay for it cannot be excluded from using it (non-excludable). Second, one's enjoyment of the climate does not diminish the capacity of others to enjoy it (non-rivalrous). (Perman, Ma, Common, Maddison, & Mcgilvray, 2011, pp. 113-115)

Another key characteristic of the public good of the climate is that of an externality. An externality arises when in an exchange the action of one agent, producer or consumer, affects others that are absent or incompletely represented in the exchange. Therefore, they do not reward the actor for the benefits or penalize him or her for the costs. The market then does not provide an optimal level of resource allocation, which is called a market failure. Externalities fall into two categories. The first category is called positive externalities. These externalities are those where production or consumption decisions of one agent have a positive impact on others in an unintended way, and when no compensation is made. An example of a positive externality is the outcome of Research & Development (R&D). The second category is called negative externalities. This means that producers or consumers do not pay compensation to those who bear the negative effect of action. (Perman et al., 2011, pp. 121-1214)

Economic activities based on the burning of fossil (or carbon-based) fuels involve the emission of CO_2.[1] When CO_2 accumulates in the atmosphere, the temperature increases, and the climatic changes that result, such as changes in temperature extremes, precipitation patterns, rise of sea level, storm location and frequency, snow packs and water availability, impose costs (and some benefits) on society. However, the full costs of CO_2 emissions, in terms of climatic changes, are not immediately borne by the emitter. As a consequence, the emitter faces little or no (economic) incentive to reduce emissions. Similarly, emitters do not have to compensate those who are affected by climatic changes, now or in the future. In this sense, one can describe anthropogenic, i.e. human induced, climate change as (the result of) a negative externality.

Within economics, whenever externality or market failure occurs, there is a potential role for a central decision maker or social planner to internalize the externality. The model of the social cost-benefit analysis is an important economic tool to support the decision maker, often the government, in answering the question of how to internalize the externality. In choosing among alternative trajectories, SCBA attempts to balance objectively the costs of reducing CO_2 emissions with the perils of inaction to a socially optimal level.

The SCBA is built upon the critical assumptions of neoclassical economics. Samuel Bowles calls this the conventional framework within economics (Bowles, 2004, pp. 99-101). The reason for this is that the neoclassical school of thought dominates economics. I use the terms 'neoclassical' or 'conventional' economics interchangeably. In the following I explicate the assumptions underlying the conventional framework. The first assumption of the conventional framework is that knowledge is objective, in other words knowledge is independent of an observer's viewpoint or bias (Horowitz, 2005, p. 1657). The decision maker is able to maximize utility or satisfaction of needs by choosing objectively the optimal alternative, which is preferable to every alternative available to them. The second assumption is that the

---

1   In this study CO_2 is used as shorthand for greenhouse gases (GHGs) that include carbon dioxide (CO_2), nitrous oxide (N_2O), and halocarbons (a group of gases including chlorofluorocarbon (CFC).

unit of analysis is one dynasty of households. This dynasty includes all interests involved, not only those of the present generation, but also those of the next generation. In order to keep the analysis simple the interests of the members of one dynasty are commonly assumed in terms of a 'representative individual'. This is an attempt to 'microfound' macroeconomics, which means that "… all general outcomes need to be explained in terms of the rational choices of isolated individuals" (Skidelsky, 2020, p. xiv). In other words, this dynasty fiction is not a standard element of conventional economics, but rather a working hypothesis to allow working on long-term intertemporal utility optimization. The third assumption is about fixed preferences. This means that what people want among the alternatives in the world is exogenously given, and therefore fixed within the model.

Within SCBA, the Ramsey rule is an important organizing concept for thinking about intertemporal decisions. The reason for this is that in choosing among alternative trajectories for CO_2 reduction, future costs need to be translated into present values. In order to increase consumption in the future, economies invest today in capital, education and technologies. By doing so, they abstain from today's consumption. The Ramsey rule is a mathematical approach to intertemporal decision-making. In the following, I try to explain this rather mathematical rule.

In choosing among alternative trajectories of CO_2 reduction, a key economic variable in the Ramsey rule is the real return on capital, r. The real return on capital measures the net, i.e. subtracting all expenses, yield on investments. Within the context of climate change, the Ramsey rule models the real return on capital, real interest rate or the opportunity costs of capital, r, as the sum of three components:

$$r = \rho + \alpha g$$

where ρ is the time discount rate. This parameter expresses the importance of the welfare (or more precisely, consumption) of future generations relative to the present. When the time discount rate is zero it means that future generations are treated like present generations. A positive discount rate means that the weight placed on the welfare of future generations is reduced compared with nearer generations. The real return on capital depends also on the elasticity of the marginal utility of consumption, α. This consumption elasticity can be seen as a societal preference for consumption smoothing, inequality aversion or risk aversion. The last parameter of the equation is the growth of consumption per generation, g. This parameter includes not only economic growth, but more implicitly also, for example, expectations about the development of technology. (Gollier, 2018, p. 85)

In SCBA, including the Ramsey rule, key questions are: How much should countries reduce CO_2 emissions? When should they reduce emissions? How should the reductions be distributed across industries and countries? What may be the costs of a reduction of CO_2?

Espagne, Nadaud, Fabert, Pottier and Dumas (2012) rightly argue that SCBA becomes controversial in answering these questions. Controversies about the Ramsey rule have been central to responses to climate change for many years (Gollier, 2018, p. 161). One controversy stands out, the Stern/Nordhaus-controversy. In the next section this controversy is discussed in detail in order to trace the hidden dimension of uncertainty in the economics of climate change.

2.4 Stern/Nordhaus-controversy

Two of the most prominent and respected economic studies in the discourses around climate change are those of William Nordhaus and Nicolas Stern. Since the late 1970s Nordhaus has been developing his DICE model. In 2018 Nordhaus received the Nobel Prize in Economic Sciences for his pioneering work on the economics of climate change. Here we focus on his DICE-2007 model. (Nordhaus, 2008) This is a global model that aggregates different countries into a single level of capital, technology and emission. The world is assumed to have a well-defined set of preferences, which ranks different paths of consumption. In his SCBA Nordhaus tries to integrate the main components of society, economy, biosphere and atmosphere, in order to determine the social cost of carbon. Such an analysis is called an Integrated Assessment Model. One assumption of the model is that economic and climate policies should be designed to optimize consumption over time, up to about 200 years ahead. Different strategies for climate change will yield different patterns of consumption. Consumption is viewed broadly and includes besides food and shelter also nonmarket environmental amenities and services.

In 2005, the Stern Review was commissioned by the government of the United Kingdom, and named after the head of the team, Nicholas Stern. Stern was asked to lead a major review on the economics of climate change in order to understand more comprehensively the challenges of climate change and how to respond to them. The Stern Review, which appeared in 2006, uses the PAGE model, which has the same framework of SCBA as Nordhaus' DICE model. However, within the model they proceed from different parameters. The Stern Review uses a discount rate of 0.1 percent per year. Stern argues that the welfare of future generations should be treated on a par with our own (Stern, 2006, p. 35). Nordhaus argues for a discount rate of 1.5 per year (Nordhaus, 2008, p. 178). The Stern Review assumes a consumption elasticity of 1, Nordhaus one of 2. The Stern Review adopts a consumption growth rate of 1.3%. Nordhaus argues for a growth rate of 2%. We have seen that the real return on capital is given by $r = \rho + \alpha g$. As a consequence, the Stern Review results in a real return on capital of 1.4 percent per year. Nordhaus presents a real return of 5.5 percent per year. The real return and its components as presented in the Stern Review and Nordhaus are summarized in table 2.1.

Table 2.1   **Real return on capital and its components for Stern (2006) and Nordhaus (2008)**

	Stern Review	Nordhaus
ρ	0.1	1.5
α	1	2
g	1.3	2
R	1.4	5.5

Using a real return of 1.4 percent, Stern arrives at a present value of future climate damages of around \$85 per ton of emissions. This means that an action to reduce CO_2 should be undertaken if it costs less than \$85 per ton of emissions. Under these conditions, most environmental projects (such as carbon sequestration, wind power, photovoltaics, and biofuels) are socially desirable. However, Nordhaus, using a real return of 5.5 percent, arrives at a much lower present value of future damages of around \$8. (Gollier, 2018, p. 73) As a result, the principal conclusion of the Stern Review is that strong and early actions should be taken to reduce CO_2. One of the main results of Nordhaus' DICE model is that the best response to climate change is not to invest heavily using current technologies, but rather to invest in R&D of more efficient technologies before attempting to reduce CO_2. The different outcomes of the models of Nordhaus and Stern lead to different, even conflicting, advice to a decision maker about how to respond to climate change. Espagne et al. (2012) even argue that the Stern/Nordhaus-controversy has polarized the question about how to respond to climate change.

The Stern/Nordhaus controversy has mainly focused on the role played by the choice of the discount factor. Nordhaus points to the fact that, because of the assumption about discounting, the results of the Stern Review differ dramatically from those of earlier economic models that use the same basic data and analytical structure (Nordhaus, 2008, p. 169). He argues that a time discount rate of 0.1 percent per year represents a shift from mainstream economic theory. But, as indicated in table 2.1, there is also disagreement about the consumption elasticity and the growth rate per capita consumption. In the latter, in both cases the question can be raised as to how such growth rates of 1.3%. (Stern) and 2% (Nordhaus) relate to the expected environmental dangers. Espagne et al. (2012) also highlight the importance of disagreement between Nordhaus and Stern on two other parameters: technical progress on abatement costs and the climate sensitivity.

2.5   Uncertainty

The reason why Stern and Nordhaus disagree so strongly, while using the same conventional economic model, has to do with the fact that the used model does not represent uncertainty. The aim of a SCBA is to support a decision maker objectively in the question of how to internalize an externality. The question is whether it is possible to compensate for this lack of objective probabilities. When there is a lack of objective knowledge, conventional economic theory proceeds by assigning 'subjective' probabilities to each of the possible outcomes that it has identified. There is no single tool to deal with 'subjective' probabilities. Economists use a variety of techniques, for example decision theory (game theory), Bayesian judgements (an estimation of the probability of an event occurring by an individual or a group of individuals), betting markets (predicting markets) and expert elicitation (judgement of more experts together) (Hulme, 2009, p. 85; Nordhaus, 2008, p. 125).[2] Generally speaking, especially in a 'small world', when there is a lack of objective knowledge, "… economists have been able to provide decent enough estimates to facilitate decision making" (Van Kooten, 2013, p. 217). However, in the large world, controversies related to the discount rate, in particular the one between Stern and Nordhaus, show that these techniques inevitably contain subjective elements, which lead to different, even contrasting

---

2   Another way to deal with uncertainty in SCBA is to incorporate a risk premium into the discount rate. This risk premium is supposed to reflect the uncertainty involved. See for example Lemoine (2020).

outcomes. Subjective knowledge is the knowledge an individual has about a situation or phenomenon based on personal opinions, biases, and preferences (Bunnin & Yu, 2004, p. 663).

Van Kooten argues that uncertainty within the context of climate change poses a particular challenge to the economics on externalities (2013, p. 217). In climate change there is not just one uncertainty, but climate change is surrounded by many uncertainties (Heal and Kriström, 2002; Quiggin, 2008; Van Kooten, 2013, p. 9). There is for example uncertainty about climate sensitivity. This is about the relationship between the human-caused emissions and the temperature changes that will result from these emissions. There is also uncertainty about emission scenarios; this is the future growth or reduction of CO_2 emissions. Uncertainty can also refer to the impact of feedbacks. The effects of global warming have created all kinds of feedbacks in the atmosphere, ocean and land, for example acidification of the oceans, rise of the sea level, increased droughts and floods, more intense storms and more extreme heat episodes. Finally, even if we were able to know accurately and in detail how the climate is going to change, we would still not be able to fully describe the effect on human behaviour.

Due to the many uncertainties involved, economists and their studies often disagree strongly with one another about estimations and value judgements like economic growth and the discount rate, as illustrated by the Stern/Nordhaus-controversy. When uncertainty is at centre stage it appears impossible to make decent enough estimations to guide collective decision-making. This leads to questions like the following: How to proceed if an economic model, that should guide collective decision-making, leads to contrasting outcomes? How should uncertainty affect a collective response to climate change?

Haurie, Tavoni and Van der Zwaan argue that much progress has been made in the economics on climate change over the past decade:

> The formulation of climate policy is increasingly becoming reliant on the adequacy of economic analysis, yet many of its aspects are left poorly understood... Among the subjects that deserve further in-depth investigation, the issue of uncertainty emerges as, perhaps the most prominent. (2012, p. 1)

The focus of this study is on uncertainty in the context of climate change. The next step is to define which uncertainty of the many possibilities we wish to examine.

2.6 Radical uncertainty

Within the context of climate change there is not just one uncertainty. Climate change is surrounded by many uncertainties. There is, for example, uncertainty about climate sensitivity. This turn of phrase deals with the relationship between the human-caused emissions and the temperature changes that will result from these emissions. There is also uncertainty about emission scenarios; here lies the pressing concern regarding the future growth, or reduction, of CO_2 emissions. Finally, even if we were able to know accurately, and in detail, how the climate is going to change, we would still not understand fully the implications for social and economic activity. In addition, there is also uncertainty about how technology will develop, for example in areas of green energy and climate engineering.

Uncertainty in the context of climate change is attributed to two main sources by Heal and Millner (2013). The first source is scientific uncertainty, an incomplete understanding of the climate system and related parameters. One can refer here for example to climate sensitivity (relation between atmospheric CO_2 concentration and global average temperature). The second source of uncertainty is socio-economic uncertainty, an incomplete understanding of the impacts of climate change on people and societies, how people and societies will respond, and related parameters. One can refer here for example to parameters related to future policies such as economic growth.

I am adding a third source of uncertainty, which might best be termed 'radical uncertainty'. It is a source of uncertainty inherent in what Hannah Arendt has called 'the human condition of existence'. Hannah Arendt (1906–1975) is considered as one of the most important and original political philosophers of the twentieth century. Although Arendt did not subscribe to a specific school of thought, she did describe herself as a sort of phenomenologist. By this she means that her point of departure is lived experience (Hayden, 2014, p. 10). To put it in her own words from the prologue of *The Human Condition*: "What I propose in the following is a reconsideration of the human condition from the vantage point of our newest experiences and our most recent fears" (Arendt, 1958, p. 5). Arendt insists on taking seriously the basic conditions of human existence, namely life itself, birth and mortality, natality (the capacity to bring something new into the world), worldliness, plurality and the earth (Arendt, 1958, p. 11). Arendt's concept includes the recognition that humans have the freedom for speech and action, which means that there is always the possibility that people can do or say new, unexpected and unprecedented things. As a consequence, the future cannot be predicted in advance. By making the human condition her starting point, Arendt argues against the mainstream Western philosophical tradition, in particular Platonic and Christian worldviews with their emphasis on non-earthly matters and an abstract conception of 'man' (Hayden, 2014, p. 30).

Arendt's concept of the human condition is highly relevant in the context of this study. It shows that we live in a world of radical uncertainty in which our understanding of the present is imperfect, while our understanding of the future is even more limited. As a consequence, this source of uncertainty permeates the two other sources of uncertainty: scientific uncertainty and socio-economic uncertainty. Therefore, human knowledge is limited, and the future cannot be predicted.

Van Kooten points explicitly to the fact that radical uncertainty cannot be ignored in the context of climate change, especially when it comes to long-term decision making. He argues that one hundred year ago automobiles, electricity, airplanes and computers were largely unknown, but that today we cannot envision doing without them. He then wonders: "How can we predict potential damages (or benefits) from climate change in 2050 or 2100, much less 2200, without knowing the technical, social and economic changes that will occur on a global scale during that period?" (Van Kooten, 2013, p. 218). In this research I place radical uncertainty within the context of climate change at the core of the investigation.

2.7   Economics on radical uncertainty

In this research I employ an approach to economics as expressed in Dan Rodrik's *Economics Rules* (section 2.2). Following Rodrik's approach, an economic model is a way to organize our thinking. An economic model is useful when its assumptions capture only the most relevant aspects of reality. In section 2.3 we have seen that the SCBA, part of conventional economics, is an important economic model to support the decision maker in the question of how to respond to climate change. The underlying assumptions of the SCBA are: (1) objective knowledge, (2) the unit of analysis is one dynasty of households, represented in terms of a 'representative individual', and (3) fixed preferences. However, we have seen above that critical assumptions underlying SCBA do not sufficiently address radical uncertainty in the context of climate change, especially the first and third assumption.

The first assumption refers to objective knowledge. However, when it comes to radical uncertainty in the context of climate change, one cannot determine objectively the optimal level of decision making. Economists use a variety of techniques to substitute for a lack of objective knowledge. However when it comes to climate change, uncertainty is at centre stage. As a result, the outcomes of different SCBA, developed to guide objective collective decision-making, can differ widely due to the subjective elements in the estimated parameters, as illustrated by the Stern/Nordhaus-controversy.

The second assumption is a unit of analysis that includes the interests of the members of one dynasty of households. At first sight, this assumption does not run into serious limitations when it comes to radical uncertainty in the context of climate change. However, from chapter 4 onwards we will see that the commonly assumed simplification of representing the interests of one dynasty in terms of a 'representative individual' does not sufficiently address radical uncertainty.

The third assumption refers to the fact that what people prefer is given. However, due to radical uncertainty, it is also impossible to know in advance, especially over long-time horizons, what people will prefer. There is imperfect knowledge about the scope and impact of climate change, but also about future economic growth, including the development of technology.

In addition, although implementation is not part of the SCBA, when externalities arise, a social planner, often the government, intervenes by law, taxes or/and subsidies to internalize the externality. In the context of climate change as a global issue, such a planner, a global authority, does not exist. Even if it were possible to develop objectively an optimal level, there is no global authority that can intervene. In other words, in the context of climate change there is also a governance problem.

How then should we formulate a response to climate change? Employing Rodrik's approach to economics requires not only that we question a model's efficacy when its critical assumptions do not sufficiently cover the given context, here radical uncertainty in the context of climate change. It also challenges us to contribute to more fitting critical assumptions.

In the research tradition of economics in the 20th century[3], there are several prominent economists that acknowledge uncertainty as a fundamental source in economic theory: (1) Frank Knight (1885-1972), (2) John Maynard Keynes (1883-1946) and (3) Friedrich von Hayek (1899-1992).

(1) Knight started the debate in the 1920's by distinguishing, in his classic book *Risk, Uncertainty and Profits* (1921), the difference between risk and uncertainty as two different types of imperfect knowledge about the

---

3   For an account of the role of uncertainty in early modern economics, see Köhn (2017, Chapter 2).

future. For Knight, risk is a known change, quantitatively measurable, while uncertainty is unmeasurable. Köhn argues that the key distinction between the two types is not about the availability of probabilities but about the limits of human knowledge. Some knowledge imperfections can be overcome, as in a classic risk situation like gambling. Other situations of imperfect knowledge cannot be overcome due to human limitations and people's freedom of action and speech. This has consequences for decision-making under conditions of uncertainty. It is meaningless to develop subjective probability calculus in the face of uncertainty. Knight argues for intelligible, wise, creative and entrepreneurial decisions to guide actions in situations of uncertainty. (Köhn, 2017, p. 98) To complete Knight's argument, uncertainty leads to imperfection competition–as opposed to perfect knowledge and perfect competition–which is the cause and ground of profit. Profit is the reward the entrepreneur gains for bearing uncertainty. (Köhn, 2017, p. 100) By referring to the limits of human knowledge, Knight classifies the distinction between risk and uncertainty in terms of epistemology, i.e. it is about limits and reliability of claims to knowledge. What is more, to Knight this distinction is not only a result of cognitive limitations of human actors (epistemological), but lies also in the nature of the real world (ontological).

(2) Keynes states that in a radically uncertain world investors may become pessimistic about the future and reduce their investments. For Keynes, when investments fall, overall spending falls. Government intervention is required to achieve full employment and price stability. Keynes thought that investment will be high enough for full employment only when the animal spirits of the potential investors are stimulated by new technologies, financial euphoria and other unusual events. The term 'animal spirits' is used by Keynes in chapter 12 *The State of Long-Term Expectation* concerning entrepreneurship and long-term investment. Keynes does not define 'animal spirits' precisely, but he associates it with spontaneous optimism, confidence, hope, nerves, hysteria, whim, sentiment or chance. 'Animal spirits' is not used here as a technical term, but much more literally. It is an umbrella term for ingredients for investments on the long term which are not 'reasonable calculations'.

(3) Hayek rejects government intervention. First, because the central planner, the government, does not have all the relevant information. Second, the centrally planned economic model provides too little incentive for effort and creativity. (Hayek, 1945; 1989) For Hayek, it is only through the spontaneous order of the competitive market that the diverse and ever-changing plans of numerous economic actors, responding to unpredictable and complex

shifts of the world, can be reconciled with one another. In other words, for Hayek, the spontaneous order of the free market is the best economic system to deal with radical uncertainty.

In the following I will use the term 'Knightian uncertainty' as a shorthand to bundle uncertainty as a fundamental type of uncertainty in economics, expressed by classical economists like Knight, Keynes and Hayek. I will use 'Ramseyan uncertainty' to refer to uncertainty defined as a risk by attaching subjective probabilities to it, as done in conventional economics.

To sum up, within economics, generally speaking, we can distinguish two types of uncertainty. On the one hand there is the acknowledgement of uncertainty as a fundamental source proposed, although with different accents, by Knight, Keynes and Hayek. On the other hand there is a tradition based on Ramsey which assumes that the knowledge issue related to uncertainty can be overcome on the basis of subjective probabilities, so that decision-making under conditions of uncertainty can be reduced to decision-making under conditions of risk.

In the course of the 20th century the work of Knight, Keynes and Hayek, with their fundamental distinction between risk and uncertainty, was largely side-tracked by conventional economics (Köhn, 2017, p. 4). Ramsey won, and Knight, Keynes and Hayek lost the debate over the interpretation of uncertainty.

The financial crisis of 2007-09 drew attention back to this old debate about the interpretation of uncertainty. Since then, several economists have been rediscovering the theme of radical uncertainty. A prominent voice is Mervyn King, Governor of the Bank of England during the crisis and currently professor of Economics and Law (New York University) and School Professor of Economics (London School of Economics). In his book *The End of Alchemy: Money, Banking and the Future of the Global Economy* (2017), King argues that the financial crisis of 2007-09 was not just a failure of individuals or institutions, but primarily a failure of the ideas that underpin economic policymaking. "There was a general misunderstanding of how the world economy worked" (King, 2017, p. 3). Therefore, King states: "Unless we go back to the underlying causes we will never understand what happened and will be unable to prevent a repetition and help our economies truly recover" (King, 2017, p. 2). In King's view, the failure to incorporate radical uncertainty, in the sense of Knightian uncertainty, into economic theories was one of the factors responsible for the misjudgements that led to the crisis. King argues that it is not always possible to identify all possible future events, attach probabilities to them, estimate their potential impacts on wellbeing or utility and seek to optimise that utility. He considers radical uncertainty as part of 'the human condition', to use Arendt's phrase.

In recent years other economists have also highlighted uncertainty besides risk. To describe this uncertainty, they use terms like 'deep uncertainty', 'ambiguity', 'fundamental uncertainty' and 'uncertainty in a wide sense' (Wakker, 2011; De Grauwe, 2012, p. 27; Roos, 2015; Trautmann and van de Kuilen, 2015; Li, Müller, Wakker and Wang, 2017; Gollier, 2018, pp. 88-89). According to Koppl and Luther, economists rediscover the theme of radical uncertainty either from a more or less Keynesian or Hayekian perspective, respectively government or market. These perspectives are then regarded as two diametrically opposed forms of governance. It has to be government or market, one or the other. (Koppl and Luther, 2012, p. 224) In this study I go beyond an 'either-or' perspective. I will come back to this in section 6.5.1.

When it comes to climate change in particular, the last decade also shows the emergence of economic literature that seeks to incorporate ambiguity or radical uncertainty. One can mention here non-probabilistic approaches, like the Maxmin approach of picking the strategy whose worst possible outcome (min) is least bad (max). There are also probabilistic approaches like the Maximum Expected Utility, which is a probabilistic equivalent of the Maxmin. (Millner, Dietz and Heal, 2010; Lemoine & Traeger, 2012; Heal & Millner, 2013, p. 14)

In this research I follow a different track to cover radical uncertainty in the context of climate change. I focus on a conversation between economics and theology in order to investigate a response to radical uncertainty in the context of climate change.

2.8   Theology on radical uncertainty in climate change

Climate change is not only a challenge for economics, but also for (Christian) theology. Eco-theology is a new branch of theology that has emerged as theologians have wrestled with challenges like (1) the failure of traditional theologies to respond to the problems of the eco-system, and (2) the criticism of traditional theologies, which are considered anthropocentric. Today there are centres, handbooks, websites and many books and articles on religion and ecology. When it comes to the North Atlantic context, in which I live, one can refer, for example, to the *T&T Clark Handbook of Christian Theology and Climate Change* (2020), the Forum on Religion and Ecology and the Amsterdam Centre for Religion and Sustainable Development (Vrije Universiteit).[4]

Several categorisations within eco-theology can be made. In the following I give two examples.

(1) Kim identifies four different approaches of eco-theology: social ecology, creation theology, eco-feminism and eco-spirituality (Kim, 2011, p. 61). *Social ecology* follows a liberation theology methodology and seeks to liberate nature from the bondage of socio-political structures. *Creation theology* views the original creation as the perfect model for God's relationship with humanity and the natural world. *Eco-feminism* identifies women and nature as victims of the dominating, male structures resulting in oppression and exploitation. *Eco-spirituality* starts with the interconnectedness of human beings and nature, and includes resources from primal (and other) religions. Primal religions are regarded as yielding deep eco-theological insights.

(2) Deane-Drummond reviews something of the diversity of eco-theological thought by distinguishing eco-theology from different global contexts: North, South, East and West. *Eco-theology from the North*, focuses on writers in the Northern hemisphere like Aldo Leopold, Matthew Fox, Teilhard de Chardin and Thomas Berry. *Eco-theology from the South* refers to various forms of liberation theology, including Leonardo Boff and Sean McDonagh. *Eco-theology from the East* focuses on theologians from the Eastern Orthodox tradition, for example John Zizioulas and Sergii Bulgakov. In *Eco-theology from the West,* Deane Drummond highlights writers with a concern for socio-political issues, like Michael Northcott and Murray Bookchin.

Eco-theology, as a new development within theology, broadens the scope of theology beyond human society to include nature. However, eco-theology has not yet dealt with the specific problem of radical uncertainty within the context of climate change, especially in interaction with economics. The above mentioned *T&T Clark Handbook of Christian Theology and Climate Change*, includes a critique of an article by Eaton on uncertainty in climate change from the perspective of eco-theology, maintaining that it pays too much attention to uncertainty in climate science itself or its computer models (scientific uncertainty) and overlooks uncertainty regarding to human decision-making by individuals, governments and political parties and leaders (socio-economic uncertainty). According to Hayhoe and Hayhoe

---

4   Forum on Religion and Ecology: https://fore.yale.edu/; Amsterdam Centre for Religion and Sustainable Development: https://vu.nl/en/about-vu/research-institutes/amsterdam-centre-for-religion-and-sustainable-development (accessed 6 December 2022).

the answer to the question of whether the goals of the Paris Agreement will be achieved is not a matter of scientific uncertainty, but will be determined by politics and economics and ideologies that drive our nations. (Hayhoe & Hayhoe, 2020, p. 30). Above I have argued for adding radical uncertainty, derived from Arendt, as a third source of uncertainty. Radical uncertainty permeates both scientific uncertainty and socio-economic uncertainty.

Theology on climate change has not yet dealt with the specific problem of radical uncertainty within the context of climate change. Jonathan Sacks has extensively written on radical uncertainty. Therefore, I propose to use his work to study radical uncertainty in the context of climate change. I will come back to this in chapter 4. First I will discuss a possible conversation between theology and economics.

2.9   Conclusion

In this chapter I have stated the problem of this research, namely that radical uncertainty in the context of climate change is insufficiently covered by the critical assumptions of conventional economics. In economics on climate change the SCBA, an attempt to balance objectively the costs of reducing CO_2 emissions with the perils of inaction to a socially optimal level, is an important model to support a central decision maker. In the chapter it was shown that in the Ramsey rule, an organizing concept for thinking about intertemporal decisions, there is no space for uncertainty. This leads to a polarization in the debate about how to respond to climate change, as illustrated by the Stern/Nordhaus-controversy. It is argued that the critical assumptions of conventional economics run into serious limitations when uncertainty is involved. This study puts radical uncertainty center stage. As used by Hannah Arendt, radical uncertainty refers to a source of uncertainty that is inherent in the human condition. Radical uncertainty implies that human knowledge is limited, and the future cannot be predicted. It is argued in the chapter that this source of uncertainty permeates two other sources of uncertainty in climate change, namely scientific uncertainty and socio-economic uncertainty. Since the financial crisis of 2007-09 economists are rediscovering the theme of radical uncertainty. In this study I follow a different track and focus on an interaction between economics and theology in order to address radical uncertainty in the context of climate change. Eco-theology has not yet addressed radical uncertainty. The chapter proposes using the work of Jonathan Sacks to address radical uncertainty, but first I will explore the possibility of an interaction between theology and economics.

Bibliography

Arendt, H. (1958, 1998). *The Human Condition* (2nd. ed.). Chicago, IL: The University of Chicago Press.

Bowles, S. (2004). *Microeconomics: Behavior, Institutions, and Evolution*. Princeton, NJ: Princeton University Press.

Bunnin, N., & Yu, J. (2004). *The Blackwell Dictionary of Western Philosophy*. Malden, MA: Blackwell publishing. http://dx.doi.org/10.1002/9780470996379

Deane-Drummond, C. (2008). *Eco-theology*. London, United Kingdom: Darton, Longman and Todd. De Grauwe, P. (2012). *Lectures on Behavioral Economics*. Princeton, NJ: Princeton University Press.

Espagne, E., Nadaud, F., Fabert, B.P., Pottier, A., & Dumas, P. (2012). *Disentangling the Stern/Nordhaus Controversy: Beyond the Discounting Clash*. Milan, Italy: FEEM Working Paper (61.2012). http://dx.doi.org/10.2139/ssrn.2160751

Gollier, C. (2018). *Ethical Asset Valuation and the Good Society*. New York, NY: Columbia University Press.

Hauri, A., Tavoni, M., & Van der Zwaan, B.C.C. (2012). Modeling Uncertainty and the Economics of Climate Change: Recommendations for Robust Energy Policy. *Environmental Modeling and Assessment, 17*, 1-5. https://link.springer.com/article/10.1007/s10666-011-9271-5

Hayden, P. (Ed.). (2014). *Hannah Arendt: Key Concepts.* Oxon, United Kingdom: Routledge.

Hayek, F.A. (1945). The Use of Knowledge in Society. *The American Economic Review, 35*(4), 519-530. Retrieved from http://www.aeaweb.org/journals/aer

Hayek, F.A. (1989). The Pretence of Knowledge. *The American Economic Review, 79*(6), 3-7. Retrieved from https://fee.org/resources/the-pretense-of-knowledge/

Hayhoe, K. & Hayhoe, W.D. (2020). A response to Heather Eaton. In E.M. Conradie & H.P. Koster (Eds.), *T&T Clark Handbook of Christian Theology and Climate Change* (pp. 27-30). London, United Kingdom: T&T Clark.

Heal, G., & Millner, A. (2013). *Uncertainty and Decision in Climate Change Economics*. Cambridge, MA: National Bureau of Economic Research Working Paper (18929).

Horowitz, M.C. (Ed.). (2005). *New Dictionary of the History of Ideas*. Vol. 4. Detroit, MI: Charles Scribner's Sons.

Hulme, M. (2009). *Why We Disagree About Climate Change: Understanding Controversy, Inaction and Opportunity*. Cambridge, United Kingdom: Cambridge University Press.

Keynes, J.M. (2008). *The General Theory of Employment, Interest and Money* (later edition). Middletown, RI: BN Publishing.

Kim, S.C.H. (2011). *Theology in the Public Sphere: Public Theology as a Catalyst for Open Debate*. London, United Kingdom: SCM Press.

King, M. (2017). *The End of Alchemy: Money, Banking and the Future of the Global Economy*. London, United Kingdom: Abacus.

Köhn, J. (2017). *Uncertainty in Economics: A New Approach*. Cham, Switserland: Springer.

Kooten, C.G. van (2013). *Climate Change, Climate Science and Economics: Prospects for an Alternative Energy Future*. Dordrecht, The Netherlands: Springer.

Koppl, R., & Luther, W.J. (2012). Hayek, Keynes, and Modern Macroeconomics. *The Review of Austrian Economics, 25*(3), 223–241. http://dx.doi.org/10.2139/ssrn.1580145

Lemoine, D.M., & Traeger, C.P. (2012). *Tipping Points and Ambiguity in the Economics of Climate Change*. Cambridge, MA: National Bureau of Economic Research Working Paper (18230).

Lemoine, D.M. (2020). The Climate Risk Premium. How Uncertainty Affects the Social Cost of Carbon. *Journal of the Association of Environmental and Resource Economists, 8*(1): 27-57. https://www.journals.uchicago.edu/doi/10.1086/710667

Li, Z., Müller, J., Wakker, P.P., & Wang, T.V. (2017). The Rich Domain of Ambiguity Explored. *Management Science*, published online in Articles in Advance 17 August 2017. https://dx.doi.org/10.1287/mnsc.2017.2777

Millner, A., Dietz, S. & G. Heal (2010). *Ambiguity and Climate Policy*. Cambridge, MA: National Bureau of Economic Research Working Paper (16050).

Nordhaus, W. (2008). *A Question of Balance: Weighing the Options on Global Warming Policies*. New Haven, CT: Yale University Press.

Perman, R., Ma, Y., Common, M., Maddison, D., & McGilvray, J. (1996, 2011). *Natural Resource and Environmental Economics* (4th. Ed.). Harlow, United Kingdom: Pearson Education Limited.

Rodrik, D. (2015). *Economics Rules: Why Economics Works, When It Fails, and How To Tell The Difference*. Oxford, England: Oxford University Press.

Roos, M. W. M. (2015). *The Macroeconomics of Radical Uncertainty*. Essen, Germany: Ruhr Economic Papers (592). http://dx.doi.org/10.2139/ssrn.2721683

Skidelsky, R. (2020). *What's Wrong with Economics? A Primer for the Perplexed*. New Haven, CT: Yale University Press.

Stern, N. (2006). *The Economics of Climate Change: The Stern Review*. Cambridge, United Kingdom: Cambridge University Press.

Trautmann, S. & Kuilen G. van de. (2015). Ambiguity Attitudes. In G. Keren & G. Wu (Eds.), *The Wiley Blackwell Handbook of Judgement and Decision Making* (pp. 89-116). Oxford, United Kingdom: Blackwell.

Wakker, P.P. (2011). Jaffray's ideas on ambiguity. *Theory and Decision, 71*(1), 11–22. http://dx.doi.org/10.1007/s11238-010-9209-4

3. Theology and Economics in Conversation

Abstract

This chapter aims to develop a methodology that allows an interaction between theology and economics. A short review shows that there has hardly been any equal conversation between theology and economics in recent times. Therefore the chapter explores van Huyssteen's postfoundational approach as a methodology for enabling a conversation between theology and economics. The key to a postfoundational interdisciplinary interaction is expressed in the notion of transversal reasoning (TR). TR has facilitated a conversation between theology and science, especially theology and natural sciences. Nevertheless, the point made here is that this approach is appropriate for any interdisciplinary conversation as long as the three guidelines for TR are mutually honoured. Radical uncertainty in climate change is then defined in depth, using work of Hannah Arendt. Drawing on insights obtained from the work of Jonathan Sacks, the author proposes that interaction with economics can lead to a fruitful interpretation of radical uncertainty. The chapter ends by arguing for TR between Jonathan Sacks and the economists Bart Nooteboom, Samuel Bowles, Dan Ariely and John Kay & Mervyn King.

Keywords: Wentzel van Huyssteen, postfoundational approach, transversal reasoning, Hannah Arendt, Jonathan Sacks

3.1 Introduction

The aim of this chapter is to explore an interaction between theology and economics when it comes to climate change. I proceed in five steps. First, I introduce interactions between theology and economics by providing a short review. This review will show that there has been hardly any interaction between theology and economics in contemporary times, either in general

Hasselaar, J.J., *Climate Change, Radical Uncertainty and Hope: Theology and Economics in Conversation*. Amsterdam: Amsterdam University Press, 2023

DOI 10.5117/9789048558476_CH03

terms or specifically on climate change. Then I discuss Van Huyssteen's postfoundational approach, based on the science and religion debate, to explore whether, how and in what sense it is possible to construct a conversation between theology and economics. Thereafter, third, I define radical uncertainty in climate change as a shared problem in theology and economics. The fourth step provides a reflection on how some theologians have started to work with the notion of hope and its relation to climate change. Fifth, I offer my contribution to bridging the gap between contemplative and action-oriented approaches to climate change by focusing this study on the understanding of hope in the work of the British intellectual Jonathan Sacks. His work will be used to study an interpretation of radical uncertainty in the context of climate change in interaction with economics. These five steps allow me to formulate the research question and sub-questions. A final summary concludes this chapter.

3.2   Theology and economics

Climate change is a public issue studied by theology as well economics. Nevertheless, there has been hardly any interaction between theology and economics on this issue. Within the work of the Intergovernmental Panel on Climate Change (IPCC) "the significance of economics in tackling climate change is widely recognized" (IPCC, 2014, p. 213). However, a contribution from theology is nowhere to be found in this document. Nor does theology participate in the Integrated Assessment Model. This model, using input from several academic disciplines, seeks to link, within a single and consistent framework, the main components of society and economy with the biosphere and the atmosphere (section 2.4). Within theology, a special 2010 issue of the International Journal of Public Theology was devoted to climate change and the common good. The contributions came from different theological and ecclesial traditions and address several levels of climate change. However, the contributions hardly interacted with a broader audience. (Pearson, 2010, p. 270)

What is more, generally speaking, there has been almost no interaction between theology and economics.[1] In the view of Kim, "[although] theology

---

[1]   It is worthwhile to mention here a new and promising development in the interaction between economics and theology, namely the recently founded Erasmus Economics and Theology Institute (2019) at the Erasmus University Rotterdam (The Netherlands). What is more, in 2020 the institute launched 'The Journal of Economics, Theology and Religion'. For more information see: https://www.eur.nl/en/eeti/

is prepared to [be] (or already has been) engaged with politics, economics, sociology and other subjects, the interest tends to be one-way" (Kim, 2011, p. 231). One can illustrate this with Tanner's *Economy of Grace* (2005). Tanner uses a method of comparative economy to develop a conversation between theology and economics. In short, a method of comparative economy means that the relation between theology and economics is based on the discourse on economy, e.g. principles for the production and circulation of goods. She defines theology and economics normatively. Tanner's method of comparative economy allows her to create "… the maximum possible contrast between the economic principles the world follows and those involved in the Christian story of creation, fall, and redemption" (Tanner, 2005, p. xi). She states "[w]ouldn't it indeed be wonderful if Christianity had its own vision of economic life, one opposed to the inhumanities of the present system and offering direction in trying times, a practical path to a better world?" (Tanner, 2005, p. x). Tanner provides a Christian vision of economic life, expressed in a theological economy based on principles of unconditional giving and noncompetition. I appreciate Tanner's point of departure, namely human experience, exemplified by workers in Singapore, in the context of global capitalism and the economic system in the United States. But her method of comparative economy creates a straw-man argument in the understanding of economics and, I would also argue, theology. As a consequence, her method doesn't allow for a learning exchange and a real conversation between the two disciplines, although her stated aim is to encourage such interaction.

This contribution of Tanner might be described as one of the theological contributions to economics, that "… may have provided valuable insights for fellow theologians, yet they have not always been well received by economists" (Wijngaards, 2012, p. 31). On a more profound level, Brennan and Waterman argue that theologians and economists often talk past one another, partly because their attitudes towards epistemic and methodological issues are so different (2008, p. 89).

The insight that there has been hardly any interaction between theology and economics in recent times raises the question whether it is possible to develop a framework that allows equal interaction.[2]

---

2   Of course, in the compendium of the social doctrine of the Roman Catholic Church, for example, there is a whole chapter on economic life (Chapter 7): http://www.vatican.va/roman_curia/ pontifical_councils/justpeace/documents/rc_pc_justpeace_doc_20060526_compendio-dott-soc_en.html However, in this study the focus is not on an interaction between church doctrine and economic life, but on (developing) a conversation between the academic disciplines of theology and economics. See section 1.4 and 2.7.

3.3   Van Huyssteen's postfoundational approach

This section discusses van Huyssteen's postfoundational approach in order
to explore whether, how and in what sense it is possible to construct a
conversation between theology and economics. This interest will shape
my reading of van Huyssteen. As a consequence, I will not focus e.g. on the
evolutionary origins of van Huyssteen's approach.[3] As argued above, there
has been virtually no interaction between theology and economics in recent
times. However, since the nineteenth century, there has been a long debate
on the relation between theology and natural sciences, often described as the
religion and science debate. Core issues associated with this debate go back
much further. Scholars have claimed that the second part of the twentieth
century saw the emergence of a new interdisciplinary field of science and
religion. (Reeves, 2019, p. 8) One of the leading scholars in this field is J.
Wentzel Van Huyssteen. (Reeves, 2019, p. 22; Lovin & Mauldin, 2017, p. xiv)
Van Huyssteen has extensively published on this relation between religion
and science. He became the first James I. McCord Professor of Theology and
Science at Princeton Theological Seminary (1992-2014).

For van Huyssteen, a widely accepted inheritance of modernity is that
science is often considered a superior kind of knowledge. Religion then
is seen as a privatized form of subjective, if not irrational experience.
Van Huyssteen argues that the idea that science and religion have always
been in conflict is increasingly seen as an invention of the late nineteenth
century. (van Huyssteen, 1999, p. 17-18) He states that the question of how
theology and science relate to each other is neither a theological nor a
natural scientific question. It is rather an epistemological question, a
question about how two different claims of knowledge are related. Over
the years, Van Huyssteen has developed what he calls a postfoundational
approach, one that views theology and science as different but equal faces
of human rationality. In the following I give an overview of his line of
thought. While this approach was already present in his inaugural lecture
at the Princeton Theological Seminary, *Theology and Science: The Quest for
a New Apologetics* (1993), his definitive work on this topic is *The Shaping
of Rationality: Toward Interdisciplinarity in Theology and Science* (1999).
Van Huyssteen presents his postfoundational approach as a middle path
between what he calls (1) a foundational and (2) a nonfoundational form
of rationality.

---

3   For detailed secondary literature on van Huyssteen's postfoundational approach see Reeves
(2019).

(1) A foundational approach to rationality states that there is only one universal form of knowledge, i.e. objective knowledge. This view of rationality can be found both in theology and in science. It holds that in the process of justifying knowledge there is a claim resting on a foundation that is beyond doubt, self-evident and incorrigible. Foundational approaches are associated with notions of positivism, objectivism, true scientific knowledge, universal rationality and absolute principles. (van Huyssteen, 1993, p. 434) In natural sciences, a foundational approach gave rise to the thesis that knowledge rests on objective chains of justification. A foundational approach in theology is related to notions like divine revelation and biblical literalism. A foundational approach makes an interdisciplinary interaction between theology and science impossible, because its justification allows for no communication with other disciplines. The mistake of foundational approaches is, for van Huyssteen, that they neglect that "... all our inquiry and reflection, whether scientific or theological, is indeed highly contextual and already presupposes a particular theoretical, doctrinal, or personal stance and commitment" (van Huyssteen, 2014, p. 210). Van Huyssteen argues that "... indubitable beliefs that can justify all other knowledge claims do not exist" (Reeves, 2019, p. 79). Van Huyssteen associates a foundational approach closely with modernism.

(2) For van Huyssteen, a foundational approach to rationality is often rejected in favour of a nonfoundational approach, which deconstructs the claim of an objective rationality. Such an approach takes seriously the contextuality of rationality. It argues that "... every historical context, and every cultural or social group, has its own distinct rationality" (van Huyssteen, 1999, p. 63). This nonfoundational approach seems to avoid the dangers of foundational approaches. However, van Huyssteen argues that a view of many rationalities often leads to an extreme relativism of rationality. The contextualism of rationality offers a picture of human knowledge in which there is no authority in reason, as if science is just another opinion. This makes it virtually impossible to speak with authority about theology and science, and therefore does not allow interdisciplinary interaction. Van Huyssteen closely associates a nonfoundational approach with postmodernity.

Over against the objectivism of foundationalism and the extreme relativism of some nonfoundational approaches, van Huyssteen has developed an epistemological middle path. He calls this middle path a postfoundational approach to rationality. Van Huyssteen has developed four key characteristics of this approach (van Huyssteen, 1999, p. 8; 2006, p. 18):

(1) *Embeddedness of rationality.* A postfoundational approach to rationality recognizes the contextuality and the embeddedness of all human

reflection in human culture, and therefore in specific scientific and confessional traditions.

(2) *Interpreting reality by all forms of inquiry.* A postfoundational approach points to the interpretation of one shared reality as common ground of rationality in theology and science. All theology and science is an interpretation of reality. Above we have seen that in Van Huyssteen's view an inheritance of modernity is that science is often viewed as rational and religion as subjective, if not irrational. However, in a postfoundational approach the difference is based on the epistemological focus and the experiential scope that inform the reflection (van Huyssteen, 1999, p. 13). As a consequence, the postfoundational notion of rationality considers human rationality to be multidimensional.

(3) *Critical reflection.* As a theologian or scientist, one comes to interdisciplinary interactions with questions, assumptions and arguments shaped by a certain research tradition or a confessional tradition. Therefore, one can pose different questions, perceive various facts differently, and favour different explanations. For van Huyssteen, a critical reflection on one's own embeddedness is a *precondition* for going beyond one's own borders and the borders of one's epistemic community and participating in interdisciplinary interaction.

(4) *Problem-solving.* Van Huyssteen defines problem-solving as "… the most central and defining activity of all research traditions" (van Huyssteen, 2014, p. 221). Different research traditions working together on a shared problem might provide a fuller understanding of the problem and a better practical response.

With regard to these characteristics, at least one criticism can be made. For van Huyssteen, a critical reflection on one's own embeddedness, the third characteristic above, is a precondition for participating in interdisciplinary interaction. In my view, for theologians and scientists to engage in TR, having postfoundational characteristics is not a precondition per se. Developing postfoundational characteristics can also flow from participating in transversal reasoning. The reason for this is that collaborative praxis can result in greater awareness of the assumptions one lives by. In other words, postfoundational characteristics need not be a precondition, but can also be developed in practicing transversal reasoning.

To sum up, a postfoundational approach to rationality views rationality not as beyond doubt, but as embedded and self-critical, in dialogue seeking pragmatic and defensible solutions in and for the benefit of a common reality.

3.4 Transversal reasoning

The key to postfoundational interdisciplinary interaction is expressed in the notion of transversal reasoning (van Huyssteen, 2006, p. 19; 2014, p. 214). This notion is derived from the philosopher Calvin Schrag. Transversal reasoning facilitates a performative, dynamic and multi-levelled interaction between theology and science. In transversal reasoning, different disciplines "... can learn from one another and actually benefit by taking over insights presented in interdisciplinary dialogue" (van Huyssteen, 2006, p. 20). At the same time, in transversal reasoning there is not a fusion of different reasoning strategies, but a conversation between them. It is a conversation of approaches in order to solve a shared problem. In this conversation, the integrity of each of the different reasoning strategies is respected by the participants (van Huyssteen, 2014, p. 218). One can wonder how this respect for integrity relates to solving a shared problem. In my view, it is not always easy for different reasoning strategies to understand one another. It may take time to become aware of one's own assumptions and to understand the reasoning strategy of the other. Only respect for the integrity of each reasoning strategy allows participants to open up to one another and to develop a fuller understanding of the shared problem. This fits with the insight of van Huyssteen that transversal reasoning is a skill that has to be learned. At the same time, the interaction with other reasoning strategies might create the opportunity to enrich one's own discipline. Lovin and Mauldin argue that van Huyssteen's approach takes the usual interdisciplinary dialogue a step further. The reason for this is that "[a]s researchers assimilate the results of other methods of inquiry, revise their own methods and formulate new questions in the light of what they have learned, the lines drawn when disciplines set their own boundaries begin to blur" (Lovin & Mauldin, 2017, p. xxiii).

Van Huyssteen's postfoundational approach is one of the leading approaches relating theology and (natural) science. The question has to be answered whether this approach can also be used to develop a conversation between theology and economics. According to van Huyssteen, a postfoundational notion of rationality is not limited to the debate of science and religion. The reason for this is that van Huyssteen's approach is not just a description of the knowledge in science and religion, but a description of human rationality, understood as being constantly under construction in its engagement with reality. Van Huyssteen's approach aims to promote cross-disciplinary conversation (Reeves, 2019, p. 84). Van Huyssteen considers his postfoundational approach appropriate for any interdisciplinary interaction as long as the guidelines for a postfoundational approach are mutually honoured (van Huyssteen, 1993, p. 439; 2014, p. 2019). The question is then what are the guidelines that need to be honoured for possible successful transversal reasoning between theology and science, in this case between theology and economics? The guidelines can be traced in the following quotation:

> ... the rather a-contextual terms "theology and science" should be replaced by focussing our attention on specific theologians, engaging in specific kinds of theologies, who are attempting to enter the interdisciplinary dialogue with very specific scientists, working within specific sciences on clearly defined, shared problems. (van Huyssteen, 2014, p. 227)

Based on this quotation, I identify three guidelines for successfully employing transversal reasoning:
(1) there is a focus on specific theologians and scientists instead of the rather a-contextual terms 'theology and science'.
(2) the work of these theologians and scientists should be able to be constructed in a postfoundational manner.
(3) the interaction has to be on a clearly defined and shared problem.

These three guidelines need to be honoured to allow for a successful interdisciplinary interaction. Successful means here that the shared problem is more adequately addressed. After sharing the resources of interdisciplinarity, a postfoundational approach points back to the natural boundaries of one's own discipline (van Huyssteen, 2014, p. 220). This creates the opportuinity to impact one's own discipline with the gained result of the interdisciplinary interaction.

In the sections above, I have discussed van Huyssteen's postfoundational approach. Like Reeves, I consider Van Huyssteen's description of human rationality to be generally convincing (2019, p. 88). Doubts can be raised as to whether van Huyssteen has decisively answered Enlightenment challenges to religious belief (Reeves, 2019, p. 88; Reeves, 2013, 150; Schoen, 2000, pp. 122/123). Dealing with these doubts is beyond the scope of this research. The reason for this is that van Huyssteen's postfoundational approach fits for its part in this study, namely to serve as a framework that allows for exploring a conversation between theology and economics in order to solve shared problems.

The next step in this study is to honour the guidelines for a postfoundational approach. In the remainder of this chapter I start with the last guideline, identifying a clearly defined and shared problem between theology and economics. Thereafter a start is made with discussing the other two guidelines, (1) a focus on specific theologians and economists, and (2) engaging in postfoundational approaches to theology and economics.

3.5   A shared problem: radical uncertainty in the context of climate change

A postfoundational interaction requires a clearly defined and shared problem between specific theologians and economists. In chapter 2 we have seen that the conventional assumptions underlying the economic model of social cost-benefit analysis (SCBA) run into serious limitations when it comes to uncertainty in the context of climate change. However, uncertainty is still too broad to function as a shared problem. In section 2.6 a distinction was made between two main sources of uncertainty, namely (1) scientific uncertainty, an incomplete understanding of the climate system and related parameters, and (2) socio-economic uncertainty, an incomplete understanding of the impacts of climate change on people and societies and related parameters. It is possible to reduce uncertainty. However, in chapter 2 I have argued that there will always remain a residual of uncertainty due to the human condition. I have called this residual of uncertainty 'radical uncertainty'. 'Radical' is derived from 'radix', which is a Latin word for 'root'. I define radical uncertainty as rooted or inherent in what Hannah Arendt has called 'the basic human condition of existence'. In contrast to Heidegger's elevation of mortality as the defining characteristic of human existence, Arendt accentuates natality. For Arendt, we are not solely human because of physical birth and mortality. People become fully human on the basis of the natality of their second, 'political' birth. In the view of Arendt, natality is based on the human capacity for speech and freedom of action (Hayden, 2014, p. 14). Taking seriously the basic human condition as described by Arendt means that human knowledge is limited and that humans have the freedom for speech and action, so that there is always the possibility that people say and do new, unexpected and unprecedented things. As a consequence, the future cannot be predicted in advance. Radical uncertainty permeates the two other sources of uncertainty: scientific uncertainty and socio-economic uncertainty. In this study I consider radical uncertainty in climate change a shared problem as required by van Huyssteen's transversal reasoning.

3.6   Hope in climate change

Radical uncertainty in the context of climate change can easily be associated
with tragedy. The French philosopher Pascal Bruckner argues that fear and
a sense of apocalypse are widespread with regard to environmental issues,
including climate change (Bruckner 2013, p. 2). Clive Hamilton, an Australian
public intellectual, has even written a Requiem for a Species—that species being humankind. It is as if hope has been abandoned. For Hamilton
"despair is a natural human response to the new reality we face and to
resist it is to deny the truth" (Hamilton, 2015, p. 226). But he further argues
that it is unhealthy and unhelpful to stop here. "Emerging from despair
means accepting the situation and resuming our equanimity; but if we go
no further we risk becoming mired in passivity and fatalism" (Hamilton,
2015, p. 226). Hamilton takes advice from Pablo Casals: "The situation is
hopeless; we must now take the next step" (Hamilton, 2015, p. 222). He is
willing to concede that "finding meaning in adverse circumstances is one
of the most remarkable human qualities" (Hamilton, 2015, p. 222). Hamilton
acknowledges the role of religion and wonders whether abandoning the
lesser gods like money, growth and optimism will lead people to turn to
the sacred for protection (Hamilton, 2015, p. 221). Let's turn to religion and
from there to theology.

In the view of Jonathan Sacks there are at least two possibilities for interpreting this type of uncertainty, namely tragedy and hope. Sacks was a
leading British public intellectual and Chief Rabbi of the United Hebrew
Congregations of the Commonwealth (1991-2013). According to Sacks, ancient
Greece offered the West the concept of tragedy. Tragedy is a view of the
future in which fate controls human beings. As indicated above, it is not
difficult to see how this tragic sense of fate can readily flow from the kind of
radical uncertainty that climate change projects. Sacks makes the case for
a more hopeful interpretation of radical uncertainty. It is one which stands
in a long tradition that goes back to the Hebrew Bible and gave Western
civilization, via Christianity, a concept of hope in which the state of the
world is not inevitable (Sacks, 2009b, p. 249).

In section 1.1 we have already seen that Eagleton considers hope as a
curiously neglected notion in an age which confronts us with the felt loss of
a future. Jürgen Moltmann has long argued that hope is a neglected aspect
within theology too, in the sense that there are theological traditions on
love and faith, but there is no tradition '… shot through by hope' (Moltmann,
2015. p. 177). Nevertheless, it is true that in recent years some theologians

have started to reflect on hope and its relation to climate change. Albert Nolan, South African Dominican priest and well known for his work against the apartheid system, argues for developing a perspective of hope in this context that is not based on signs, but on trust in God (2010, p. 5). Borgman has developed a Catholic perspective through his interaction with the papal encyclical *Laudato Si'*. He argues for a politics of contemplation in order to find hope where only hopelessness seems to remain (Borgman, 2017, p. 102). Borgman states that looking with eyes of love, the world becomes visible as the place of promise that it essentially is (2017, p. 76). The essence of this perspective is to see where the light of love presents itself, to let it in, and to put oneself in the service of this light (Borgman, 2017. p. 35). With his politics of contemplation, Borgman argues against an overly activist approach in Dutch policies. In the wake of the Fifth Assessment Report of the IPCC, suggesting that exceeding the critical threshold of two degrees Celsius before the end of the century may be unavoidable, Stefan Skrimshire emphasizes that an attitude of hope "that denies despair in the face of such epic failures, and encourages action in the face of the death that such failures will bring, may be an extremely welcome one in the light of such a report" (Skrimshire, 2014, p. 5).

This study aims to contribute to an understanding of hope that allows for a bridging of the gap between contemplative and action-oriented approaches. For this purpose I limit myself to Jonathan Sacks' understanding of hope as a way to interpret radical uncertainty in the context of climate change. Sacks' work is clearly embedded in Orthodox Judaism. One can argue that he did not actually work within the research tradition of theology because, generally speaking, Orthodox Judaism maintains that it doesn't have a theology in the sense of a separate academic or intellectual discipline. The reason for this is that it considers theology as defining God in words. Orthodox Judaism regards God as essentially unknowable. In line with this, Sacks uses the term 'philosophy of the human condition under the sovereignty of God' instead of 'theology' to define his reasoning strategy, at least as related to the book of Genesis. Arguably this is also the case for Exodus, which plays a key role in the present study, because both books of the Torah, Genesis and Exodus, are part of the same literary unit. In this unit theology is almost always implicit rather than explicit. (Sacks, 2009a, p. 6) As a consequence, Sacks calls his own approach 'public philosophy' and not 'theology' (Tirosh-Samuelson & Hughes, 2013, p. 106). Nevertheless, most theologians are also aware that words will always fall short of describing God (Ten Kate & Poorthuis, 2017, p. 552). Therefore, I consider Sacks as a representative of the research tradition of theology.

It is not uncommon within theology to refer to Jewish public thinkers. In 2013 The International Journal of Public Theology devoted a special issue to Jewish Public Theology. This issue paid particular attention to Rabbi Abraham Joshua Heschel, one of the leading Jewish thinkers of the twentieth century. What is more, Tomáš Halík, a leading Christian theologian and professor of sociology of Charles University (Prague), considers Sacks' understanding of hope very promising for the understanding of hope within Christian theology (Halík, 2019, p. 11). This is in line with the statement of the Dutch Roman Catholic bishops that an interaction on hope with Judaism can be fruitful for the church:

> Catholics have come increasingly to realize that we share a common messianic mission to make the earth inhabitable.... Slavery and death [do not] have the last word but liberation and life in God's presence is our common conviction.... Jews and Christians live from one and the same hope. With this hope as a solid basis, modern man does not necessarily have to experience the future as an ominous void. (The Roman Catholic Bishops of the Netherlands, 1999)

In this study I develop an understanding of hope based on the work of Jonathan Sacks.[4]

Before we can situate Sacks' understanding of hope in the context of climate change, it needs extensive decoding. The reason for this is that hope is often used glibly in everyday language. Take for example the following remark: I hope that tomorrow the sun will shine. Sacks' understanding of hope is completely different. When Sacks uses the concept of hope, he is giving a commentary on the Torah, especially the Exodus, which in turn gives a commentary on present reality. In the Exodus, the concept of hope is not just an expectation, wish or emotion. Hope orientates us to the possibility

---

4   Although this research touches upon the relation between Judaism, in particular Jonathan Sacks, and Christianity, an explicit elaboration on this relation is beyond the scope of this research. Nevertheless, there are already some examples of an interaction between Jonathan Sacks and Christianity. In the Vatican, in 2014, Jonathan Sacks gave an address at the colloquium on the complementarity of man and woman. In 2008 Sacks spoke at the Lambeth Conference of the Anglican Community. An example of a Christian theologian reflecting on some lines of thought of Sacks is Thabo Makgoba, Archbishop of Cape Town and Metropolitan of the Anglican Church of Southern Africa, see Makgoba (2009). What is more, Justin Welby, Archbishop of Canterbury and *primus inter pares* of the worldwide Anglican Communion, states that Sacks had a powerful influence on Anglican social thought over the last decades. (Sacks, 2021, p. vii)

of gradually starting something new and liberating in the midst of radical uncertainty. Sacks' reading of hope, derived as it is from the experience of the Exodus, offers several key ingredients to address radical uncertainty, namely *emunah* (a special kind of trust), *chessed* (a special kind of love) and a change of identity. The next chapter extensively develops an overview of Sacks' understanding of hope in relation to his general approach of *Torah veḥokmah*, which means the relation between Torah and secular wisdom (including natural and social sciences).

In the pilot study of transversal reasoning comprising chapters 5 through 8, I will construct a conversation on radical uncertainty and hope between Sacks and five economists, namely Bart Nooteboom, Samuel Bowles, Dan Ariely, and John Kay & Mervin King, a kind of intellectual pop-up salon. The reason for choosing these economists is twofold. The first reason is that their scientific approach can be constructed as what I call a postfoundational approach to economics. The second reason is that concepts in their work seem good candidates for interacting with Sacks' understanding of hope in TR.

3.7 Central question and structure of the research

Now that the framework required for an interaction between theology and economics has been described, the central question for the interaction can be formulated:

> *What is the relevance of a conversation between the theologian Jonathan Sacks and the economists Bart Nooteboom, Samuel Bowles, Dan Ariely and John Kay & Mervin King for a social response to radical uncertainty in the context of climate change?*

The term conversation is here defined as transversal reasoning (TR). A social response refers, in line with SCBA, to collective decision-making. A social response is distinguished from the private decision-making of consumers and producers. Radical uncertainty is defined as uncertainty inherent in the human condition. In the remainder of this study, the terms 'uncertainty' and 'response' are used as both abbreviations and synonyms for radical uncertainty and social response, respectively. To be able to answer the research question in chapter 9, I have broken it down into three sub-questions:

1. Whether, how and in what sense is it possible to construct a conversation between theology and economics?

2. What is the meaning of Jonathan Sacks' understanding of hope?
3. How can a conversation between Jonathan Sacks and the economists
    Bart Nooteboom, Samuel Bowles, Dan Ariely and John Kay & Mervin
    King be constructed in such a way that it leads to the creation of a fuller
    understanding of a social response to radical uncertainty in the context
    of climate change?

The first sub-question is answered in this third chapter. The second one is
answered in chapter 4 and the last one in chapters 5 through 8. The figure
below gives a thematic overview of the structure of this study, beyond the
introduction.

Figure 3.1   Overview of the thematic structure of the research

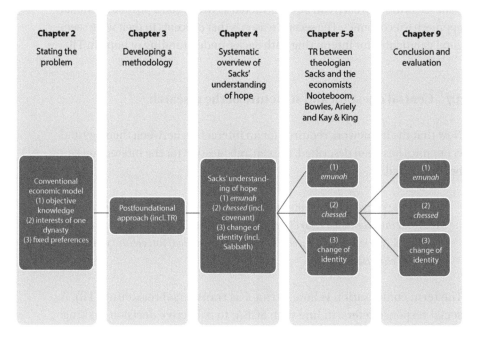

3.8   Conclusion

In this chapter I have developed van Huyssteen's postfoundational approach,
originally created to facilitate the interaction between theology and natural
sciences, into a methodology that could possibly provide a framework for a
conversation between theology and economics—a conversation scarcely

attempted in recent times. According to van Huyssteen, a postfoundational approach is appropriate for any interdisciplinary interaction as long as it mutually honours the three guidelines of a postfoundational approach. These guidelines are: (1) a focus on specific theologians and scientists (instead of the rather a-contextual terms 'theology and science'), (2) whose work can be constructed as specific kinds of theologies and sciences with postfoundational characteristics, and (3) who work together on a clearly defined and shared problem. In the chapter I argued that one can consider radical uncertainty, the uncertainty inherent in the human condition, in the context of climate change a clearly defined and shared problem (satisfying the third guideline of TR). In the chapter it is argued that radical uncertainty can easily call up a tragic sense of fate. However, climate change does not carry with it its own interpretation. In recent years, some theologians have started to work with the notion of hope and its relation to climate change. In the chapter Jonathan Sacks' understanding of concept of hope is highlighted as a possibly promising theological contribution to this shared problem of radical uncertainty in climate change. By selecting Sacks and focusing on his understanding of hope, the chapter has also taken a first step in honouring the first and second guidelines of TR and pointed ahead to chapters 5 through 8, where five economists will interact with Sacks in TR. Subsequently, the central research question was formulated and divided into three sub-questions.

Bibliography

Borgman, E. (2017). *Leven van wat komt: Een katholiek uitzicht op de samenleving.* Utrecht, The Netherlands: Meinema.

Brennan, G., & Waterman, A. (2008). Christian theology and economics: convergence and clashes. In I. Harper & S. Gregg (Eds.), *Christian Theology and Market Economics* (pp. 77-93). Cheltenham, United Kingdom and Northampton, MA: Edward Elgar Publishing.

Bruckner, P. (2013). *The Fanaticism of the Apocalypse: Save the Earth, Punish Human Beings.* Cambridge, United Kingdom: Polity Press.

Halík, T. (2019). *Niet zonder hoop: Religieuze crisis als kans.* Utrecht, The Netherlands: KokBoekencentrum Uitgevers.

Hamilton, C. (2015). *Requiem for a Species: Why We Resist the Truth about Climate Change.* London, United Kingdom: Routledge.

Hayden, P. (Ed.). (2014). *Hannah Arendt: Key Concepts.* Oxon, United Kingdom: Routledge.

IPCC. (2014). *Climate change 2014: Mitigation of Climate Change. Contribution of Working Group III to the Fifth Assessment Report of the Intergovernmental Panel on Climate Change*. Cambridge, United Kingdom and New York, NY: Cambridge University Press.

Kate, L. ten, & Poorthuis, M. (Eds.). (2017). *25 Eeuwen theologie: Teksten/toelichtingen*. Amsterdam, The Netherlands: Boom uitgevers.

Kim, S.C.H. (2011). *Theology in the Public Sphere: Public Theology as a Catalyst for Open Debate*. London, United Kingdom: SCM Press.

Lovin, R.W., & Mauldin, J. (Eds.). (2017). *Theology as Interdisciplinary Inquiry: Learning with and from the Natural and Human Sciences*. Grand Rapids, MI: Wm. B. Eerdmans Publishing.

Makgoba, T. (2009). Politics and the Church—Acting Incarnationally: Reflections of an Archbishop. *Journal of Anglican Studies, 7*(1), 87-91. http://dx.doi.org/10.1017/S1740355309000175

Moltmann, J. (2015). *The Living God and the Fullness of Life*. Geneva, Switzerland: World Council of Churches.

Nolan, A. (2010). *Hope in an Age of Despair*. New York, NY: Orbis Books.

Pearson, C. (2010). Editorial: Special Issue–Climate Change and the Common Good. *International Journal of Public Theology, 4*. Leiden, The Netherlands: Brill, 269-270.

Reeves, J. (2013). Problems for Postfoundationalists: Evaluating J. Wentzel van Huyssteen's Interdisciplinary Theory of Rationality. *The Journal of Religion, 93*(2), 131-150. http://dx.doi.org/10.1086/669209

Reeves, J. (2019). *Against Methodology in Science and Religion: Recent Debates on Rationality and Theology*. Abingdon, United Kingdom: Routledge.

Sacks, J. (2009a). *Covenant & Conversation, Genesis: The Book of Beginnings*. Jerusalem, Israel: Maggid Books.

Sacks, J. (2009b). *Future Tense: Jews, Judaism, and Israel in the Twenty-First Century*. New York, NY: Schocken Books.

Sacks, J. (2021). *Morality: Restoring the Common Good in Divided Times*. London, United Kingdom: Hodder & Stoughton.

Schoen, E.L. (2000). Review: The Shaping of Rationality: Toward Interdisciplinarity in Theology and Science by J. Wentzel van Huyssteen. *International Journal for Philosophy of Religion, 48*(2), 121-123. http://dx.doi.org/10.1023/A:1004080214599

Skrimshire, S. (2014). Eschatology. In M. S. Northcott & P. M. Scott (Eds.), *Systematic Theology and Climate Change: Ecumenical Perspectives* (pp. 157-174). London: United Kingdom: Routledge.

Tanner, K. (2005). *Economy of Grace*. Minneapolis, MN: Augsburg Fortress.

The Roman Catholic Bishops of the Netherlands, (1999 November 1). *Living with One and the Same Hope: On the Meaning of the Meeting with Judaism for Catholics*. Retrieved from https://www.lucepedia.nl/dossieritem/antisemitisme/

levend-met-een-zelfde-hoop-over-de-betekenis-van-de-ontmoeting-met-het-jodendom-

Tirosh-Samuelson H., & Hughes A.W. (Eds.). (2013). *Jonathan Sacks: Universalizing Particularity.* Leiden, The Netherlands: Brill.

van Huyssteen, J.W. (1993). Theology and science: The quest for a new apologetics. *HTS Teologiese Studies / Theological Studies, 49*(3), 425-444. http://dx.doi.org/10.4102/hts.v49i3.2501

van Huyssteen, J.W. (1999). *The Shaping of Rationality: Toward Interdisciplinarity in Theology and Science.* Grand Rapids, MI: Wm. B. Eerdmans Publishing.

van Huyssteen, J.W. (2006). *Alone in the World: Human Uniqueness in Science and Theology (Gifford Lectures).* Grand Rapids, MI: Wm. B. Eerdmans Publishing.

van Huyssteen, J.W. (2014). Postfoundationalism in Theology: The Structure of Theological Solutions. *Ephemerides Theologicae Lovanienses, 90*(2), 209-299. http://dx.doi.org/10.2143/ETL.90.2.3032676

Wijngaards, A.E.H.M. (2012). *Worldly Theology: On Connecting Public Theology and Economics* (Doctoral dissertation). Retrieved from http://mobile.repository.ubn.ru.nl/bitstream/handle/2066/93624/93624.pdf?sequence=1

4.   Jonathan Sacks' Understanding of Hope

Abstract

The aim here is to answer the twofold question: What is the meaning and possible societal impact of Jonathan Sacks' understanding of hope? The chapter opens, however, by demonstrating that Sacks meets the requirements for entering into transversal reasoning (TR) with economists in succeeding chapters. Then the first question is answered by developing a systematic overview of Sacks' approach of *Torah veḥokmah,* a term that refers to an ongoing conversation between *Torah* (theology and philosophy) and *ḥokmah* (secular wisdom, including natural and social sciences). Particular attention is given to Sacks' interpretation of the narrative of the Exodus, because his understanding of hope is derived from this narrative. To answer the second question, the chapter shows that the Exodus as a narrative of hope provides a particular perspective on reality, accessible for all. This perspective has not only been the subject of an ongoing conversation within Judaism. The chapter highlights examples of earlier societal impacts of retelling the Exodus story. Contemporary debates argue directly or indirectly for such a retelling in times of climate change. The chapter concludes that the key ingredients of Sacks' understanding of hope lend themselves to address radical uncertainty: *emunah* (a form of trust), *chessed* (a form of love, including the institution of the covenant) and change of identity (including the institution of a public Sabbath).

Keywords: Jonathan Sacks, hope, *Torah veḥokmah,* Exodus, climate change, radical uncertainty

4.1   Introduction

The aim of this chapter is to answer the twofold question: What is the meaning and possible societal impact of Jonathan Sacks' understanding of hope?

Hasselaar, J.J., *Climate Change, Radical Uncertainty and Hope: Theology and Economics in Conversation.* Amsterdam: Amsterdam University Press, 2023
DOI 10.5117/9789048558476_CH04

The reason for raising this twofold question is, as indicated in section 3.6, to interpret radical uncertainty in the context of climate change through the lens of Sacks' understanding of hope. This will take the form of TR as presented in the following chapters. Answering the twofold question in this chapter demands extensive decoding of Sacks' understanding of hope, which differs significantly from our use of the word in everyday language. For Sacks, hope is not just an expectation, wish or emotion. When Sacks uses the concept of hope, he is giving a commentary on the Torah, especially the Exodus, and the Torah in turn gives a commentary on present reality. This understanding of hope orients us to the possibility of gradually starting something new and liberating in the midst of radical uncertainty.

To decode Sacks' understanding of hope, I develop a systematic overview of Sacks' approach of *Torah veḥokmah* or Torah and *ḥokmah*.[1] *Torah veḥokmah* refers to an ongoing interaction between Torah (theology and philosophy) and *ḥokmah* (secular wisdom, including natural and social sciences). Within *Torah veḥokmah* particular attention is given to Sacks' interpretation of the narrative of the Exodus. The reason for this is that Sacks' understanding of hope is derived from this narrative. I proceed then to highlight key ingredients of Sacks' understanding of hope as a way to address radical uncertainty, namely *emunah* (a special kind of trust), *chessed* (a special kind of love), a change of identity, and the related institutions of covenant and Sabbath. Then I explain that for Sacks the biblical God represents a particular view on reality. I discuss briefly examples of earlier societal impacts of this view and contemporary debates in climate change that directly or indirectly argue for adopting such a view when addressing climate change.

The systematic overview of Sacks' *Torah veḥokmah* that I develop in this chapter is based on an extensive study of the literature, largely the study of Sacks' own work. My intention here is not to give an overview of his complete work. In this study we have the central question of radical uncertainty. This interest will drive my engagement with Sacks and will, no doubt, shape my reading of Sacks. This study of the literature has both risks and advantages. Its main risk is that it puts together passages from various works of Sacks without doing full justice to differences in genre, context or audience, which may affect their meaning. Another risk is that in some work concepts like *Torah veḥokmah*, hope, radical uncertainty and their cognates are sometimes the main focus, but they can also be mentioned by

---

1   In this study the Hebrew word *ḥokmah* is also written as *chokhmah* when Sacks' own work is cited.

Sacks in passing, when the main concern of Sacks is elsewhere. This may affect the meaning of the concepts. The main advantage of this study is that it provides a systematic overview of Sacks' understanding of hope, so that it can be used in the following chapters with regard to radical uncertainty in the context of climate change and brought into interaction with economics.

4.2   A postfoundational approach to theology

To allow for successful TR in the chapters 5 through 8, Sacks' theological contribution should potentially meet the four key requirements of van Huyssteen's postfoundational approach (section 3.3). In the following I will assess whether Sacks' work can be constructed as a postfoundational approach to theology:

(1) *Embeddedness of rationality*. This characteristic recognizes the contextuality and the embeddedness of all human reflection in human culture, and therefore in specific scientific and confessional traditions.

Sacks has a background in the research traditions of philosophy and theology (Judaic studies). It was only at the end of his study of philosophy that Sacks came to realize the embeddedness of philosophy. He had almost given up philosophy, because "... British philosophy had reached a dead end. It was linguistic, it was dry... All it told you was what words meant. And it was also tone deaf to the history of what words mean" (Tirosh-Samuelson & Hughes, 2013, p. 106). It was Alasdair MacIntyre's book *After Virtue* (1981) that reignited Sacks' interest in philosophy. "He gave philosophy back its history, and that was tremendously liberating. The return to history gave philosophy its credibility, its depth, and its substance" (Tirosh-Samuelson & Hughes, 2013, p. 106). MacIntyre showed Sacks that philosophy is a series of traditions. Sacks recognised instantly where this applied to Judaism as well. (Tirosh-Samuelson & Hughes, 2013, p. 106) Sacks' work is embedded in Orthodox Judaism, one of the main traditions within in Judaism.

Sacks thus recognizes the embeddedness of rationality.

(2) *Interpreting reality in all forms of inquiry*. This characteristic points to the interpretation of reality as common ground of rationality in all theology and science.

Sacks distinguishes two complementary epistemologies, Torah and *ḥokmah*. For Sacks, Torah (theology) and *ḥokmah* (natural and social sciences) represent two domains of knowing that uncover different dimensions of reality. He considers these two domains of interpreting reality as complementary in creating a fuller understanding of reality. (Sacks, 2012, p. 291)

Sacks thus recognizes the interpretation of reality as common ground in all forms of rationality.

(3) *Critical reflection.* This characteristic refers to a critical investigation of one's own embeddedness by the participant of an interdisciplinary interaction, embeddedness for example in a certain research tradition or a confessional tradition.

Sacks' work provides autobiographical data which refer to a critical reflection on his own assumptions, those of his community (religion) and research tradition (theology). I give one example of each. First, Sacks credits the philosopher and atheist Bernard Williams, his doctoral supervisor, for challenging him to articulate the rationality of his religious belief. According to Sacks, Williams rightly argued that if you have to believe something that is impossible, "… once you start down this road, there is no way of distinguishing between holy nonsense and unholy nonsense. If a belief cannot be stated coherently, then what is it to believe in it?" (Sacks, 2012, p. 82). Second, Sacks is critical of traditional commentaries within Judaism, which often concentrate on the detail, the fragment of a text in isolation. Sacks tries to explain the biblical text in an intertextual setting and the wider contexts of ideas. (Sacks, 2009a, p. 3) Third, Sacks argues against an interpretation of religion that sees God as relieving people of responsibility. For Sacks, God is a teacher instructing people how to exercise responsibility.

Sacks thus has critically investigated his own embeddedness.

(4) *Problem solving.* This characteristic of a postfoundational approach considers problem solving the most central and defining activity of all research traditions.

At the heart of Sacks' work is the quest for problem-solving. To put it in his own words: "I philosophize because I need to solve a problem" (Tirosh-Samuelson & Hughes, 2013, p. 122). In several of his writings Sacks contributes explicitly to problem solving, in Hebrew *Tikkun Olam* (repairing the world). One can refer here to his bestseller *The Dignity of Difference* (2002, 2011), which tries to make room in society for ethnic and religious differences. One can also refer to his *The Home We Build Together* (2007), in which Sacks offers a new paradigm of 'integrated diversity' for British citizenship. In *Not in God's Name* (2015) Sacks explores the roots of violence and its relationship to Judaism, Christianity and Islam. He argues that these religions should become part of the solution, living together as sisters and brothers. Finally, Sacks argues in *Morality* (2021) that Western societies have outsourced morality to the markets and the state. In the book he challenges society to rebuild our common moral foundation.

Sacks thus considers problem solving the key activity of his work.

To conclude this section, I have shown above that Sacks' work displays the four characteristics of van Huyssteen's postfoundational approach. Therefore, Sacks can be regarded as employing a postfoundational approach to theology that allows him to enter into TR with economists in chapters 5 through 8. In the following, I develop a systematic overview of Sacks' *Torah veḥokmah*.

4.3 Developing a middle ground: *Torah veḥokmah*

In his book *Future Tense* Sacks describes a crisis of Jewish continuity. "Jews are either engaging with the world and losing their Jewish identity or preserving their identity at the cost of disengaging from the world" (Sacks, 2009b, p. 2). Sacks describes this first position as assimilation and the second one as segregation. Assimilation seeks to merge into society. Segregation is an inward turn. Sacks argues that both positions have good historical reasons. In the nineteenth and twentieth centuries assimilation made sense in a world of anti-Semitism. Segregation made sense after the Holocaust when the tradition in Eastern Europe had been almost entirely obliterated. But according to Sacks Judaism lives today in different realities. "*The two dominant strands in the Jewish world today are fighting the battles of the past, not those of the future*" (Sacks, 2013a, p. 20).

Jonathan Sacks is convinced that the challenge of today is to turn outward and to engage with the world. Therefore he seeks a middle ground between the two extreme positions of engaging with the world and losing one's identity or preserving that identity at the cost of disengagement with the world. He has called this middle ground *Torah veḥokmah*. *Torah veḥokmah* is about engaging with the world and contributing to its common good, while at the same time proudly maintaining one's own particularity and a self-understanding expressed in one's own terms.

According to Sacks, there is much overlap between his *Torah veḥokmah* and the outlook of some earlier Orthodox thinkers, like Rabbi Samson Raphael Hirsch and Rabbi Norman Lamm:

> In nineteenth century Germany the favored phrase among disciples of Rabbi Samson Raphael Hirsch was *Torah im derekh eretz*, "Torah and general culture." In the United States, the preferred principle was *Torah umada*, "Torah and science." Neither of these rubrics is particularly helpful. *Torah im derekh eretz* is a quotation from the teachings of Rabban Gamliel III (third century CE), who used it to mean something else, "Torah together with a worldly occupation." *Torah umada* is a modern coinage

with no source in tradition. *Ḥokhma*, by contrast, is a biblical category. One book, Proverbs, is devoted to it, and several others – notably Job and Ecclesiastes – belong to what is generally known as the "wisdom literature." *Ḥokhma* is human wisdom as such: the universals of mankind's intellectual quest. (Sacks, 2013b, p. 8)

Sacks prefers the term *Torah veḥokmah*, because both *Torah* and *chokmah* are biblical categories. He argues that in the Hebrew Bible there is a basic duality in relating to the world, expressed in two epistemologies or forms of knowledge, *Torah* and *ḥokmah*. Because of the tendency in Judaism to disengage *Torah* and *ḥokmah*, especially since the nineteenth century, Sacks considers his *Torah veḥokmah* as studying, teaching and writing Torah in an 'old-new way'.

4.4   The meaning of *Torah veḥokmah*

What does Sacks exactly mean by *Torah veḥokmah*? Sacks regularly uses an ideal type analysis to define *Torah* and *ḥokmah*. Take for example the following quotation:

> *Chokhmah* is the truth we discover; Torah is the truth we inherit. *Chokhmah* is the universal heritage of humankind; Torah is the specific heritage of Israel. *Chokmah* is what we attain by being in the image of God; Torah is what guides Jews as the people of God. *Chockmah* is acquired by seeing and reasoning; Torah is received by listening and responding. *Chokmah* tells us what is; Torah tells us what ought to be. *Chokhmah* is about facts; Torah is about commands. *Chokmah* yields descriptive, scientific laws; Torah yields prescriptive, behavioural laws. *Chokhmah* is about creation; Torah about revelation. (Sacks, 2009b, p. 221)

Torah here is associated with terms like heritage of Israel, what ought to be and prescriptive laws. *Chokhmah* or *ḥokmah* refers to facts as well as descriptive and scientific laws. Sacks defines *chokhma* as secular wisdom, including natural and social sciences (Sacks, 2016a, p. xxxix). He considers *chokhma* not only a biblical category. He relates it strongly to ancient Greece. "The West owes its development to two cultures, ancient Greece and ancient Israel...They were the first two cultures to make the break with myth, but they did so in different ways, the Greeks by philosophy and reason, the Jews by monotheism and revelation" (Sacks, 2012, p. 58).

Sacks uses Jerome Brunner's book *Actual Minds, Possible Worlds* (1986), to argue that *Torah* is about narrative and *chokhma* about argument. Narrative can kindle the awareness that reality could have been and still can be and become otherwise. Therefore it is possible to act anew and differently in the present. Narratives can offer a perspective of possible worlds we would or wouldn't like to inhabit. Argument comes together with objective knowledge, scientific detachment, analysis and verifiable truths. "You can test an argument. You cannot test a story, but it can still convey powerful and revelatory truths" (Sacks, 2012, p. 53). I return to the narrative in section 3.5.

In his work Sacks uses a kind of ideal type analysis as an analytical tool to describe what he considers the essential features of phenomenon. For Sacks the ideal type analysis is useful when it comes to describe distinctive features of the epistemology of Torah and science. In this paragraph I explain this usefulness at some length, before mentioning some disadvantages in the next paragraph. In the view of Sacks, Jewish philosophy in the past had conformed too closely to Western philosophy. In interaction with modernity and the social processes in its wake, the meanings of many of the key terms of Judaism have been lost or forgotten (Tirosh-Samuelson & Hughes, 2013, p. 8). The result was that Jewish philosophy failed to express what was unique to Judaism (Sacks, 2012, p. 90). The God of the Hebrew Bible became confused with a Greek concept of God:

> Words like "knowledge" and "truth" do not mean in Judaism what they mean for Plato and Aristotle. Da'at [*sic*] (knowledge) in the biblical Hebrew does not mean detached, clear-sighted cognition. It means intimacy, physical and emotional. (Tirosh-Samuelson & Hughes, 2013, p. 117)

Sacks credits Bernard Williams for clarifying and strengthening Sacks' understanding of the difference between the Jewish and the Greek conception of God. Williams said that believers were called to believe two things that cannot be true at the same time. Williams referred to Christianity, but for Sacks, the same is true for Judaism. Williams said it cannot be true that God is on the one hand eternal, unchangeable and beyond time and on the other hand is involved in history. Bernard Williams considered this a contradiction within faith. However, Sacks recognized it as a contradiction between the Jewish and the Greek conception of God. "The changeless, unmoved mover was the God of Plato and Aristotle. The God of history was the God of Abraham. They simply did not belong together" (Sacks, 2012, p. 83). Sacks' ideal type analysis is thus useful to make a clear epistemological distinction between a Jewish and Greek conception of God.

Sacks' ideal type analysis also has some disadvantages. A first disadvantage is that it does not do full justice to the types involved. In chapter 6 I will argue that when it comes to Torah and economics, a richer account of economics is needed. But a richer account of the Greek tradition is also possible. For example, ancient Greece is not only about what Sacks calls *chokhma*. Teresa Morgan argues in her *Roman Faith and Christian Faith* that trust for the Greeks and Romans was considered a virtue as well. This virtue was perceived to be basic to family, friendships and more broadly to society as a whole. Nevertheless, it was not the core of Greek and Roman religiosity. (Morgan, 2015, p. 306) A second disadvantage of this ideal type analysis is that it *contrasts* two types in order to create clarity. If, for example, Torah and economics are understood in terms of a contrast, it may be hard, if not impossible, to create an interaction on the issue of radical uncertainty in the context of climate change. These two criticisms of his ideal type analysis are acknowledged by Sacks himself when he argues that, although the distinctions remain useful, he actually embraces both sides of the dichotomies he makes (Sacks, 2012, p. 10). Following the lead of the great medieval Jewish philosophers, especially Maimonides, Sacks is convinced that Torah (religion) and secular wisdom (science) need one another. In his view religion and science uncover dimensions of reality that are compatible with another. Science and religion are "... two essential perspectives that allow us to see the universe in its three-dimensional depth" (Sacks 2012, p. 2).

In chapter 5 I come back to *chokhma*, which will then be limited to economics. In the remainder of this chapter I focus on Torah and its distinctive features. This means we now have to enter the book of Torah.

4.5   Torah

For Sacks, to understand the book of Torah, the first five books of the Hebrew Bible, one has to know to which genre it belongs. Sacks stresses that Torah is not about history, legend, chronicle or myth, even though it includes all that. Nor does Torah answer the question: how did the universe come into being? Torah should be understood as instruction, teaching or guidance. For Sacks, "one of the key questions the Torah addresses is: how do we create associations that honour both self and the other, 'I' and 'Thou'?" (Sacks, 2005, p. 53). According to Sacks the focus of Torah is on normative questions: What should one do? How should one live? What kind of person should one strive to become? "Torah is a commentary on life, and life is a commentary on Torah. Together they constitute a conversation, each shedding light on the other. The Torah is a book not only to be read but to be lived" (Sacks, 2009a, p. 2).

Sacks explains why the Torah is not just a book of history, but one that remains relevant and incisive for our time. Essential is the idea of dual Torah, which consists of the Written Torah (the Mosaic books) and the Oral Torah (the ongoing work of commentary and application). Sacks refers to the Written Torah with the notion of Torah *min hashamayim*, which means 'Torah from heaven'. He defines this as 'what the text meant then' (*peshat*). *Midrash* is for Sacks what the text means now. "The susceptibility of Torah to new interpretation in every generation derives from our belief that, through its words, God is communicating with us, here, now" (Sacks, 2010, p. 263). Therefore, the idea of 'Torah from heaven' is far more than a belief about the origin of a text. It reverses the idea of people being the author of their own texts. It suggests that the text was the author of the people.

In line with this understanding of Torah, Sacks began in 2004 a weekly commentary on Torah readings in the publication, *Covenant and Conversation*. Covenant and Conversation is in essence what Torah learning is for Sacks:

> The *text* of Torah is our covenant with God... The *interpretation* of this text has been the subject of an ongoing conversation for as long as Jews have studied the divine word, a conversation that began at Sinai thirty-three centuries ago and has not ceased since. Every age has added its commentaries, and so must ours. Participating in that conversation is a major part of what it is to be a Jew. For we are the people who never stopped learning the Book of Life, our most precious gift from the God of life. (Sacks, 2009a, p. 3)

Sacks' commentary on Torah is a voice in a long tradition. This tradition of a new interpretation in every generation becomes clearly visible in, for example, the *Miqra'ot Gedolot*, a commentary used by Sacks. It was first published around 500 years ago and is known as the Rabbinic Bible. A page of this Rabbinic Bible consists of the Hebrew biblical text (the Masorah text), one or more Aramaic translations of the text, and the most prominent commentaries on the text from the medieval period—Rashi (1040-1105, Northern France); Rashbam, Rashi's grandson (ca. 1085-ca. 1174, Northern France); Ibn Ezra (1089-1164, lived in Muslim Spain for 50 years and spent the rest of his days wandering through Christian Europe); Nahmanides, also known as 'Ramban' (1195-1270, born in Spain and died in Israel)—often accompanied by explanatory notes. In this Rabbinic Bible the reader is encouraged to join the conversation.

Figure 4.1   A page of the *Miqra'ot Gedolot*[2]

NJPS   saying, "Every boy that is born you shall throw into the Nile, but let every girl live."

OJPS   people, saying: "Every son that is born ye shall cast into the river, and every daughter ye shall save alive."

2   A certain man of the house of Levi went and married a Levite woman. ²The woman conceived and bore a son; and when she saw how beautiful he was, she

לְכָל־עַמּוֹ לֵאמֹר כָּל־הַבֵּן הַיִּלּוֹד הַיְאֹרָה תַּשְׁלִיכֻהוּ וְכָל־הַבַּת תְּחַיּוּן : ס

בַ וַיֵּלֶךְ אִישׁ מִבֵּית לֵוִי וַיִּקַּח אֶת־בַּת־ לֵוִי : ²וַתַּהַר הָאִשָּׁה וַתֵּלֶד בֵּן וַתֵּרֶא אֹתוֹ

2   And there went a man of the house of Levi, and took to wife a daughter of Levi. ²And the woman conceived, and bore a son; and when she saw him that he was a

RASHI   was born today. We do not know whether he is an Egyptian or an Israelite. But we can see that his end will come by means of water." So Pharaoh issued his decree that very day, against the Egyptians as well as against the Israelites. Read carefully! It does not say, "every boy that is born *to* the Hebrews," but "every boy that is born." What the astrologers did not understand was that the "waters" through which Moses would come to harm were the waters of Meribah. [C]

2:1 Married a Levite woman.   Rather, "took the daughter of Levi." He had separated from her in order not to conceive children who would then fall victim to Pharaoh's decree. Now he brought her back and "took" her to wife a second time. She was even turned back into a young woman, though she was 130 at the time. For she had been born on the journey down to Egypt, just as they arrived, and the Israelites were in Egypt for 210 years. Since Moses was 80 when they left, she must have been 130 when she got pregnant with him. But she also became young again, for the text calls her "daughter" of Levi. [D]

2 How beautiful he was.   When he was born, the whole house filled with light. [E]

[C]   For striking the rock there to get water, Moses is punished by not being allowed to live long enough to cross into the land of Israel. See Num. 20:1–13 and Deut. 32:50–51.   [D]   When the descendants of Jacob who came down to Egypt are listed in the book of Numbers, Jochebed is included with the note that she "was born to Levi in Egypt" (Num. 26:59), having presumably been conceived in Canaan or on the journey down. The fact that Moses has older siblings implies that Amram and Jochebed had already been married before the marriage described in 2:1.   [E]   Rashi's source, B. Sotah 12a, is based on the resemblance of our verse—literally, "She saw him, that he was good"—to Gen. 1:4, "God saw the light, that it was good."

NAHMANIDES   is quite plentiful in Egypt. The Israelites would get them from those who caught them at the king's order, and would get cucumbers and melons from the gardens, "with no one to molest them" (Judg. 18:7). For it was the king's command. But our Sages say that they were slaves to the kings themselves, not to the subjects of the kings. If so, then **the Egyptians** who **imposed upon** them were Pharaoh's taskmasters.

2:1 A certain man of the house of Levi went.   Our Sages said that he "went" to get her back after taking his daughter's advice to end their separation (see below). Ibn Ezra says that the Jews lived in many different cities, and he "went" from his own city to hers in order to marry her. But what point would there be for the text to mention this? In my opinion, the text is emphasizing that he ignored the danger posed by Pharaoh's decree and got married with the intention of having children. For the text uses the expression "went and did" about everyone who bestirs himself to do some new action: e.g., "Reuben *went* and lay with Bilhah" (Gen. 35:22); "he *went* and married Gomer" (Hosea 1:1). This man too "went" and **married a Levite woman**. The text does not mention either of their names, because if it did so it would have had to give their entire genealogies right back to Levi. But at this point, in a hurry to get to the birth of Israel's savior, the text wished to be brief. Afterward, in 6:14–25, the text will give the complete genealogy of Reuben and Simeon in order to get down to Levi and to the parents of Moses. According to the

RASHBAM   2:1 A certain man of the house of Levi.   It was Amram. **Married** Jochebed, **a Levite woman.** Literally, with OJPS, "a daughter of Levi"; we know from Num. 26:59 that she "was born to Levi in Egypt." He married her some years before the birth of Moses. For according to 7:7, Aaron was 83 and Moses was 80 when they spoke to Pharaoh, making Aaron, their first child, three years older than his younger brother.

2 The woman conceived   at the time of Pharaoh's decree about casting the boys into the Nile **and bore a son; and when she saw how beautiful he was, she hid him.**   One who explains this to mean that she hid him *because* she saw he was beautiful is a liar. For the mothers of all newborns have maternal instincts toward them. So "saw" must be explained as we explained it in Gen. 1:31, "God saw all that He had made, and found it very good." He looked at all He had made and at all the actions He had performed to see whether any of them needed repair. It turned out that everything was fine and in good repair. The same applies here. Moses was presumably born at the end of six months—just as Samuel was

IBN EZRA   2:1 Went.   Apparently she lived in another city. All the Israelites lived in Rameses, but there were a number of different cities there. **A Levite woman.** Literally, with OJPS, "a daughter of Levi" the son of Jacob. This is clear from Num. 26:59, where she is referred to as "Jochebed daughter of Levi, who was born to Levi in Egypt." Thus she is the sister of Kohath. That is why 6:20, naming her husband Amram, calls her "his father's sister." This demonstrates that those who say inbreeding

produces defective offspring are wrong; the prohibitions against incest are not for practical reasons, but to make Israel a holy people. [F]

2 The woman conceived.   We know that Aaron was older than Moses. This passage does not mention him because nothing happened to him in his youth, as it did to Moses. A similar phenomenon is found in 2 Sam. 12:24, where Solomon appears to be David's first living child; yet, according to 2 Sam. 5:14, Shammua, Shobab, and Nathan had already been born to him. Miriam, too, was older; our ancestral tradition identifies her with Puah, the midwife, and v. 4 says explicitly that Moses' sister stationed herself to watch over him. Ben Zuta reads Num. 26:59, "she bore ... Aaron and Moses and their sister Miriam," as implying that Miriam was the youngest; but this

[F]   Lev. 18:12 prohibits sex with the sister of one's father. But the examples of Aaron, Miriam, and Moses show that the reason for the prohibition is not that the children will be defective.

ADDITIONAL COMMENTS   appropriate reward for giving life, for the mark of a complete leader is that he provides for the welfare of those whom he leads (Gersonides).

22 Let every girl live.   Pharaoh assumed the girls would marry Egyptians and be assimilated (Gersonides).

2:1 A Levite woman.   The tradition quoted by Rashi says that Jochebed was 130 when Moses was born. My own calculations, according to the rabbinic assumption that she was born just as the sons of Jacob entered Egypt, make her 145. In either case, this would be a greater miracle than happened to Sarah; one would think the Torah would have mentioned it. But the whole assumption is the height of absurdity. If she was born at the end of Levi's life, long after he arrived in Egypt, she would have been 58 at Moses' birth, which is a good deal less strange (Gersonides).

2 She hid him for three months.   The Egyptians did not realize she was pregnant for three months, at which point they began to

The typography of the *Miqra'ot Gedolot* above already shows how the Judaic tradition combines here an inexhaustible creativity with received inheritance from earlier generations. In itself a typography of the Talmud and the *Miqra'ot Gedolot* is image and map of the process of tradition (Poorthuis, 1992, p. 2). Using this typography, the commentary of Sacks on Torah can be seen as a contemporary voice in an enduring conversation. At the same time, Sacks argues that he differs from many traditional commentaries, which often concentrate on the detail, the fragment of a text in isolation. According to Sacks, they look at the biblical texts through a microscope. Sacks tries to look through a telescope, to see "the larger picture and its place in the constellation of concepts that make Judaism so compelling a picture of the universe and our place within it" (Sacks, 2009a, p. 3). Sacks tries to explain the biblical text in an intertextual setting and the wider contexts of ideas, for example the concept of the stranger (Sacks, 2015c, p. 187).

4.6 Torah and the narrative

A characteristic of Torah, for Sacks, is that it conveys its truths through narratives (Sacks, 2012, p. 54). Sacks considers three characteristics of storytelling essential for Torah (Sacks, 2009a, pp. 7-8):

(1) *A story is universal.* This universality of a story has to be understood against the background that for Sacks Judaism is about the creation of a society in which everyone has access to religious knowledge. Hence the importance of stories which everyone can understand. The Torah is a book written for all and therefore it is written in the mode of a story, so that everybody, even children, have access to it.

(2) *A story contains several levels.* Stories can be understood by everyone, but not by all on the same level. Each of the stories in Genesis and Exodus has layer upon layer of meaning and significance, which one can only grasp after repeated readings. That says something significant about the Torah's view of human knowledge: the truths of the human condition are simply too deep to be understood at once and on the surface. Only stories have this depth, this ambiguity, this multiplicity of meanings.

(3) *Only stories adequately reflect what it is to be free human beings.* "Our fate does not lie in the stars, nor in the human genome, or in any other form of determinism. We become what we choose to be. Therefore, we don't know what will happen next... and the best way of showing this is by way of stories, in all of which the outcome is in doubt" (Sacks, 2009a, 8). This element of

openness, not knowing what will happen next, reflects a central theme of Genesis and Exodus: God's gift of freedom to humanity.

According to Sacks, the Torah did adopt a very specific mode of storytelling, to which Sacks refers as the 'concealed counter-narrative' (Sacks, 2015a, p. 5). What does this mean? First, the notion of 'concealed' means that each narrative has a layer under the surface. The meaning and significance of this layer can only be grasped by closely reading or listening. Second, the notion 'counter' means that the layer below the surface is not only concealed. It usually also turns out to be radically different from the layer on the surface. The layer under the surface often moves in the opposite direction. Hence the term '*counter*-narrative' (my emphasis). Following clues present in the biblical text itself, one will discover an unexpected counter-narrative.

> The Torah signals this by giving us clues, discrepancies in the text, not obvious enough to be noticed at first glance but sufficient to make the thoughtful reader go back and read the text again and discover that the real story the Torah is telling us is richer and more complex than we first thought. (Sacks, 2015a, p. 5)

To conclude, in the last two sections I have discussed Sacks' interpretation of Torah. He accentuates that Torah has adopted a mode of storytelling, called a concealed counter-narrative, in order to gain counter-intuitive knowledge about the human condition. In the next section I limit myself to Sacks' interpretation of the concealed counter-narrative in the book of Exodus.

4.7   The Exodus

In Sacks' view, many readers may think that the narrative of the Exodus is primarily about the divine intervention liberating the Israelites by ten plagues from slavery in Egypt. God can then be seen as an external force or energy that delivers a people from evil or radical uncertainty. For Sacks, such a reading misses the complete meaning of the narrative. Sacks insists that, in order to understand the Exodus, it is critical to delve beneath the surface of the biblical text itself. There is a second layer which tells another story. Sacks shows that the Exodus contains a number of double narratives, whose significance becomes clear when we put them together (Sacks, 2010, p. 15):

1. *There are two battles*, one immediately before, the other immediately after the crossing of the Reed Sea, the first against Pharaoh and his chariots, the second against the Amalekites.
2. *There are two sets of stone tablets recording the revelation at Mount Sinai*, one before the episode of the Golden Calf (broken by Moses on his descent from the mountain), the second after the people have been forgiven for the Calf.
3. *There are two times that God is revealed in a cloud of glory*, once at Mount Sinai (24:15-18), the other, at the end of Exodus, in the Tabernacle (40:34-35).
4. *The Sinai covenant was declared twice*, once by God (20:1-14), the second time by Moses, reading from the book of the covenant he had written to record God's words (24:1-11).
5. *There are two accounts of the construction of the Tabernacle*, one before (25-30), the other (35-40) after the Golden Calf.

Sacks argues that in all these cases, the same shift of responsibility takes place. It is a movement from divine initiative to human endeavour. Exodus tells a double story. The first of the paired episodes tells about an act done by God alone. The second one involves human participation. In the first example the Israelites did not fight against the Egyptians, but they did fight against the Amalekites. In the second example, first Moses was passive, but then shared in the making of the second set of stone tablets. In each of the first of the paired episodes it is God who delivers the people by a set of miracles. In each of the second ones people are participating. Why this process from divine initiative to human endeavour?

To describe this process, Sacks uses two types of divine-human encounter drawn from Kabbala, Jewish mysticism, namely *itaruta de-leyah* (an awakening from above) and *itaruta de-letata* (an awakening from below) (Sacks, 2010, p. 272). The first term represents the divine intervention, e.g. the ten plagues in Egypt, the division of the Reed Sea and so on. Sacks writes that each of these supernatural events was an intrusion of God into the natural order:

> An "awakening from above" may change nature, but it does not, in and of itself, change human nature. In it, no human effort has been expended. Those to whom it happens are passive. While it lasts, it is overwhelming; but only while it lasts. Thereafter, people revert to what they were. An "awakening from below," by contrast, leaves a permanent mark. (Sacks, 2010, p. 272)

According to Sacks the transition of an awakening from above towards human responsibility is the underlying argument of the Exodus. If there is an overarching theme in the Hebrew Bible then it is this story of the transfer from divine initiative to human initiative (Sacks, 2005, p. 155). Humans are called to freedom by internalizing conflicting forms of interest. God wants humans to learn to fight their own battles, because only then can people change their identity and become liberated from an identity that holds them captive. Identity is seen by Sacks as the images people live by—images of themselves, others and the world. For Sacks, the journey of the Exodus is about individual and societal transformation of the identity people live by.

Sacks' understanding of hope, derived from the Exodus, means that people are not determined by their past. "There is a difference between 'is' and 'ought', between the world we observe and the world to which we aspire, and in aspiring begin to make" (Sacks, 1997, p. 266). For Sacks, Hope is not the same as optimism in the sense of a passive virtue that things will get better. Hope is expressed in a long journey in which people gradually learn how to take responsibility for making things better (Sacks, 2011, pp. 206-207).

4.8 Key ingredients of Sacks' understanding of hope

Sacks' understanding of hope, derived as it is from the Exodus, is of crucial importance for this study, because it offers several key ingredients to deal with radical uncertainty. Sacks describes the uncertainty inherent in the human condition as "... the constitutive uncertainty of our lives as we walk towards the undiscovered country called the future" (Sacks, 2012, p. 96). Sacks' reading provides the following ingredients to address radical uncertainty: the Hebrew word *emunah*, a certain type of trust, the Hebrew word *chessed*, a certain type of love (including the institution of the covenant) and change of identity (including the institution of the Sabbath).

4.8.1 *Emunah*

Emunah. Sacks considers *emunah* to be the human response to the human condition of radical uncertainty (Sacks 2012, p. 96). *Emunah* is often translated in a propositional way, for example belief or faith in God with a connotation of certainty or a set of creeds one has to belief in. Sacks considers it more appropriate to translate it with words like trust, faithfulness, loyalty and affirmation. The question is then: In what or whom do we have trust or show loyalty?

Emunah orientates us to trust in a certain perspective on, or epistemology of reality. Sacks describes this epistemology with the words 'philosophy of the human condition under the sovereignty of God'. What does that mean? In an effort to clarify this, I make use of a metaphor of 'the biblical God as light' given by the Czech Roman Catholic theologian Tomáš Halík (2016, p. 24).[3] Halík argues that the biblical God is not just in front of people, just as light is not in front of people. People cannot see the light, they can only see things in the light. When it comes to the biblical God, people cannot see God as an object that exists independently of human beings just as they cannot see light as an object. All that people can do, is see the world in the light of God.[4] In my view, this metaphor coincides with Sacks' approach to Torah as 'philosophy of the human condition under the sovereignty of God'. In Sacks' own words, "in the Bible, people talk to God, not about God" (Sacks, 2012, p. 72). God is here referred to as a focal point. God is seen as a point of reference from which to perceive and understand reality. In that sense, the biblical God is a possibility, a particular perspective on reality. For Sacks, the light thematized in the narrative of the Exodus is a light of hope. God as point of reference highlights a perspective of hope towards reality. It is a perspective already there, but to claim its potential one is invited to respond by learning to see the world in this light. Learning here is not understood as just cognitive knowledge. It is a kind of relational knowledge referred to as *da'at*, which includes intimacy and engagement and only comes into being in building relations.

Da'at can be described as a form of knowledge that comes into being between subjects. Therefore Sacks calls this form of knowledge intersubjective knowledge (Tirosh-Samuelson & Hughes, 2013, p. 117). Generally speaking, intersubjective knowledge is defined as a form of knowledge that creates shared meanings developed between people with similar experiences

---

3   Halík refers to Christianity when stating that since modernity "... The failure of taking into account the consequences of the longstanding gradual replacement of the biblical God with the Aristotelian concept of God proved fateful for the Catholic theology in the modern age" (Halík, 2016, p. 58). This critique is similar to the one raised by Sacks on the relation between modernity and the concept of the biblical God (section 4.4). Therefore, although Halík proceeds from a Christian point of view in his description of the biblical God, I consider his metaphor also appropriate for Sacks' understanding of the biblical God.

4   Within contemporary Christianity and theology, Rowan Williams has made a similar point by making the useful distinction between knowledge exercised *by* God and knowledge directed *towards* God. Williams argues that religious discourses have easily slipped into an assimilation between faith, or knowledge directed *by* God and the knowledge exercised *towards* God. (Williams, 2012, p. 19) For related understandings see also Pope Francis (Spadaro, 2013) and Toine van den Hoogen (2011, p. 130).

(Chandler & Munday, 2016). A closer look shows that several understandings of the concept of intersubjectivity can be found in the literature, for example in the work of Merleau-Ponty, Wittgenstein, Habermas, Buber and Harari. (Crossley, 1996, p. viii; Harari, 2017, pp. 167-168) Sacks describes intersubjective knowledge as a third form of knowing besides objective and subjective knowledge (Tirosh-Samuelson & Hughes, 2013, p. 117). In section 2.3 we defined objective knowledge as knowledge which is independent of an observer's viewpoint or bias. In section 2.5, subjective knowledge is defined as the knowledge an individual or a group of individuals has about a situation or phenomenon based on personal opinions, biases, and arbitrary preferences. Subjective knowledge is often seen in contrast to objective knowledge, insofar as the latter requires that the facts should be able to speak for themselves. Sacks is right to consider intersubjective knowledge as a third way of knowing, in the sense that it concerns the relation between subjects, rather than beyond them (objective knowledge) or within them (subjective knowledge) (Calhoun, 2002). The relation between subjects then, is inspired by *chessed*.

4.8.2 *Chessed*

Chessed. This Hebrew word is usually translated as 'kindness' or 'compassion', in Latin it becomes *charitas*. For Sacks, *chessed* is not love as kindness, emotion or passion, but a kind of love that sees oneself and others primarily as valuable in themselves, regardless of one's merits or one's use for others. *Chessed* considers all people as made in the image of God. Not only the neighbour, who is almost like me, but also the stranger, who is completely different from me. (Sacks, 2000, p. 128; Sacks, 2007, p. 180) As a consequence, *chessed* values plurality among people: it values the dignity of difference. Everyone has to contribute something unique to the shared project of which everyone is part. For Sacks, the consequence of relations of *chessed* is joy. The Hebrew word for joy is *simhah*. Considering oneself and the other as valuable in themselves, so that both can flourish, creates a shared joy, especially when that flourishing is threatened. This meaning of joy has strong connotations of liberation.

  Chessed is the face-to-face relationship, which can also be found in the work of other Jewish thinkers like Martin Buber and Emmanuel Levinas. A criticism directed towards thinkers like Buber and Levinas, rightly or wrongly, has been that "... their thought cannot be applied beyond the sphere of the individual to that of society" (Harris, Rynhold and Wright 2012, x). For Sacks the interest in civil and political society as a specifically religious concern is central to his work. For him, *chessed* is not only about the individual, but also a societal and economic driving force. The reason for this role lies in how *chessed* creates new relationships in which new societies can be built (Sacks, 2012, p. 164).

Chessed is here not just a universal kind of love. It is more complex than that. In the notion of *chessed*, there is a special affinity to particular relationships, for example kin or family. Sacks states that in these particular relationships, the first 'moral bonds' are formed. The particular love is not a form of narrowness, but a school of life. It is for this reason that Sacks points out the importance of the education of young people, the next generation. "As we grow, our sense of obligation widens to include friends, neighbors, community members, and fellow citizens" (Sacks, 2016b, p. xxx).

Sacks' understanding of *chessed* is not a naïve invitation to a better world in the midst of radical uncertainty. His interpretation of the Exodus is critical of the superficial use of *chessed*, given that *chessed* is constantly in danger of being undermined by pure self-interest, fear, doubt, rebellions, false turns and so on. *Chessed* can never be taken for granted. It can develop and degrade. For this reason Sacks highlights the importance of two institutions to support *chessed*, namely the institutions of covenant and Sabbath. Here I focus on the covenant. I will return shortly to the Sabbath.

Covenant. The covenant of the Exodus has several characteristics. I mention two characteristics that are of particular value when it comes to radical uncertainty.

(1) *The covenant is an exchange of promises.* The covenant enters into being when two or more parties voluntarily promise to take responsibility for a shared future, the common good (Sacks, 2009b, 164). The covenant of the Exodus is not primarily a top-down treaty between leaders or governments. The covenant is made between people, from the bottom up.

(2) *The covenant values the dignity of difference or the plurality among people.* Each participant becomes part of the covenant on his or her own terms. As a consequence, to be part of the same covenant does not mean that everybody agrees with one another. A covenant is an argumentative association; it does not seek the affirmation of one position, but stimulates opposition as a way to open the identities of the ones involved in order to create a new and common identity. What the members of a covenantal society share is a future-oriented responsibility. "In the short term, our desires and needs may clash; but the very realization that difference is a source of blessing leads us to seek mediation, conflict resolution, conciliation and peace – the peace that is predicated on diversity, not on uniformity." (Sacks, 2011, p. 203).

4.8.3   A change of identity

A change of identity. Sacks assumes that there are two kinds of identity in
the Exodus. Identity refers to who people are, i.e. the images people live
by—images of themselves, others and the world. The first is referred to
with the Hebrew word *am.* This is an identity based on a shared history.
Individuals feel bound to one another because they share, for example,
the same past, the same ethnic origin or the same suffering, like slavery in
Egypt. They are, as Sacks puts it, a community of fate. The second potential
form of identity he refers to with the Hebrew word *edah.* This is an identity
based on where a people are going; it is a shared vision of the future that
includes all involved. In this case people are defined by the social order
they are called on to create. Sacks identifies this society as a community
of faith. The driving force behind a change of identity from *am* to *edah* is
chessed. Chessed calls for an opening up of one's identity and learning to
see oneself and the other, especially the one not like me, as valuable in
themselves, regardless of merits or use for others. In the Exodus, the new
identity is expressed in the ten words or principles of the covenant, called
by some the Ten Commandments, and easily understood by everybody,
including the children. Even when the people have actively adopted a new
identity, the ten words are accompanied by the memory that 'Remember
that you were slaves in Egypt'. The reason for this call to remember is
to ensure that the covenant remains open and does not become a new,
settled, status quo. That openness to a yet-to-be-disclosed is evident in the
injunction: 'do not harm the stranger because you were once where he is
now. See the world from his perspective because it is where your ancestors
stood' (Sacks, 2015c, p. 184).

The Exodus is the journey of the Israelites from Egypt to the promised
land. Literally speaking, it is a journey of a few days. However, for Sacks,
there is no short cut of a few days to the promised land. Why not? The
promised land stands for a free society, one that will be the opposite of the
slavery in Egypt. Sacks refers to the 12th-century Jewish thinker Moses
Maimonides to explain the need for time in periods of transition. It takes
time to change the identity or images people live by. Therefore, it is impossible for the Israelites to abandon in a few days everything that they have
been accustomed to in Egypt, especially their own identity as slaves. Sacks
appropriates Maimonides' assertion that God wanted humans to abolish
slavery. God cannot, or chooses not to, change human nature. People must
abolish slavery by their own choice, if they are to be free at all. As a result,
a journey of a few days takes 40 years (Sacks, 2005, p. 77).

Sacks refers to Maimonides, who points to the fact that during the 40 years in the wilderness another generation grew up that had not been accustomed to degradation and slavery. Therefore it was no accident that the generation that left Egypt was not the generation that entered the promised land. "It takes a generation born in freedom to build a society of freedom" (Sacks, 2010, p. 100). Therefore in Sacks' interpretation, education, especially of the next generation, is crucial when it comes to radical uncertainty.

Sacks' interpretation presents the narrative of the Exodus as a transitional pathway in which the images or identity people live by change only gradually. Sacks calls this 'a redemption of small steps'. The emphasis of the Exodus is not on the promised land, but on the way to it. The focus is on the future tense between the 'yet' of the Promised Land and the 'not-yet' of the present. However, in order not to lose one's way in times of transition, the key to the process is an institution called Sabbath, not as a religious institution, but one for all involved in the transition.

Sabbath. The key to the transitional pathway is the Sabbath. Above we have seen that God cannot or chooses not to change human nature. However, the narrative of the Exodus provides a very specific architecture to support decision-making in periods of transition. The covenant above is one element of the architecture, the ritual of the Sabbath is even more important. In the narrative of the Exodus the Sabbath signals that slavery is wrong, but that it has to be abolished by the people themselves, in their own time and through their own understanding. After Egypt slavery was changed from an ontological condition to a temporary circumstance. "The most powerful force tending in this direction was the Sabbath" (Sacks, 2010, p. 331).

Sacks' interpretation of the Exodus as a narrative about individual and societal transformation has implications for our understanding of the Sabbath. The Sabbath is then not just a religious institution, but also and essentially a 'political' institution (Sacks, 2000, p. 136). The case could be made for it being a public rather a political institution: the Sabbath is not about politics in particular but, rather, the wider public sphere. The Sabbath here is an institution for all involved. Therefore, I will use the phrase 'public Sabbath' instead of 'political Sabbath'. The way in which Sacks understands the Sabbath possesses four meanings which are of relevance for the problems posed by the question of radical uncertainty.

(1) *The Sabbath is Utopia Now.* After Egypt, the first mark of the free people of Israel was the installation of the Sabbath. After Egypt, no Israelite was allowed to see herself/himself any longer as a slave. They might have been reduced to slavery for a period of time, but this was a passing plight,

not an identity. The Sabbath became the antithesis of Egypt, the utopia in the present, presenting a way of life that people may yet barely glimpse. At the Sabbath people celebrate closeness to God and, by doing so, reveal and receive connectivity with oneself, the other, and—in all of that—with God. The Sabbath is a rehearsed utopia that breaks into the present, upending its logic and defying its priorities. Sacks calls this 'Utopia Now' (Sacks, 2010, p. 16). The Sabbath is practising, contemplating and enacting the promised land of freedom, while being on the way.

(2) *The Sabbath is a neutral space.* Although the Sabbath is public, it is free of one dominant ideology. The reason for this is that it orients people to a mystery greater than their own beliefs and ideology. The Sabbath stimulates putting oneself in the position of the other. It promotes a willingness to listen respectfully to those with whom one disagrees. The idea of neutral spaces is that they bridge differences. They bring people together who would not otherwise meet (Sacks, 2007, p. 190). What is more, the Sabbath values the dignity of differences. The reason for this is that only the experience of sharing a common world with others who look at it from different perspectives can make people aware of their own identity and open up to the possibility of developing an alternative, new and common identity. Without others with whom one disagrees, people are limited to their own perspective, in which only their own feelings, wants and desires have reality.

(3) *The Sabbath practices of chessed.* Relations of *chessed* can never be taken for granted, because they are never untouched by for example fear, doubt or scepticism. The relations have room to develop, but also to degrade. The Sabbath is what it literally means: 'to stop' daily life, not out of laziness, but in order to practice ways to protect, strengthen and reset relations of *chessed*. At the Sabbath, people can become awakened, inspired and creative again by *chessed,* the driving force towards a new inclusive identity.

(4) *The Sabbath is an embodied truth.* The Sabbath brings in the power of symbol, music, sharing, eating together, memory, narrative, poetry, prayer, art and imagination in order to shape identity and to refer to realities that cannot be expressed in reflections and arguments. "It is one thing to have an abstract conception of ecological responsibility, another to celebrate the Sabbath weekly ... Prayer, ritual and narrative are ways to shape what De Tocqueville called the 'habits of the heart'. They form character, create behavioural dispositions and educate us in patterns of self-restraint" (Sacks, 2011, p. 171).

Above we have seen that it takes time to change the identity or images people live by. Sacks' derives his insight about the time people need to change their identity, or the images they live by, from the Exodus—because this story presents us with people of flesh and blood. There are no perfect characters in the Bible. Everybody tries, fails, stands up, resets and tries again. This makes it clear that people will never fully complete their tasks. Therefore the Sabbath is not simply a pause that refreshes, but a regular and crucial pause that transforms.

To sum up, in this section I have explored the key ingredients which are used in Sacks' interpretation of the Exodus to address radical uncertainty: *emunah, chessed,* (including covenant) and change of identity (including Sabbath). However, one can raise the question: So what? Why should this narrative with these ingredients be of any relevance beyond Judaism? What is more, why should this religious story be of any relevance for serious questions related to radical uncertainty in climate change?

4.9 God, a particular light in a universal world

Sacks' understanding of *emunah* reminds us that we are not alone in the midst of radical uncertainty. (Sacks, 2009b, p. 2). The patriarchs Abraham, Isaac and Jacob were the first who discovered that they were not alone in this world. They discovered what Sacks has called an 'intersubjective' dimension in reality. Sacks refers to this dimension with the word 'God'.

A deeper understanding of the biblical God emerges from the encounter in the Exodus between Moses and God in the burning bush. When Moses asks what name he should use when people ask him who the voice in the burning bush is, the voice replies in a cryptic phrase: *Ehyeh asher Ehyeh* (Exod. 3:14). In Judaism, the phrase *Ehyeh asher Ehyeh* is treated with enormous respect and reverence, because it is considered the name of God. For this reason the phrase is not pronounced, but referred to as *Hashem,* 'the name' par excellence, G'd or God. (Sacks, 2009a, p. 287). In the Hebrew Bible a name often represents characteristics. Therefore one can ask what this name reveals about God.

Sometimes the cryptic phrase is read as 'I am that I am', as in the King James Version. For Sacks, such a translation is a mistranslation, because it associates the biblical God with a Greek notion of God, for example the unmoved mover or the ultimate reality. Sacks argues that the proper translation is 'I will be what I will be'. This name of God is a statement about the future. This statement is an assurance that the future is not an ominous void. God will be there in the radically uncertain future, but how God will be there cannot be known in advance.

At the same time, Sacks states, trust in God has solid foundations. By referring to the past, "I am the God of your father, the God of Abraham, the God of Isaac, and the God of Jacob" (Exod. 3:6), God shows that He can be trusted. He is the one who has been liberating in the past and awaits us in a radically uncertain future. Trust in God, Sacks argues, is therefore not blind trust and does not demand an unreasoned leap of faith.

In section 3.5 I pointed out that 'radical' in 'radical uncertainty' is derived from 'radix', which is a Latin word for 'root'. Radical uncertainty is then inherent in what Hannah Arendt has called 'the basic human condition of existence'. By referring to God, Sacks orients us to another layer in the notion of 'radical' when applied to uncertainty. Radical can also be seen as referring to a rooted dimension in reality that can be trusted in the midst of deep uncertainty.

For Sacks, the biblical God is particular in the sense that He sheds a particular light on reality, namely one of hope. The ingredients of this light are: *emunah*, *chessed* and change of identity supported by covenant and Sabbath. On the other hand, God is universal in the sense that He or She is larger than any nation, group, culture or creed. God lives within one's own group, but he also lives beyond. Therefore Sacks' concept of hope is not limited to Judaism; he considers hope a particular message thematized by Judaism, but available for all (Sacks, 2009b, p. 7). Sacks uses several phrases to describe this message of hope, for example 'ethics of responsibility', 'politics of hope' and 'political theory of society'.

4.10 Retelling the narrative of hope

The Exodus story, through being told and retold over and over again, has become engrained in Western societies (Sacks, 2007, p. 97; 2009b, p. 15; 2010, p. 1). Each retelling is about appropriating the light of Torah in a specific context. In this recurring narrative, oneself and the other, especially the one not like me, are seen as valuable in themselves, regardless of merits or use for others. Sacks considers the Exodus the meta-narrative of hope in western civilization.

The Exodus has been interpreted by many generations within Judaism. What is more, every year Jews re-enact the Exodus by celebrating Passover. The reason for this is that each generation has its own pharaohs who have to be defeated. The Exodus has not only been the subject of an ongoing conversation within Judaism. It has also inspired Christians. Studies of the

New Testament show that the theme of the Exodus is extensively repeated in the New Testament:

> Exodus' story of the giving of the covenant, the tabernacle whereby God's dwelling presence among his people is both seen and felt, and the wilderness experience itself—both the good and the bad—established patterns and typologies by which Jesus and his teaching successors understand what has taken place in their time and are able to articulate a theology and an ethic that will guide the Church in the centuries to come. The Exodus takes its place alongside Genesis as a book that contributes major theological ideas to the thinking of Jesus and his early followers. (Evans, 2014, p. 460)[5]

Nor does the story of the Exodus end in the New Testament or in Christianity. It has also been told and retold in the public domain. In the twentieth century the biblical story of the Exodus inspired African Americans in their struggle for civil rights. The speeches of Martin Luther King were full of quotations from Exodus.

Recently, several scientists have proposed, directly and indirectly, a retelling of the Exodus in the context of climate change. Ted Nordhaus and Michael Shellenberger refer indirectly to a retelling of the Exodus in their essay *The Death of Environmentalism* (2004), where they argue that climate change requires a more radical reframing than past environmental issues such as acid rain. This essay brought immediate front-page coverage in *The New York Times* and *The Economist*. In their follow-up book, *Break Through*, they stated that the most quoted lines of their 2004 essay were the following:

> Martin Luther King Jr.'s "I have a dream" speech is famous because it put forward an inspiring positive vision that carried a critique of the current moment within it. Imagine how history would have turned out had King given an "I have a nightmare" speech instead. (Nordhaus and Shellenberger, 2007, p. 1)

In their *Break Through* Nordhaus and Shellenberger tried to articulate a new policy framework. However, their effort was nipped in the bud by those who brushed aside the effort of the young authors as 'youthful indiscretion' (Visscher, 2014, p. 45). Nevertheless, the lines of Nordhaus and Shellenberger resurfaced thanks to Maarten Hajer, by then director of the Netherlands

5   See for example also Keesmaat (1999).

Environmental Assessment Agency (PBL), in his quest to find a new governance framework:

> The policy changes lie not only in understanding the nature and extent of global environmental problems, but also in finding a better response. The discourse on 'limits' ... is of little help: constantly highlighting the complexity and scope of an almost impossible task has a paralysing, rather than motivating, effect. This is therefore a governance view of the world that is inadequate when it comes to mobilising society. A fundamental reassessment of environmental policy therefore requires the radical reframing of the issue. 'Martin Luther King did not say, "I have a nightmare". He said, "I have a dream", and he created a movement'. (Hajer, 2011, p. 28)

Hajer emphasizes the need for a new and inspiring narrative. According to him the broad outlines of questions like climate change are sufficiently well known. It is not a question of people not hearing the message, "... rather it seems to be that there is a lack of a convincing route for action" (Hajer, 2011, p. 16). Ronald Heifetz even refers directly to a retelling of the Exodus as a useful narrative in the context of climate change (Sacks, 2015b, p. xviii).

Sacks, especially in his later work, was outspoken in his view that civil and political society is a specifically religious concern. In several of his writings he sought to formulate a perspective of hope on contemporary questions. After 11 September 2001, Sacks pleaded in his bestseller *The Dignity of Difference* (2002) for a society that makes room for ethnic and religious differences instead of one based on Huntington's clash of civilizations. In his *The Home We Build Together* (2007), Sacks offers a new paradigm of 'integrated diversity' for British citizenship to replace previous models of assimilation and multiculturalism. His *Not in God's Name* (2015) is an exploration of the roots of violence committed in the name of religion between the three Abrahamic faiths: Judaism, Christianity and Islam. *Morality* (2021) discusses the rebuilding of a common moral foundation in Western societies.

Sacks has touched only slightly upon climate change (Sacks, 2005, p. 7; 2007, p. 237; 2011, p. 173). The link between Sacks, hope, the Sabbath, radical uncertainty and climate change thus becomes more indirect. Even though Sacks' own writing on climate change is not extensive, the principles underpinning his understanding of hope from his reading of Exodus can be helpful. In this chapter we have discovered that these principles, key ingredients or critical assumptions are *emunah*, *chessed* (including the covenant) and change of identity (including the Sabbath). In TR in the following chapters I will bring these ingredients into interaction with economists and investigate the relevance of this interaction for addressing radical uncertainty in the context of climate change.

4.11 Critical assumptions of hope

Sacks' understanding of hope as derived from the Exodus can be described as a model of hope. Gustavo Gutiérrez, a leading pioneer of liberation theology, describes the Exodus as a model that highlights key ingredients of a certain way of life, namely one "… in which a people learns to live its freedom in the service of love" (Gutiérrez, 2003, Chapter 5). Such a model is not a mathematical one, in the sense of a technical model, but is closely related to my understanding of an economic model, based on Rodrik. In section 2.2 we have seen that a strength of economics is that it creates knowledge by capturing in a model, simply and formally, the most relevant aspects of reality in a given context. Rodrik refers to the most relevant aspects of reality in a given context with the term 'critical assumptions'. He argues that models can be seen as fables in the sense that they work in the same way, namely as a template to understand reality (Rodrik, 2015, pp. 19-20). Fables are then short and to-the-point stories:

> These short stories often revolve around a few principal characters who live in an unnamed but generic place (a village, a forest) and whose behaviour and interaction produce an outcome that serves as a lesson of sorts…. They take no chance that their message will be lost. (Rodrik, 2015, pp. 18-19)

In this chapter we have seen that Exodus is also a story, but not a short and to-the-point one like Rodrik's understanding of a fable. The Exodus is composed as a multi-layered story, and its meaning can only be understood by reading it as a concealed counter-narrative. Interpreted with this key of concealed counter-narrative, the Exodus appears as a story about individual and societal transformation, in which people gradually learn to take responsibility in 'the service of love', to use the phrase of Gutiérrez. This interpretation of the Exodus can serve as a non-mathematical model with several critical assumptions in the context of radical uncertainty: *emunah*, *chessed* (including the covenant) and change of identity (including the

Sabbath). In the following chapters I will indicate these key ingredients of Sacks' understanding of hope as 'critical assumptions'. The reason for this is to make it clear that in Sacks' understanding of hope these ingredients are seen as the most relevant aspects of reality in the given context of radical uncertainty.

4.12 Conclusion

In this chapter I have answered the twofold question: What is the meaning and possible societal impact of Jonathan Sacks' concept of hope? First I argued that Sacks meets the four requirements for van Huyssteen's post-foundational approach. Then, turning to the first question of this chapter, I investigated the meaning of Sacks' understanding of hope by developing a systematic overview of Sacks' approach of *Torah vehokmah* based on an extensive study of Sacks' own work. *Torah vehokmah* refers to an ongoing conversation between two complementary domains of knowing, Torah (theology) and secular wisdom (natural and social sciences). The study pays particular attention to Sacks' interpretation of the Exodus as part of Torah. Sacks' understanding of hope, derived from the Exodus, means that people have the possibility to change their identity—images of themselves, others and the world—and by doing so to create something new and liberating in the midst of radical uncertainty. Sacks' interpretation of the Exodus highlights several key ingredients for dealing with radical uncertainty: *emunah, chessed*, change of identity, and two supporting institutions, namely covenant and Sabbath. The overview of Sacks' approach of *Torah vehokmah* also offers an answer to the second question, about the possible societal impact of Sacks' understanding of hope. In the view of Sacks, Torah sheds light on reality, including society, and reality sheds light on Torah. The key ingredients of the light on reality are: *emunah, chessed* and change of identity supported by covenant and Sabbath. Over the centuries, the Exodus story has been told and retold over and over again in Judaism, Christianity and beyond. Recently, several scientists have proposed a retelling of the Exodus in the context of climate change. I argued that the key ingredients of Sacks' understanding of hope can be seen as critical assumptions, because they refer to the most relevant aspects of reality in the given context of radical uncertainty. The next four chapters investigate how a conversation, constructed along the lines of van Huyssteen's TR, between Sacks' understanding of hope and five economists can contribute to fuller and better responses to radical uncertainty in the context of climate change.

Bibliography

Calhoun, C. (2002). *Dictionary of the Social Sciences*. New York, NY: Oxford University Press. http://dx.doi.org/10.1093/acref/9780195123715.001.0001

Carasik, M. (Ed.). (2005). *The Commentators' Bible: The JPS Miqra'ot Gedolot: Exodus*. Philadelphia, PA: The Jewish Publication Society.

Chandler, D., & R. Munday (2016). *A Dictionary of Media and Communication* (2nd. ed.). Oxford, United Kingdom: Oxford University Press. http://dx.doi.org/10.1093/acref/9780199568758.001.0001

Crossley, N. (1996). *Intersubjectivity: The Fabric of Social Becoming*. London, United Kingdom: SAGE Publications.

Evans, C.A. (2014). Exodus in the New Testament: Patterns of Revelation and Redemption. In T.B. Dozeman, C.A. Evans. & J.N. Lohr (Eds.), *The book of Exodus: Composition, reception, and interpretation* (pp. 440-464). Leiden, The Netherlands: Brill.

Gutiérrez, G. (2003). *We Drink from Our Own Wells: The Spiritual Journey of a People*. Maryknoll, NY, Orbis Books.

Hajer, M. (2011). *The energetic society: In search of a governance philosophy for a clean economy*. The Hague, The Netherlands: pbl Netherlands Environmental Assessment Agency.

Halík, T. (2016). *I Want You to Be: On the God of Love*. Notre Dame, IN: University of Notre Dame Press. Harari, Y.N. (2017). *Homo Deus: A Brief History of Tomorrow*. London, United Kingdom: Vintage.

Harris, M.J., Rynhold, D., & Wright, T. (Eds.). (2013). *Radical Responsibility: Celebrating the Thought of Chief Rabbi Lord Jonathan Sacks*. New Milford, CT: Maggid Books.

Hoogen, T. van den (2011). *A Taste of God: On Spirituality and Reframing Foundational Theology*. Münster, Germany: LIT Verlag.

Keesmaat, S.C. (1999). *Paul and His Story: (Re)Interpreting the Exodus Tradition*. Sheffield, United Kingdom: Sheffield Academic Press.

Morgan, T. (2015). *Roman Faith and Christian Faith: Pistis and Fides in the Early Roman Empire and Early Churches*. Oxford, United Kingdom: Oxford University Press.

Nordhaus, T., & Shellenberger, M. (2004). *The Long Death of Environmentalism*. Retrieved from http://www.thebreakthrough.org/images/Death_of_Environmentalism.pdf

Nordhaus, T., & Shellenberger, M. (2007). *Break Through: From the Death of Environmentalism to the Politics of Possibility*. New York, NY: Houghton Mifflin Company.

Poorthuis, J.H.M. (1992). *Het gelaat van de Messias: Messiaanse Talmoedlezingen van Emmanuel Levinas*. Zoetermeer, The Netherlands: Boekencentrum.

Rodrik, D. (2015). *Economics Rules: Why Economics Works, When It Fails, and How To Tell The Difference*. Oxford, England: Oxford University Press.

Sacks, J. (1997). *The Politics of Hope*. London, United Kingdom: Jonathan Cape.

Sacks, J. (2000). *A Letter in the Scroll: Understanding Our Jewish Identity and Exploring the Legacy of the World's Oldest Religion*. New York, NY: Free Press.

Sacks, J. (2005). *To Heal a Fractured World: The Ethics of Responsibility*. New York, NY: Schocken Books.

Sacks, J. (2007). *The Home We Build Together: Recreating Society*. London, United Kingdom: Continuum.

Sacks, J. (2009a). *Covenant & Conversation, Genesis: The Book of Beginnings*. Jerusalem, Israel: Maggid Books.

Sacks, J. (2009b). *Future Tense: Jews, Judaism, and Israel in the Twenty-First Century*. New York, NY: Schocken Books.

Sacks, J. (2010). *Covenant & Conversation, Exodus: The Book of Redemption*. Jerusalem, Israel: Maggid Books.

Sacks, J. (2011). *The Dignity of Difference: How to Avoid the Clash of Civilizations* (Rev. ed.). London, United Kingdom: Continuum.

Sacks, J. (2012). *The Great Partnership: God, Science and the Search for Meaning*. London, United Kingdom: Hodder & Stoughton.

Sacks, J. (2013a). *A Judaism Engaged with the World*. Retrieved from http://www.rabbisacks.org/a-judaism-engaged-with-the-world/

Sacks, J. (2013b). *The Jonathan Sacks Haggada: Collected Essays on Pesaḥ*. Jerusalem, Israel: Maggid Books.

Sacks, J. (2015a). *Covenant & Conversation, Leviticus: The Book of Holiness*. Jerusalem, Israel: Maggid Books.

Sacks, J. (2015b). *Lessons in Leadership: A Weekly Reading of the Jewish Bible*. Jerusalem, Israel: Maggid Books.

Sacks, J. (2015c). *Not in God's Name: Confronting Religious Violence*. London, United Kingdom: Hodder & Stoughton. Sacks, J. (2016a). *The Koren Sukkot Maḥzor*. Jerusalem, Israel: Koren Publishers.

Sacks, J. (2016b). *Essays on Ethics: A Weekly Reading of the Jewish Bible*. Jerusalem, Israel: Maggid Books.

Sacks, J. (2021). *Morality: Restoring the Common Good in Divided Times*. London, United Kingdom: Hodder & Stoughton.

Spadaro, S. (2013, September 30). *A Big Heart Open to God: An Interview with Pope Francis*. Retrieved from https://www.americamagazine.org/faith/2013/09/30/big-heart-open-god-interview-pope-francis

Tirosh-Samuelson H., & Hughes A.W. (Eds.). (2013). *Jonathan Sacks: Universalizing Particularity*. Leiden, The Netherlands: Brill.

Visscher, M. (2014, 13 December). Ecomodernisten: de nadruk op veerkracht. *Vrij Nederland*, 42-47.

Williams, R. (2012). *Faith in the Public Square*. London, England: Bloomsbury.

5. Transversal Reasoning on *Emunah*

Abstract

This chapter aims to initiate transversal reasoning (TR) between Sacks' understanding of *emunah* (a type of trust) and Nooteboom's understanding of trust. This TR is part of the larger TR presented in consecutive chapters. First, it is argued that Nooteboom, Bowles, Ariely and Kay & King largely meet the requirements for entering into TR with Sacks in these chapters. The reason for employing TR is to explore its relevance for a social response to radical uncertainty in the context of climate change. The relevance of TR between Sacks and Nooteboom on *emunah* appears in their treatment of what can be described as relational knowledge, a third form of knowledge, besides objective and subjective knowledge. Relational knowledge allows to embrace radical uncertainty in the context of climate change. In discourses on climate change, elements of this kind of knowledge can already be found in pleas for post-normal science.

Keywords: Transversal reasoning, Jonathan Sacks, Bart Nooteboom, *emunah,* trust, relational knowledge

5.1 Introduction

In this chapter and the next three chapters I develop TR between Jonathan Sacks and the economists Bart Nooteboom, Samuel Bowles, Dan Ariely and John Kay & Mervyn King. The point of departure in this TR is Sacks' understanding of hope with the critical assumptions of *emunah, chessed* (including the covenant) and change of identity (including the Sabbath), and its narrative mode. There are two reasons for selecting the economists mentioned above. The first reason, as I will argue shortly, is that their work can be constructed as, what I have called in section 3.4, a postfoundational approach to economics. The second reason is that concepts in their work relate to the critical assumptions or narrative mode of Sacks' understanding of hope. These concepts are trust and relational contracting (Nooteboom);

Hasselaar, J.J., *Climate Change, Radical Uncertainty and Hope: Theology and Economics in Conversation.* Amsterdam: Amsterdam University Press, 2023

DOI 10.5117/9789048558476_CH05

ethical and other-regarding motives, which I call social preference 1; the social embeddedness of people's preferences, which I call social preference 2, (both preferences are derived from Bowles); the Sabbath (Ariely); and the narrative (Kay & King). Due to limitations of space, I focus on Nooteboom's *Trust* (2002), Bowles' *The Moral Economy* (2016), Ariely's *The (Honest) Truth About Dishonesty* (2012) and Kay & King's *Radical Uncertainty* (2020). Let me be clear, this TR should be seen as a pilot study for constructing a conversation between theology and economics on radical uncertainty regarding climate change. Beyond this study, some other economists can be added to this conversation, for example Daniel Kahneman with his *Thinking, Fast and Slow* (2011) and Raghuram Rajan with his *The Third Pillar* (2019).

TR follows the structure as displayed in figure 5.1 below.

Figure 5.1   Thematic structure of the transversal reasoning

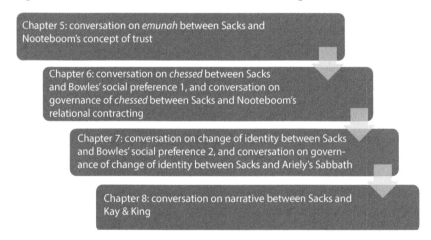

Each turn within TR consists of two parts.

Part 1 is about the question whether a critical assumption or the narrative mode of Sacks' understanding of hope and the concept of the economist concerned can interact. And if so, to what extent similarities and differences can be found. Do the concepts used by Sacks and the economist supplement or deepen one another? Can we find obvious areas of disagreement, and do we find specific issues that need to be discussed further?

Part 2 concerns the relevance of the conversation in part 1 for a social response to radical uncertainty in the context of climate change.

Before entering into TR, the economic contribution in TR will be explored: Nooteboom on trust (5.3), Bowles on social preference 1 (6.2), Nooteboom on relational contracting (6.4), Bowles on social preference 2 (7.2), Ariely on the Sabbath (7.4) and Kay & King on narrative (8.2).

5.2 A postfoundational approach to economics

In order to allow for a successful TR between Sacks and the economists, the first question that has to be addressed is whether the work of the economists can be constructed as a postfoundational approach to economics. Therefore their work must, to a large extent, meet the four key requirements of van Huyssteen's postfoundational approach (section 3.3). I have already argued that Sacks exhibits the four required characteristics of this approach (section 4.2). In the following I will assess the extent to which the work of Nooteboom, Bowles, Ariely and Kay & King may also contain these required postfoundational characteristics:

(1) *Embeddedness of rationality.* This characteristic recognizes the contextuality and the embeddedness of all human reflection in human culture, and therefore in specific scientific and confessional traditions.

Nooteboom has a background in mathematics and econometrics. He was professor of Innovation at several universities in the Netherlands, until his retirement in 2008. In his view, trust is included in the roots of the modern economic research tradition, namely in Adam Smith's *Theory of Moral Sentiments* (1759). However, he argues that the attention to trust was later sidetracked because of the dominance of the neoclassical school within economics (Nooteboom, 2002, p. 7). Such an argument shows that for Nooteboom economic thinking is not based on universal laws, but embedded in certain contexts, here expressed in different schools of thinking.

Bowles has a background in economics. He directs the Behavioral Siences Program at the Santa Fe Institute and taught economics at Harvard University. Bowles maintains that one cannot talk abstractly about the phenomenon of rationality within economics. He traces the origins of what he calls the 'conventional economic assumptions' of objective knowledge, self-interest and fixed preferences back to thinkers like David Hume, Jeremy Bentham and Adam Smith, to the (religious) wars in seventeenth-century in Europe, and the insufficiency of the civic virtues (Bowles, 2016, pp. 16-21).

Ariely has a background in cognitive psychology and business administration. He is director of the Center for Advanced Hindsight and the James B. Duke Professor of Psychology and Behavioral Economics at Duke University. In addition, he holds several other appointments. Ariely recognizes the usefulness of what we have called the 'conventional economic assumptions' in economics (section 2.3). At the same time, Ariely argues that these assumptions are of limited use when it comes to dishonesty. In his view these assumptions have to be extended in order to better understand human behaviour and achieve better outcomes (Ariely, 2012, p. 5).

Kay and King have a background in economics. Kay was dean of Oxford's Said Business School. He has held chairs at London Business School, the University of Oxford, and the London School of Economics. Kay is a Fellow of the British Academy and the Royal Society of Edinburgh. King was Governor of the Bank of England (from 2003 to 2013) and is currently professor of economics and law at New York University and school professor of economics at the London School of Economics. Kay and King recognize both the contextuality and embeddedness of all human reflection, for example by stating that "the meaning of rational behavior depends critically on the context of the situation and there are generally many different ways of being rational" (Kay & King, 2020, p. 16).

Nooteboom, Bowles, Ariely and Kay & King thus recognize the embeddedness of rationality.

(2) *Interpreting reality in all forms of inquiry.* This characteristic points to the interpretation of a shared reality as common ground of rationality in all theology and economics (hermeneutical dimension of rationality).

Nooteboom considers knowledge as always based on a not objective, mental framework. He argues that knowledge includes perception and interpretation of reality. He refers to this approach as the 'interpretative' or 'hermeneutic view' (Nooteboom, 2002, p. 24).

Bowles argues at length that when it comes to designing laws, policy and business organizations, it is anything but prudent to let the behavioural assumptions of conventional economics about the economic agent (employee, student or borrower) be the only ones to interpret human behaviour. The main point in his *The Moral Economy* is that this set of assumptions and related institutions are not objective assumptions of human behaviour, but should be supplemented with ethical and other-regarding assumptions and related institutions (Bowles, 2016, p. 2).

Ariely does not consider the assumptions of conventional economics objective assumptions of human behaviour. He uses insights, for example, from psychology and real-life experiments to supplement the conventional assumptions and interpret reality.

Kay and King criticize modern economics for having lost a great deal in seeking axiomatic rationality, meaning a rationality based on a priori assumptions about human behaviour. By doing so, Kay & King are criticizing, to use van Huyssteen's distinction, a foundational approach to economics. In their view, such an approach fails "... to acknowledge the importance of the human ability to interpret problems in context" (Kay & King, 2020, p. 387). According to them, there are several ways to interpret reality.

Nooteboom, Bowles, Ariely and Kay & King thus recognize interpretation of a shared reality as common ground of rationality.

(3) *Critical reflection.* This characteristic refers to a critical investigation of one's own embeddedness by the participant of an interdisciplinary interaction, embeddedness for example in a certain research tradition or a confessional tradition.

Nooteboom has investigated the assumptions of economics. On the one hand, he criticizes a positivistic, what Huyssteen calls foundational, approach to economics. On the other hand, he rejects, to use van Huyssteen's terms, an extreme relativistic nonfoundational approach to economics. (Nooteboom, 2002, pp. 24-25) Nooteboom seeks to employ what we have called a postfoundational approach to economics.

Bowles argues at length in his *The Moral Economy* for relaxing the conventional economic assumption of self-interest and including ethical and other-regarding assumptions in the economic analysis.

Ariely outspokenly criticizes the assumptions of conventional economics. He contends that these assumptions should be supplemented with insights from other research traditions to achieve a better understanding of human behaviour and achieve better outcomes.

Kay and King oppose a foundational approach to economics connected to a particular school of thought (e.g. neoclassical, neo-Keynesian, Austrian or behavioural). They argue for a willingness "... to draw on any or all of these schools of thought if they offer relevant insight in the context of a particular problem. We are suspicious of all 'schools' which claim to provide a wide range of answers to problems based on a priori assertions of a general kind about the world" (Kay & King, 2020, p. 397).

Nooteboom, Bowles Ariely and Kay & King have thus critically reflected on the assumptions of their own research traditions.

(4) *Problem solving.* This characteristic of a postfoundational approach considers problem solving the most central and defining activity of all research traditions.

Nooteboom is inspired by the American pragmatism of authors such as Dewey, James and Peirce, in the sense that this pragmatism does not claim absolute truths. In later work, Nooteboom has argued in line with this pragmatism that "ideas evolve in adaptation to reality, as a function of their success in action... Truth is not something eternal that we contemplate, as in Platonic philosophy, but something that develops in the world, in action" (Nooteboom, 2012, p. 66).

Bowles argues in his *The Moral Economy* for including ethical and other-regarding motives (social preference 1) on grounds of prudence. For Bowles, prudence is the virtue of pragmatic wisdom, and includes problem solving. He maintains that a synergy between self-interest and ethical and other-regarding motives is necessary for effective policy (Bowles, 2016, p. 7).

Ariely aims to contribute to an understanding of what causes dishonest behaviour in daily life. At the end of his book, as a next task, he points to some mechanisms to combat dishonesty (Ariely, 2012, p. 9).

For Kay and King, the role of an economist is to be a problem solver. In their view, economics is a problem-solving science (Kay & King, 2020, pp. 398-399). But, they continue, if economics is a problem-solving science, the relevant test of economics is its problem-solving capabilities. Kay and King point out that when the financial crisis struck in 2008, economic models were of little help because they describe a stable and unchanging structure of the economy. Kay and King insist on including radical uncertainty as fundamental in economics in order to make it a problem-solving science (again) (Kay & King, 2020, p. 340).

Nooteboom, Bowles, Ariely and Kay & King thus consider problem solving the central activity of their work.

To conclude this section, I have shown above that Nooteboom, Bowles, Ariely and Kay & King largely meet the four requirements of van Huyssteen's postfoundational approach. Therefore they can be regarded as employing a postfoundational approach to economics that allows them to enter into TR with Sacks. Now I continue with the economic contribution of Bart Nooteboom on trust.

5.3   The economist Bart Nooteboom on trust

In this section I focus on the concept of trust in Bart Nooteboom's book *Trust* (2002). One can argue that the focus of *Trust* is on relationships within and between firms. However, Nooteboom also goes beyond this focus. In *Trust* he seeks to provide "... a comprehensive and systematic treatise of trust, covering all its requisite complexity, while trying to achieve coherence and conceptual clarity" (Nooteboom 2002, p. x). This book can be seen as an example of economists paying attention to the role of trust in economic analysis in recent decades.[1] The reason I choose explicitly for *Trust* is that Nooteboom combines trust with the uncertainty inherent in the human condition (Nooteboom, 2002, p. 188).[2] In the following I give a description of Nooteboom's concept of trust.

Nooteboom describes trust as a complex and slippery notion, although this "... does not necessarily make it diffuse in the sense of unclear or imprecise" (Nooteboom, 2002, p. 7). In order to give a comprehensive and systematic analysis of trust, he ascribes to trust a four-place predicate. This predicate is based on Aristotle and can be described as follows: (1) someone, the trustor, trusts (2) someone (or something), the trustee, (3) in some respect, (4) depending on the external conditions. (Nooteboom, 2002, p. 38) I will now consider the four elements of this predicate in more detail:

(1) *Trust entails a subject, i.e. someone or something that trusts (the trustor).* Nooteboom describes this subject primarily as a person who trusts, but he argues that the subject can also be a group of people, for example an organization (2002, p. 59).

(2) *There is an object, i.e. someone or something that is trusted (the trustee).* For Nooteboom, the object of trust can have two meanings, (A) people or (B) things and institutions. (A) Trust with regard to people is about trust in individuals or in a group of people, such as an organization. (B) By trust in things Nooteboom refers to trust in material objects like a car. By trust in institutions he refers for example to God, the law, the government. Nooteboom defines an institution as enabling, constraining and guiding action and being durable and more or less inevitable (Nooteboom, 2002, p. 55). When it comes to trust in institutions, Nooteboom uses the term institutional confidence instead of trust. For Nooteboom, an important difference between trust in people (trust) and trust in institutions (confidence) is that confidence refers to bigger or wider systems or entities that can hardly be influenced by (a group of) individuals and are more or less inevitable. Nooteboom gives the example of a judge to refer to confidence. Usually, people are not in a position to choose a judge or to influence his or her judgement. People can only submit to what is imposed on them. If people choose to bribe a judge, we might speak of trust, according to Nooteboom.

---

1   Since Nooteboom wrote his book, the field of study has grown further. See for example Lewis (2008) and Sapienza, Toldra-Simats & Zingales (2013).

2   More recent work of Nooteboom related to the topic of trust is his philosophical book *Beyond Humanism* (2012) and a more popular book in Dutch *Vertrouwen* (2017).

(3) The third element of the predicate is about the internal conditions or reasons for trust in people. Nooteboom distinguishes two internal conditions: trust in someone's skills (competence trust) and trust in someone's motivations (intentional trust). Competence trust relates to the other's willingness to behave to the best of his or her competence. Intentional trust relates to the other being cooperative rather than opportunistic (Nooteboom, 2002, p. 9). According to Nooteboom, there are better and worse reasons to have trust. An evaluation of the evidence of trustworthiness may result in certain responses to increase or restore trust, like a training to improve someone's competences. Therefore, in Nooteboom's view, "trust is, or should be, subject to development, to learning" (Nooteboom, 2002, p. 38).

(4) The fourth element of the predicate is about the external conditions of trust in people, such as the context of action. This element relates to the question if it is reasonable to expect someone to remain loyal at any cost. Examples here would be contexts like a golden opportunity offered to the trustee or the extreme case of remaining loyal to friends under torture (Nooteboom, 2002, p. 46).

Nooteboom has developed this four-place predicate of trust in order to give a comprehensive and systematic analysis of trust. Generally speaking, Nooteboom's view is that trust can be mutual, however he states that it is seldom completely balanced. For example, one can expect some conditions to exceed his or her competence or commitment to perform (Nooteboom, 2002, p. 38). Nooteboom argues that 'real trust' between the trustor and trustee should be added to the economic analysis of knowledge and trust. Real trust "… entails loyalty to an agreement or to a partner, even if there are both opportunities and incentives for opportunism" (Nooteboom, 2002, p. 192). Real trust can be mutual, but it doesn't have to be (completely) mutual, for example due to a difference in developed competences and external conditions. For Nooteboom, real trust reduces opportunities for opportunism on the basis of some degree of loyalty (Nooteboom, 2002, p. 113).

The above description of Nooteboom's understanding of trust provides ingredients for TR between Sacks and Nooteboom on *emunah*.

5.4   TR between Sacks and Nooteboom on *emunah*

This section develops TR between Sacks and Nooteboom on *emunah*. In 5.4.1 the question is whether and how Sacks' concept of *emunah* and

Nooteboom's concept of trust interact. Section 5.4.2 explores the relevance of this conversation for a social response to radical uncertainty in the context of climate change.

5.4.1   On *emunah*

Sacks and Nooteboom converge in their answer to the question of how to deal with radical uncertainty. They both point to the importance of trust. However, a key question that then emerges from Nooteboom's predicate of trust is the following: What or whom does one trust when it comes to radical uncertainty? Nooteboom refers especially to real trust in connection with radical uncertainty. Real trust is a type of trust based on a relationship that seeks to include the interests of both oneself and the other. People motivated by real trust are more willing to honour an agreement, even if the situation is not in their interest, than people motivated purely by self-interest. For Nooteboom real trust *reduces* radical uncertainty by limiting opportunities for opportunism on the basis of some degree of loyalty. What or who is it that Sacks has trust in when it comes to uncertainty? One can contend that Sacks' *emunah* is expressed in Nooteboom's predicate as people's trust in God. Nooteboom refers in his analysis on trust only briefly to God. He defines God as an institution. Following Nooteboom's definition of an institution, God can hardly be influenced and is more or less inevitable. Sacks would argue that Nooteboom's understanding of God is a Greek conception of God, maybe even an idol. God is then unchangeable, the unmoved mover and beyond time. Sacks highlights another concept of God related to *emunah*, namely the biblical God. It is the God of history: the God of Abraham, the God of Jacob, the God of Martin Luther King and so on. (Sacks 2012, p. 83) By using the metaphor of 'the biblical God as light' (section 4.8.1) I have tried to clarify Sacks' concept of the biblical God. The biblical God then can be seen as a point of reference from which to perceive and understand reality. This point of reference opens a perspective on a form of knowledge, an epistemology, that can be described as relational knowledge, or in the words of Sacks, *da'at* or intersubjective knowledge (Tirosh-Samuelson & Hughes, 2013, p. 117). The biblical God orients us to a perspective on reality in which people have the possibility to create meaning together. Nooteboom is right in the sense that God cannot be influenced. The biblical God orients us to a particular perspective on reality that is already there, a dimension in reality, and will not change. However, for Sacks, the biblical God is not an institution that is inevitable. The biblical God is a possibility. People are invited to claim the potential of this possibility and by doing so to start learning how to embrace radical uncertainty. They are not and cannot be forced to respond to this invitation. In essence, *emunah* allows not only for *reducing* radical uncertainty as Nooteboom's real trust does. *Emunah* makes it possible to *embrace* radical uncertainty by creating meaning based on relational knowledge in the midst of radical uncertainty.

Besides the concept of God, another diverging line is on the concept of hope. Nooteboom does not come up with the concept of hope in his book *Trust*.[3] For Sacks, hope is a fundamentally related concept that intersects with *emunah*. Hope is the foundation for trustworthiness to which Sacks' tradition refers with God. Hope can be strengthened by acts of trustworthiness, but hope remains the foundation of trustworthiness and not the other way around. Hope includes profound situations of radical uncertainty, both on a micro and macro level. Nooteboom's real trust, by contrast, relates especially to small-scale interactions within and between firms. For Sacks, hope is best expressed in the narrative of the Exodus. The Exodus includes several layers, has an open future, invites people to acts of trustworthiness, directs them towards freedom, considers human beings as having a free will, and is about individual and societal transformation. Hope, expressed in the terms of this narrative, provides a coherent framework that gives meaning to the whole of relationships. Hope takes seriously the present situation, but also shows that something better is possible. The narrative mode as such is only implicitly present in Nooteboom's book, namely in his brief part on scenarios. The reason for this is that a scenario can be seen as having a dual structure consisting of a technical and a narrative mode.

A last diverging line is that for Nooteboom the initial surrender needed for trust to face radical uncertainty is blind (Nooteboom, 2002, p. 84). He argues that in the face of radical uncertainty "... a leap of unreasoned trust is always needed" (Nooteboom, 2002, p. 44). To use another quotation: "... where the gap of uncertainty yawns, we must surrender to trust or die from inaction" (Nooteboom, 2002, p. 200). Sacks, on the contrary, argues that trust seen as *emunah* does not require an unreasoned 'leap of faith'. He maintains that *emunah* has a solid foundation, namely a dimension of hope in our reality. One can still argue that trust in this dimension demands a leap. However, Sacks would never call such a leap 'unreasoned'. For Sacks, trust in the biblical God takes place within a tried-and-tested relationship. The reason for this is that the biblical God has shown throughout history, from the patriarchs and the matriarchs to Martin Luther King and others, that He can be trusted. At the same time, the name of the biblical God 'I will

---

3   In later work, Nooteboom touches only slightly on hope (Nooteboom, 2017, p. 107).

be what I will be' is a statement about the future (section 4.9). God can be trusted that He will be there in the radically uncertain future, in a liberating perspective, but how God will be there cannot be known in advance.

TR between Sacks and Nooteboom on *emunah* limits itself to a comparison, because, in essence, Sacks' concept of *emunah* deepens and extends Nooteboom's understanding of trust regarding radical uncertainty. Therefore TR on *emunah* does not call for debate.

To conclude, Sacks and Nooteboom converge in highlighting trust in order to provide a response to radical uncertainty. However, a key question in TR is: What do they mean when they refer to trust? TR shows that Sacks' understanding of *emunah* deepens and extends Nooteboom's analysis of trust, in particular his understanding of real trust.

(1) *Emunah* highlights 'God' as a relational perspective on reality instead of considering God an object in a subject-object relationship.
(2) The relational perspective on reality is not limited to small-scale interactions, but underlies the whole of reality, including macro-scale interactions.
(3) This perspective not only *reduces* radical uncertainty, but *embraces* radical uncertainty by orienting us to something liberating beyond what we can express with our words and thoughts in the present.
(4) *Emunah* is part of a cluster with hope. Hope underlies trust, and is best expressed in the narrative of the Exodus that gives meaning to the whole.
(5) *Emunah* does not demand a leap of unreasoned faith, but refers to relational knowledge that underlies reality and has shown in history that it can be trusted and will be liberating in the future.

In section 6.5 the interaction between Sacks and Nooteboom continues with a discussion of the governance of *chessed*.

5.4.2 On climate change

What is the relevance of a conversation between Sacks and Nooteboom on *emunah* for a social response to radical uncertainty in the context of climate change?

The relevance of the interaction is that it familiarizes us with relational knowledge, a third form of knowledge besides objective and subjective knowledge, that allows people to embrace radical uncertainty in the context of climate change. In section 2.3 we defined objective knowledge as knowledge which is independent of an observer's viewpoint or bias.

In section 2.7 I argued that objective knowledge meets its limits when it comes to radical uncertainty in the context of climate change. The lack of objective knowledge can be compensated by subjective knowledge. Subjective knowledge is defined as the knowledge an individual or a group of individuals has about a situation or phenomenon based on personal opinions, biases, and arbitrary preferences (section 2.5). However, when it comes to climate change radical uncertainty is at centre stage. Therefore subjective knowledge can lead to conflicting outcomes of studies, as illustrated in the Stern/Nordhaus-controversy. How then to proceed?

The conversation between Sacks and Nooteboom opens a perspective of relational knowledge as an additional form of knowledge for dealing with radical uncertainty in the context of climate change. The conversation orients us towards hope, best expressed in the narrative of the Exodus, as a form of relational knowledge to interpret radical uncertainty. Hope belongs to a cluster with *emunah* (particular kind of trust), *chessed* (particular kind of love) and change of identity, and the related institutions of covenant and public Sabbath. Each concept in this cluster will play its role in TR in the next chapters. In discourses surrounding climate change, elements of such a form of relational knowledge can already be found, for example, in recent work of Van der Sluijs. Van der Sluijs has argued for complementing objective knowledge with post-normal science to deal with radical uncertainty (Van der Sluijs, 2012). Post-normal science, as understood by Van der Sluijs, is based on three defining features. First, it acknowledges the existence of radical uncertainty. Second, it recognizes the existence of a plurality of legitimate perspectives. Third, it requires an extended peer community that includes representatives from social, political and economic domains who openly discuss various dimensions of uncertainties in the available body of scientific evidence and the implications for all stakeholders with respect to the issue at hand. (Van der Sluijs, 2012, pp. 176-177) The relational knowledge highlighted by the interaction between Sacks and Nooteboom is related to a post–normal science in the sense that both forms of knowledge seek to complement objective knowledge with a form of knowledge that takes radical uncertainty seriously. A difference is that Van der Sluijs does not explicitly refer to hope and related critical assumptions of *emunah* and *chessed*, and the related institutions of covenant and Sabbath. At the same time, Van der Sluijs' recognition of a plurality of perspectives and an extended peer community relate to Sacks' assumption of *chessed*.

To conclude, the relevance of TR between Sacks and Nooteboom on *emunah* is that it familiarizes us with relational knowledge, a third form of knowledge besides objective and subjective knowledge. Relational knowledge, expressed in a narrative of hope, has the potential to embrace radical uncertainty in the context of climate change. TR deepens contemporary debates regarding climate change that seek to complement objective knowledge.

5.5 Conclusion

This chapter started by assessing the extent to which the work of Nooteboom, Bowles, Ariely and Kay & King allow for a postfoundational conversation. I concluded that they can be regarded as employing a postfoundational approach to economics, which makes it possible to develop TR between Sacks and these economists. I then initiated TR by developing a conversation on *emunah* between Sacks and Nooteboom's concept of trust. In TR Sacks and Nooteboom converge in highlighting the relevance of trust as a relational form of knowledge in responding to radical uncertainty. In TR it becomes clear that they diverge in their understanding of the concept of God, their use of the concept of hope, and what they consider the foundation of trust. Regarding radical uncertainty in climate change, TR familiarises us with a third form of knowledge besides objective and subjective knowledge, in order to create a fuller understanding of a social response to radical uncertainty in the context of climate change. TR deepens contemporary debates on post-normal science regarding climate change that seek to complement objective knowledge.

The following chapter continues TR with a conversation on *chessed* between Sacks and the economists Bowles.

Bibliography

Ariely, D. (2012). *The (Honest) Truth About Dishonesty: How We Lie to Everyone–Especially Ourselves*. New York, NY: Harper.

Bowles, S. (2016). *The Moral Economy: Why Good Incentives Are No Substitute for Good Citizens*. New Haven, CT: Yale University Press.

Kay, J. & King, M. (2020). *Radical Uncertainty: Decision-making for an unknowable future*. London, United Kingdom: The Bridge Street Press.

Lewis, P. (2008). Uncertainty, power and trust. *The Review of Austrian Economics*, 21, 183-198. http://dx.doi.org/10.1007/s11138-007-0038-9

Nooteboom, B. (2002). *Trust: Forms, Foundations, Functions, Failures and Figures*. Cheltenham, United Kingdom: Edward Elgar.

Nooteboom, B. (2012). *Beyond Humanism: The Flourishing of Life, Self and Other.* Basingstoke, United Kingdom: Palgrave Macmillan.

Nooteboom, B. (2017). *Vertrouwen: Opening voor een veranderende wereld.* Utrecht, The Netherlands: Uitgeverij Klement.

Sacks, J. (2012). *The Great Partnership: God, Science and the Search for Meaning.* London, United Kingdom: Hodder & Stoughton.

Sapienza, P., Toldra-Simats, A., & Zingales, L. (2013). Understanding Trust. *The Economic Journal, 123,* 1313-1332. http://dx.doi.org/10.1111/ecoj.12036

Sluijs, J.P. van der (2012). Uncertainty and Dissent in Climate Risk Assessment: A Post Normal Perspective. *Nature of Culture, 7*(2), 174-195. http://dx.doi.org/10.3167/nc.2012.070204

Tirosh-Samuelson H., & Hughes A.W. (Eds.). (2013). *Jonathan Sacks: Universalizing Particularity.* Leiden, The Netherlands: Brill.

6. Transversal Reasoning on *Chessed*

Abstract

This chapter continues transversal reasoning (TR) with a conversation on *chessed* between Jonathan Sacks and the economist Samuel Bowles, and between Sacks and Bart Nooteboom on the governance of *chessed*. The reason for this TR is to explore its relevance for a social response to radical uncertainty in the context of climate change. TR on *chessed* indicates other-regarding motives, besides self-interest, for dealing with radical uncertainty in the context of climate change. People inspired by *chessed* learn to take responsibility together, bottom-up and in the present, for a shared future. The plurality among those involved is crucial for opening up the identities people are living by in order to create a new 'we'. This new 'we' is not only between humans, but also between humans and non-humans. Joy appears as one of the results of building relationships inspired by *chessed*. TR points out that there are also negative other-regarding motivations and that seemingly positive motivations can slip into negative ones. This raises the question of whether it is possible to govern positive motivations. To answer this question, TR turns to a conversation between Sacks and Nooteboom. This conversation highlights the role of the covenant in governing positive other-regarding motivation on a micro- and macro-scale. It is argued that, in a social response to radical uncertainty in the context of climate change, the covenant can be supported by, and help to flesh out, competition (market) and hierarchy (government).

Keywords: Transversal reasoning, Jonathan Sacks, Samuel Bowles, Bart Nooteboom, *chessed,* other, regarding motives, covenant

6.1 Introduction

This chapter continues TR that started in last chapter. The focus of this part of TR is on *chessed*, one of the critical assumptions of Sacks'

Hasselaar, J.J., *Climate Change, Radical Uncertainty and Hope: Theology and Economics in Conversation*. Amsterdam: Amsterdam University Press, 2023
DOI 10.5117/9789048558476_CH06

understanding of hope. In TR Sacks' *chessed* will be brought into conversation with the concept of social preference 1 derived from the work of Samuel Bowles. Thereafter, TR is developed around the governance of *chessed*. In order to develop this, we review a conversation between Sacks and Nooteboom as set forth in section 5.4, but now looking at the governance of *chessed*. Before beginning TR, we will present Bowles' social preference 1.

6.2   The economist Bowles on social preference 1

In the last two decades behavioural experiments like the Ultimatum Game, the Trust Game, the Gift Exchange Game and Public Good Games, with economists like Ernst Fehr and Urs Fischbacher, have played an important role in weakening the exclusive reliance in economics on self-interest. Today economists consider people as more socially minded than conventional economics assumed with its assumption that individuals act solely out of self-interest. Behavioural experiments have shown that ethical and other-regarding motives are common in virtually all human populations. (Bowles, 2016, p. 4) Bowles refers to ethical and other-regarding motives with the term 'social preferences'. I refer to ethical and other-regarding motives with the term 'social preference 1'. In section 7.2 I will define 'social preference 2'. Social preference 1 is a concern, positive or negative, for the well-being of others, as well as a desire to uphold ethical norms. Concrete examples of social preference 1 are altruism, reciprocity, spite, revenge, resentment, envy, and aversion to inequity (Bowles, 2016, p. 45).

For Bowles, the human ability to cooperate is one of the main reasons humans have managed to survive. He argues in his earlier work *A Cooperative Species* (2011), co-authored with Gintis, that the driving force of evolution is not primarily about competition based on self-interest, but about cooperation. Cooperation is then defined as engaging with others in a mutually beneficial activity, which includes behaviour that takes others into account. Bowles and Gintis maintain that members of groups that sustained cooperative strategies for provisioning, childrearing and sanctioning non-cooperators had significant advantages over members of non-cooperative groups. In the course of history humans have created novel environments exhibiting similar or even greater benefits of cooperation, such as the division of labour coordinated by market exchange and respect of property rights.

To be clear, classical economists never considered economic agents as merely self-interested, but they did view self-interest as an acceptable basis for good government (Bowles, 2016, p. 18). According to Bowles, the reason for this goes back to the roots of modern economics. Bowles argues that it was in the shadow of the European (religious) wars and disorder that self-interest came to be seen as an acceptable basis of good government. Religion was used as a tool of power to define groups in terms of 'us/we' and 'them'. Bowles calls the form of altruism that creates 'us/we' and 'them' parochial altruism. It was in that time of seventeenth and eighteenth-century Europe that Adam Smith, in looking for an alternative way to serve collective benefit, formulated the idea of the market.[1] At the same time public philosophers like David Hume and Jeremy Bentham turned to the design of public policy based on what Bowles calls a 'constitution of the knaves', meaning that public policy should be designed on the assumption that every person is driven by pure self-interest. This is not to say that these philosophers believed that actors are only self-interested. Rather, self-interest had come to be seen as a less harmful motivation than those of religion and power. Since then, economists have come to adopt the motivation of self-interest as, what Rodrik calls, their benchmark assumption (2015, p. 187).

From the eighteenth century onwards, the market has been a powerful idea for increasing welfare based on the pursuit of self-interest. However, Bowles argues that a positive concern for the well-being of others is an essential requirement of economic and social life in today's societies. The reason for this is that in economic exchanges contracts are often absent or incomplete, for example in the case of employment and climate change. Where markets fail there is a task for the government. However, the government can also fail in its governance, because it is absent or has a lack of information. In these cases other-regarding motives (social preference 1) can be an additional governance mechanism, because people are intrinsically motivated to take into account the interests of those not included in the exchange (Bowles, 2016, p. 222).

---

1   In short, Smith argued that individual agents in maximizing their self-interest also create collective benefit. His famous example is that the baker who gets up early in the morning to bake bread is not acting out of altruism. He serves his self-interest, but by doing so, he is serving the well-being of consumers as well. What is good for the individual appears to be good for the whole. Initially, the triumph of the idea of the market was unprecedented. Competition between entrepreneurs led to (material) growth, reduction of poverty and extraordinary developments in technology. In the course of the twentieth century it became more and more visible that the market creates also negative external effects like environmental problems.

6.3   TR between Sacks and Bowles on *chessed*

This section develops TR between Sacks and Bowles on *chessed*. In 6.3.1 the question is whether and how Sacks' concept of *chessed* relates to Bowles' concept of social preference 1. Section 6.3.2 is about the relevance of this conversation between Sacks and Bowles for a social response to radical uncertainty in the context of climate change.

6.3.1   On *chessed*

Sacks and Bowles converge in the view that human motivation goes beyond self-interest, by arguing for *chessed* (Sacks) and for social preference 1 (Bowles). *Chessed* is an expressly positive concern for the well-being of oneself and others. It is a particular type of love that seeks, bottom-up and in the present, to create relations that honour both oneself and the other. *Chessed*, therefore, includes the critical assumption of conventional economics (self-interest) and is part of Bowles' social preference 1, a concern, positive or negative, for others.

Social preference 1 makes explicitly clear that other-regarding motives are not always positive. Prosocial behaviour towards one's own group can be antisocial behaviour towards outsiders at the same time. For every 'us/we' there is a 'them'. Bowles calls this parochial altruism. Sacks recognises the resistance heard among economists when it comes to (religiously motivated) altruism which turns into parochial altruism. Sacks describes evil committed in the name of high ideals as altruistic evil (2015c, p. 9). Sacks converges with Bowles in admitting that faith in God has often contributed to conflicts between 'us/we' and 'them', for example in seventeenth-century Europe. "It is fair to say that religion did not distinguish itself at that time. It was then that honest, thoughtful men and women began to say to themselves: if people of faith cannot live together in peace, despite their differences, then for the sake of the future we must find another way" (Sacks 2011, p. 10). At the same time, Sacks contends that there is nothing specifically religious about altruistic evil, because there are also many secular utopias that have led to violence, for example Nazi Germany and Stalinist Russia (Sacks, 2015c, pp. 9-10). Sacks goes on to argue that in the course of the centuries, God was further side-tracked in Western societies: first in science, then in the arts, then as the basis of good governance. God became quaint, something for the private sphere and not for the public. The reason for all of this, Sacks maintains, is that religion failed to meet the challenge of change (Sacks, 2011, pp. 10-11).[2]

Sacks and Bowles also converge on the need to seek a form of reciprocity that goes beyond altruistic parochialism (Bowles) or altruistic evil (Sacks). Bowles argues that '... the fact that altruism and parochialism may have a common evolutionary origin, whether cultural or genetic, does not mean that the two are inseparable" (Bowles & Gintis, 2011, p. 147). He argues that one of the main reasons humans have managed to survive is that the driving force of evolution is not primarily self-interest, but especially cooperation. He defines cooperation as engaging with others in a mutually beneficial activity, which includes other-regarding behaviour (social preference 1). Also, Sacks argues that altruism is not 'parochial' *per se*, by referring to the stranger. For Sacks, the key challenge in going beyond altruistic evil is to recognize the image of God in oneself and the other, especially the stranger. In his view, in monotheism God is God of all. Therefore the related concept of love, *chessed*, is not limited to one's own group, but includes, expressly, the stranger, the one who is not like me (Sacks, 2010, p. 186; Sacks, 2011, p. 201; 2013b, p. 32: 2015c, Chapter 8).

Chessed opens up a perspective for creating relations between people with different or even conflicting identities. Identity refers to the images people live by—images of themselves, others and the world. The reason for this is that *chessed* does not seek the affirmation of one specific position, but it stimulates opposition to open up the identities people are living by. Some identities may have been useful in the past, but that does not mean that they are still useful in the present. *Chessed* orients us to creating a new and inclusive identity, a new 'we', beyond present identities.

For Bowles, social preference 1 includes a concern for the environment. Bowles refers, for example, to other-regarding motives when Brazilian fishermen adopt more environment-friendly traps and nets (Bowles, 2016, p. 41). *Chessed* deepens this concern. *Chessed* goes further than just a concern for the environment in the sense of people taking care of the environment. The reason for this is that *chessed* bears in itself the potential to be extended to nonhumans. Sacks connects *chessed* with the 'I-Thou

---

2   In relation to the economy, the same tendency was formulated almost a century earlier by the economist Richard H. Tawney. In his view, religion had lacked "the creative energy" to reinvent its insights "in a form applicable to the needs of a more complex and mobile social order" (Tawney, 1998, p. 281). As a consequence, according to Tawney, religion took as its province the individual soul and the economy the public domain.

relationships' of Martin Buber (Sacks, 2007, p. 174). Within his poetical tract *I and Thou* (1937) Martin Buber makes the distinction between two modes of engaging the world. In the first of these modes, the mode of 'I–it', the object of experience (the It) is viewed as a thing to be utilized. In the second mode, 'I-Thou', we enter into a relationship with what or whom we encounter, and both the I and the Thou are transformed by the relation between them. For Buber, the combination I-Thou is not limited to the human sphere, but also includes our relation with nature (Buber, 1937, p. 5). In line with this is Sacks' reference to an interpretation by Rabbi Samson Raphael Hirsch of the phrase in Genesis 1, 'Let us make mankind in our image, in our likeness' (Gen 1: 26). Hirsch says that the 'us' refers to the rest of creation (Sacks, 2016b, p. 303). *Chessed* thus challenges us to go beyond a concern for the environment by inviting us to enter into a relationship with the environment.[3]

Chessed also deepens Bowles' argument about the joy in working together with like-minded people (Bowles & Gintis, 2011, p. 3). Sacks adds another dimension of joy, expressed with the Hebrew *simhah*. This dimension emphasizes that considering oneself and the other as subjects, so that both can flourish and enter in a relationship in which both are transformed, creates a shared joy, especially when that flourishing is threatened. This meaning of joy has strong connotations of liberation.

To conclude, Sacks and Bowles converge in a view on human motivation which goes beyond self-interest, by arguing for *chessed* (Sacks) and for social preference 1 (Bowles). *Chessed* is an other-regarding motive that pays special attention to the stranger, the one who is not like me. Bowles points to the fact that other-regarding motives are not only positive. What is more, he shows that there is a deep historical conflict in the legacy of the research traditions of theology and economics due to parochial altruism. However, TR between Sacks and Bowles shows that conflict need not be their destiny. Sacks and Bowles converge in seeking a new 'we' (Sacks) or cooperation (Bowles) that goes beyond altruistic parochialism. *Chessed* highlights the importance of creating relations between people with different or even conflicting identities in order to open up the identities people are living by. *Chessed* deepens Bowles' concern for the environment and his understanding of joy.

---

3   In recent decades the question emerged whether the notion 'image of God' can be extended to nonhumans as well. An explicit plea for broadening the concept of imago Dei beyond human beings has been made for example by Peterson (1999). For the discussion as a whole, see also Moritz (2015).

6.3.2   On climate change

What relevance does the conversation between Sacks and Bowles on *chessed* have for a social response to radical uncertainty in the context of climate change?

The conversation between Sacks and Bowles highlights the relevance of social preference 1 when it comes to developing a social response to radical uncertainty in the context of climate change. People inspired by *chessed* seek to create, in the midst of radical uncertainty, a new 'we' that honours both oneself and the other, especially the one still excluded, the other. Important to stress here is that *chessed* challenges us to consider the 'other'—for example, the climate, people in areas affected by climate change, climate refugees, young people and yellow vests—not in abstract terms, but to learn to know them by name and to enter into a relationship with them.

TR orients us also to creating meaning in relations between people with different and even conflicting identities, which might be expressed in conflicting interests in the present or different opinions about the time needed for a transition related to climate change. This plurality is of crucial importance for opening up identities that may have been useful in the past, but are not useful anymore. An example here would be the director of an environmental NGO and the CEO of an oil company creating meaning by learning together how to take responsibility for a shared future. Or school children skipping school to march for the climate as an expression that they want their voices to be heard. Perhaps more uncomfortable than children raising their voices by skipping school, is the example of the often less peaceful demonstrations of the 'yellow vest' movement. These demonstrations started in November 2018 in France as local protests against a planned tax on fuel, part of the French President Macron's climate plan to promote electric and hybrid vehicles. The protests quickly morphed into an angry, seemingly leaderless, nationwide protest movement demanding higher wages, a repeal of the fuel tax and even Macron's resignation. The reason for mentioning the three examples above is to accentuate that *chessed* does not seek the affirmation of one specific position, but stimulates plurality in relationships in order to open up the identities people live by.

Chessed orients us to the role that ordinary people, 'day-by-day experts', play in building new relationships in the midst of radical uncertainty, in addition to 'professional-experts' seeking to optimize objectively a social response to climate change (section 2.4). Focusing on ordinary people—mothers, fathers, singles, children, in one word citizens—coincides with recent analyses that focus on deliberative democracy, namely on non-state actors like citizens, cities and business (Hajer, 2011; Stevenson and Dryzek, 2014).

Chessed challenges the imagination to create not only relationships between humans, but also between humans and nonhumans. One can refer here to a concept like 'working together with water', as found in a report of the second Delta Committee in the Netherlands (2007-2008). The Delta committee was set up by the Dutch cabinet as a way of proactively adapting to climate change and anticipating predicted sea level rise and greater fluctuations in river discharge. The idea of the Committee is to build and develop the country as far as possible in harmony with ecological processes. (2008, p. 39) In other words, it proposes a kind of partnership between humans and nature to adapt to climate change, by working with natural processes and building with water, as the title of the reports puts it. This approach of working together with water challenges the earlier approach of managing nature. Nevertheless, one might argue that concepts like 'working together with water' or 'working together with nature' still advocate too instrumental an approach to nonhumans. The idea of extending *chessed* to nonhuman beings might be even better expressed in studies of a new field defined by Frans de Waal as evolutionary cognition. Evolutionary cognition is "... the study of all cognition (human and animal) from an evolutionary standpoint" (De Waal, 2016, p. 28). In this field the study of cognition is on a less anthropocentric footing. Evolutionary cognition tries to treat every species on its own terms, using human empathy as a way to understand other species. In this way De Waal crosses the border separating his own species from others. "True empathy is not self-focused but other-orientated. Instead of making humanity the measure of all things, we need to evaluate other species by what they are. In doing so, I am sure we will discover many magic wells, including some as yet beyond our imagination" (De Waal, 2016, p. 275).

TR shows that learning to take responsibility in the context of climate change is not necessarily a painful matter of self-sacrifice, nor feeling guilty about your ecological footprint, doing your duty or chastising conscience. It familiarizes us with a perspective which is essentially about the joy of entering into relationships with one another, especially including those yet excluded.

Thus far the good news about other-regarding motives. In TR it is especially Bowles who makes some critical remarks about it. First, he points out to the importance of not being naive about human behaviour. There are negative other-regarding motivations as well, like parochial altruism, hate, opportunism, fear, indifference or envy. Radical uncertainty in climate change can also trigger these motivations. Second, seemingly positive motivations like *chessed*, crucial for developing an inclusive new 'we', can slip into parochial altruism, creating an 'us/we' versus a 'them'. History shows that creating a new 'we' has often led to a 'them' as well. This realistic picture of human behavior raises the question of whether it is possible to govern human behaviour that seeks to stimulate relations that honour oneself and the other without creating a 'them' in the midst of radical uncertainty. In order to answer this question, we will return to a conversation with Bart Nooteboom, who has developed insights about the governance of trust.

To conclude, the relevance of TR between Sacks and Bowles on *chessed* is that it orients us to social preference 1, besides self-interest, when it comes to developing a social response to radical uncertainty in the context of climate change. People inspired by *chessed* seek to create a new 'we' that honours both oneself and the other in the midst of radical uncertainty. TR points especially to creating meaning in relations between people with different and even conflicting identities. The reason for this is that difference creates the opportunity to become aware of the views of oneself and the other that one lives by, to open up these views, and develop together an inclusive identity. *Chessed* challenges us to create not only relationships between humans, but also between humans and nonhumans. Joy is a result of developing relations based on *chessed*. It is Bowles who focuses attention on the importance of addressing negative other-regarding motivations. Radical uncertainty in climate change can trigger these motivations. This raises the question of whether it is possible to govern human behaviour that seeks to stimulate relations that honour oneself and the other without creating a 'them' in the midst of radical uncertainty.

6.4   Nooteboom on relational contracting

Nooteboom analyses in his book *Trust* not only the concept of trust, but also how trust can be used as an instrument of governance. Governance deals with the question of how to enable relations while reducing transaction costs, which are the costs of an economic exchange (Nooteboom, 2002, p. 103). Generally speaking, Nooteboom considers three forms of governance: (1) 'hierarchy', that can settle disputes with coercion or direct control of actions, (2) 'obligational contracts', to reduce opportunities for opportunism by legal contracts, a contract that can be enforced by a legal authority, and (3) 'relational contracting', a very wide form of governance based on relationships like kinship, advantage, mutual dependence and shared ownership. For Nooteboom, the three forms of governance can be seen as complementary instead of substitutes. "Governance on the basis of coercion of self-interest always has to be supplemented by trust, because future contingencies and motives are never completely known, and language cannot yield certainty of meaning, so that contracts and self-interest always leave a gap of uncertainty" (Nooteboom, 2002, p. 200). Here the focus is on the governance of real trust, which is for Nooteboom trust beyond self-interest. Nooteboom considers the governance of real trust to be part of the general form of relational contracting. The reason for this is that one can select people for an economic exchange on the basis of ex ante real trust, for example kinship or friendship. If there is no ex ante real trust in an economic relation, real trust can also be developed in a process of trust building.

6.5 TR between Sacks and Nooteboom on governance of *chessed*

This section develops TR between Sacks and Nooteboom on governance of *chessed*. In 6.5.1 the question is whether and how Sacks' covenant interacts with Nooteboom's relational contracting. Section 6.5.2 is about the relevance of this conversation for a social response to radical uncertainty in the context of climate change.

6.5.1 On governance

When it comes to governance, Sacks' understanding of hope highlights the covenant and the Sabbath. The covenant takes place at one particular moment. The Sabbath is a regular institution, and includes the renewal of the covenant. Here the focus is on the covenant; the Sabbath will be dealt with in section 7.4 and 7.5. Sacks describes the covenant as an institution that formalizes relations of *chessed*. He draws a sharp contrast between the institution of the covenant and that of the contract. He associates the covenant with an 'other-regarding' motivation, long-term relations and enforcement by moral commitment. He associates the contract with a motivation of self-interest, short-term transactions and legal enforcement. (2007, p. 109; Sacks, 2009b, p. 163) Let me recall briefly several characteristics of the covenant (section 4.8.2):

First, the covenant is a formalization of relations of *chessed* created by two or more people who voluntarily and each on their own terms exchange promises to take responsibility for a shared future.

Second, entering into a covenant does not mean that everybody agrees with one another. The covenant is an argumentative association in which the dignity of difference is valued. The differences between the people are essential for opening up one's own identity in order to be able to create a new 'we'.

Third, For Sacks, the covenant has a theological dimension. The reason for this is that one of the partners of the covenant is God. God's presence is not on the surface of things. It is in relations of *chessed* that God becomes visible.

In his work, Sacks gives a nuanced definition of the covenant, but a similar treatment of the contract is hard to find. However, in economics a more nuanced definition of the contract can be found. This definition might allow for further interaction between Sacks and Nooteboom.

In economics there is a variety of contracts. When Sacks uses the term 'contract' he seems to refer to the simplest form, a legal private contract. This contract arranges a bilateral exchange between money and goods. Both parties know what they want: I sell, and you buy, that's all. For example, I buy an apple from my greengrocer. A private contract is very specific and contains legally binding obligations which can be enforced in the courts. However, it is unlikely that my greengrocer and I will go to court. The transaction is quite complete. There is not much left to have a dispute about. If he sells me a rotten apple, the next time I will simply buy my apple somewhere else. (Kay, 1993, p. 51) Nooteboom considers such an exchange part of the general form of governance called 'obligational contracts'. For him, the most characteristic element of this form of governance seems to be that it is legally binding. However, in the example of the greengrocer the key element of the exchange is not so much the fact that it is legally binding. Most of the time we might not even be aware that the transaction has a legal component. If we are disappointed in the transaction, it is easier and more common to go to the competitor next time instead of going to court. Therefore, I consider the key element of this form of governance 'competition' instead of 'obligational contracts' (Bovenberg, 2016, p. 27).

Of course, Sacks is right that the covenant is not a contract, in terms of a private contract. However, in economics Sacks' notion of covenant can be seen as part of a particular kind of governance, which Nooteboom calls 'relational contracting'. Relational contracting is about getting the interests parallel via relationships, such as kinship and friendship. Using Nooteboom, I would say that there is more interaction possible than suggested by Sacks' contrasting of the covenant and the contract. Figure 6.1 below summarises the three general forms of governance which I define in a Venn-diagram.

Figure 6.1   The three general forms of governance

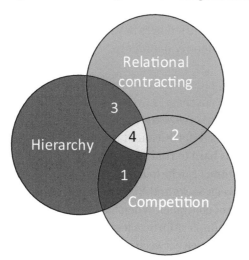

In this figure, the blue circle is the general form of competition. This form is about simple social interactions in the market between a small number of people. One can refer here to the example given above about buying an apple from a greengrocer. Interactions are based on price and reputation. The red circle in the Venn-diagram is the general form of hierarchy. This form is about simple social interactions between a small and large number of people. Coercion is exercised by institutionalized authority, for example, laws and rules (government). The green circle is the form of relational contracting and contains the governance of real trust. Following Nooteboom, real trust relates especially to small-scale interactions within and between firms. However, the covenant as a formalization of *chessed* considers the whole of reality as a network of relations of trust, both small-scale and large-scale. Figure 6.1 portrays the covenant as rooted in the general form of relational contracting, because it is based on relationships of trust. At the same time, the covenant can also be prior to parts of the other two kinds of governance, when it is described as a societal covenant expressing the kind of society in which we want to live.

In the figure I distinguish several interactions between the three general forms of governance.

Overlap 1 is about interactions between government and market. An example here would be a private legal contract.

Overlap 2 is about interaction between market and relational contracting. This refers to expressions of the market which are so complex that they are not (completely) legally contractible. Here we can think of an implicit contract like an employment contract.

Overlap 3 is about interactions between government and relational contracting. Examples of such interaction would be government stimulating the norms of civil behaviour by a message in order to prevent a weakening of support for tax-paying in society, or by messages about behaviour related to COVID-19 transmission.

Overlap 4 is about an interaction among all three forms of governance, and includes part of the covenant. An example here would be education that is founded by actors in civil society based on a certain view of the good life. The government then monitors the quality of education. Competition between schools is based on reputation (market).

A possible mix of the three forms of governance as a social response to radical uncertainty is a different outcome than generally seen in economics. In section 2.7 it was pointed out that since the financial crisis of 2007-09, several economists are not only rediscovering the theme of radical uncertainty, but are doing so from a more or less Keynesian or Hayekian perspective, respectively government or market. These perspectives are (often) regarded as two diametrically opposed forms of governance.

To conclude, in the interaction above Sacks highlights the covenant as an institution that formalizes relations motivated by *chessed*. Sacks sharply contrasts the institution of the covenant and that of the contract. However, Nooteboom deepens Sacks' understanding of the contract by arguing that there is a variety of contracts. The covenant can be seen as part of a particular kind of governance, which Nooteboom calls 'relational contracting'. The covenant can be supported by, and help to flesh out, other forms of governance.

6.5.2   On climate change

What relevance does the conversation between Sacks and Nooteboom on governance have for a social response to radical uncertainty in the context of climate change?

The conversation familiarizes us with the covenant as a possible institution of governance to strengthen new relationships inspired by *chessed* in matters related to climate change. In section 2.7 it was stated that there is no global authority that can intervene when it comes to climate change. Therefore Biermann stresses the need for more imagination and courage in our approach to the governance of the earth system, including climate change. (2014, p. 203) One way to bring about an improved architecture of governance is to redesign or reform and strengthen (top-down) intergovernmental decision-making (hierarchy), as Bierman proposes. Here the focus is on the covenant, which is part of the general form of relational contracting and can be described as a bottom-up agreement between subjects learning how to create space for one another and oneself. In a covenant, people formalize relations capable of creating a new world that includes all involved in the midst of radical uncertainty. TR shows that such a formalization can take place on several levels. The focus of Nooteboom is on radical uncertainty on a micro-level. However, Sacks argues that a covenant includes both the micro- and macro-level. What is more, he maintains that there is also interaction possible between the micro- and macro-level. One can think of a shared mission between a few people that develops into a movement. Another example would be children, who have to learn in particular settings, for example school, what it means to build relations that honour oneself and the other. When children grow up they are educated to widen their horizon to include the climate, fellow citizens and strangers.

Figure 6.1 shows that the covenant is not about creating either-or forms of governance. It shows that the covenant can influence the way competition (market) and hierarchy (government) are given shape. When it comes to climate change, competition is then important for stimulating innovations by entrepreneurs, and lower prices for increasing accessibility to energy sources like wind and solar. The role of the government then is not primarily about defining and controlling the outcome of the process by setting strict targets for the short and long term in a Climate Act. Due to radical uncertainty, the government does not have all the required information to set such strict targets for the short term and especially for the longer term. Rather than defining precisely the outcome and setting clearly defined targets, the role of the government should be to support the learning process of how to create a new 'we' that includes the interests of the climate and next generations.

In the covenant based on *chessed* nonhumans are not just represented by an environmental NGO. *Chessed* challenges us to imagine the possibility for including nonhumans on their own terms as well. However, we still do not have the slightest idea of what the consequences of including nonhumans in a covenant or 'a collective', as Latour puts it, will be (Latour, 2004, p. 82). Nevertheless, Latour argues that "to limit the discussion to humans, their interests, their subjectivities, and their rights, will appear as strange a few years from now as having denied the right to vote of slaves, poor people, or women" (2004, p. 69).

The covenant does not mean that all participants have to agree with one another or have the same interests in the short term. A director of an environmental NGO and a CEO of an oil company can be part of the same covenant, even though they sharply disagree on the question of how and when to respond to climate change. What is more, it is especially the differences between people that are essential for opening up one's own identity as a way to visualize new perspectives. Therefore one can argue that the Energy Agreement for Sustainable Growth in the Netherlands (2013) contains elements of a covenant. The agreement gives voice to the willingness of forty-seven parties, with sometimes conflicting interests—including central, regional and local government, employers' associations and unions, nature conservation and environmental organizations, and financial institutions—to work on issues related to climate change and energy. In 2018 the Dutch government initiated new discussions with approximately 100 parties from the private sector, civil society and subnational authorities to try to reach a climate agreement in order to reduce CO_2 emissions[4] by 49% by 2030. Something that comes closer to a proposal for a covenant can be found in Macron's letter to the French people launching *Le Grand Débat National* (January 2019) as a response to the 'yellow vest' movement:

> In France, and also in Europe and the world, people are not just extremely worried, they are deeply distressed… In order for hopes to dominate fears, it is necessary and legitimate for us together to return to the major questions about our future. (2019)

In this letter Macron launched a major national debate which continued until 15 March 2019. He invited the French people to provide input for a new contract for the nation. This 'Great National Debate' resulted in plans that included the following key points: Citizens' Initiative Referendums, tax cuts for a maximum number of citizens, especially the middle-class, better control of borders at the national and European level, uncompromising approach to 'political Islam' that seeks to break with the rest of the country, reforming France's civil service and elite schools.[5] Macron's national debate seems to come closer to a covenant than the Energy Agreement for Sustainable Growth in the Netherlands, because all citizens are included and not just forty-seven parties. However, some critical remarks have to

---

4   In this study CO_2 is used as shorthand for greenhouse gases (GHGs) that include carbon dioxide (CO_2), nitrous oxide (N_2O), and halocarbons (a group of gases including chlorofluorocarbon (CFC).

5   See https://granddebat.fr/

be made. First, Macron's initiative is still a kind of contract between the government and the citizens instead of a covenant that is initiated bottom up. Second, Macron's initiative is a response to the 'yellow vest' movement and includes an uncompromising approach to, what is called, 'political Islam'. It is beyond the scope of this study to elaborate on the meaning of political Islam. Nevertheless, the critical question has to be asked whether Macron's contract can be broken open in order to become more inclusive, also to Muslim minorities in France.

Also in the Netherlands proposals have been made to develop new relations of trust in society. Pieter Omtzigt, member of Parliament for the Christian Democratic Party in the Netherlands, has argued for a new social contract between government and citizens in the Netherlands (Omtzigt, 2021, pp. 183-187). Gert-Jan Segers, the parliamentary leader of the Christian Union party, has argued explicitly for renewing the idea of covenant as found in the work of Jonathan Sacks in order to rebuild an inclusive society based on trust (Segers, 2016, pp. 220-223). These proposals have a different focus than issues related to climate change and humans-nonhumans. However they can be extended to include these issues as well.

I finish this section with an example of a covenant of hope which we drafted during the symposium 'Water in Times of Climate Change. A Values-driven Dialogue', Amsterdam, 6-7 November 2019. This symposium was closely related to the Amsterdam International Water Week 2019. The water symposium investigated issues related to water and anthropogenic climate change, focussing on several interlocking dimensions: science, economy, government and religion. An aim of the symposium was to build dialogues and long-term relationships on shared issues between environmental and climate scientists, scholars in and of religion and other fields, local and national governments and international organisations, financial corporations, business and NGOs, as well as religious and worldview communities. An outcome of the symposium was the signing of a covenant of hope, expressed as one of the Amsterdam Agreements of the Amsterdam International Water Week. The text of the covenant is as follows:

Water in Times of Climate Change: A Covenant of Hope
Water: source of life, symbol of purity. But also threatening force of nature that humans have to struggle with. Life-giving friend, life-taking foe. Since time immemorial and across the globe this ambiguous relationship with water has resonated in religious narratives and technological innovations alike. Today it resonates also in several of the Sustainable Development Goals, the umbrella to address the challenges of our times.

Securing our existence and the future of our children has become more than navigating ambiguity. Water in times of climate change has become a radical uncertainty, key to the most compelling challenges of our societies. Rising sea levels, drought and desertification, shortage of drinking water and sanitation, shapes and forms our struggles with water that will be crucial to the sustainability and viability of the earth.

We can respond in various ways to this radical uncertainty and ambiguous complexity. Reckless denial ignores all the warning signs and postpones all action so that the next generation will suffer the consequences. Helpless despair lets itself be overwhelmed by the dreadful consequences so that we lose the power and courage to act. Thoughtless self-confidence believes that our technological ingenuity will suffice so that we risk overlooking moral dimensions and yet unseen complexities.

Our response is a fearless hope that acknowledges uncertainty and complexity. Hope balances the imperfections and failings of the present with the promises and possibilities of the future. Hope builds the bridge between the "what is" of reality and the "what if" of our visions. Hope is the contrary of denial, of despair, and of the self-confidence that easily turns into a new escapism. Hope is the engaged and engaging response of the people of today to the calling from the future.

This covenant of hope invites us to respond to that calling. It brings together all those of good will, ready to share our insights, visions, resources, and capabilities. The covenant respects the dignity of our differences and the responsibility for joint action. The covenant seeks to bridge our practical, technological, legal, economical, and spiritual understandings of our predicament. Together we will take the small steps needed today to reach our rich vision of living sustainably on this earth, living with water as our dangerous friend. (Hasselaar & IJmker, 2021, pp. 118-119)

The covenant was signed, by among others, the Ecumenical Patriarchate, ABN AMRO Bank, Van Oord Dredging and Marine Contractors, NWB Fund, Water & Waste Department Cape Town, DKI Jakarta, Waternet Amsterdam, United Nations Environmental Program, the Netherlands-Indonesia Consortium for Muslim Christian Relations, and Amsterdam Sustainability Institute (Vrije Universiteit Amsterdam). One might think that signing such a covenant is more about the intention to contribute to a new 'we', than about a real commitment. However, this appears not to be the case. In 2020, for example, the covenant resulted, in the weeks of the corona outbreak, in a cooperation on developing the water strategy of the city Cape Town[6], with a focus on including township residents in the process of becoming a water-sensitive city. Leading partners in the project are Water and Waste Department of the city of Cape Town, University of Western Cape, Waternet Amsterdam and Vrije Universiteit Amsterdam.

To conclude, TR Sacks and Nooteboom on the governance of *chessed* highlights the role of the covenant in governing positive other-regarding motivation in the context of radical uncertainty related to climate change. It is argued that, in a social response to radical uncertainty in the context of climate change, the covenant can be supported by, and flesh out, competition (market) and hierarchy (government). The concept of the covenant is compared to several recent and related initiatives. The chapter closes with an example of a covenant of hope.

6.6   Conclusion

In this chapter I have developed TR between Sacks and the economists Bowles and Nooteboom on *chessed* and related governance in order to create a fuller understanding of a social response to radical uncertainty in the context of climate change.

TR on *chessed* between Sacks and Bowles indicates other-regarding motives, besides self-interest, for dealing with radical uncertainty in the context of climate change. People inspired by *chessed* (Sacks) learn to take responsibility together, bottom-up and in the present, for a shared future. The plurality among those involved is crucial for opening up the identities people are living by in order to create a new 'we'. Creating a new 'we' is in line with Bowles' positive other-regarding behaviour that in the course of history has created new forms of cooperation. *Chessed* challenges us to create not only a new 'we' between humans, but also between humans and nonhumans. Joy is one of the results of building relationships inspired by *chessed*, especially when one of the subjects is threatened. Nevertheless, in the conversation it is especially Bowles who makes some critical remarks, pointing out that there are also negative other-regarding motivations and that seemingly positive motivations can slip into negative ones. This raises the question of whether it is possible to govern positive motivations. To answer this question, TR turns to a conversation between Sacks and Nooteboom.

---

6   https://resource.capetown.gov.za/documentcentre/Documents/City%20strategies,%20 plans%20and%20frameworks/Cape%20Town%20Water%20Strategy.pdf

The conversation between Sacks and Nooteboom on the governance of *chessed* highlights the role of the covenant in governing positive other-regarding motivation on a micro- and macro-scale. It is argued that, in a social response to radical uncertainty in the context of climate change, the covenant can be supported by, and help to flesh out, competition (market) and hierarchy (government).

Bibliography

Biermann, F. (2014). *World Politics in the Anthropocene.* Cambridge, MA: The MIT Press.

Bovenberg, A.L. (2016). *Economieonderwijs in balans: kiezen en samenwerken.* Tilburg, The Netherlands: Tilburg University.

Bowles, S., & Gintis, H. (2011). A *Cooperative Species: Human Reciprocity and Its Evolution.* Princeton, NJ: Princeton University Press.

Bowles, S. (2016). *The Moral Economy: Why Good Incentives Are No Substitute for Good Citizens.* New Haven, CT: Yale University Press.

Buber, M. (1923, 2013). *I and Thou.* London, United Kingdom: Bloomsbury.

De Waal, F.B.M. (2016). *Are We Smart Enough to Know How Smart Animals Are?* New York, NY: W.W. Norton & Company.

Deltacommissie. (2008). *Working together with water: A living land builds for its future.* Retrieved from http://www.deltacommissie.com/doc/deltareport_full.pdf

Hajer, M. (2011). *The energetic society: In search of a governance philosophy for a clean economy.* The Hague, The Netherlands: pbl Netherlands Environmental Assessment Agency.

Hasselaar, J.J., & IJmker, E.C. (eds.). (2021). *Water in Times of Climate Change: A Values-driven Dialogue.* Amsterdam, The Netherlands: Amsterdam University Press.

Kay, J. (1993). *Foundations of Corporate Success: How Business Strategies Add Value.* Oxford, United Kingdom: Oxford University Press.

Latour, B. (2004). *Politics of Nature. How to Bring the Sciences into Democracy.* Cambridge, MA: Harvard University Press.

Macron, M.E. (2019, January 13). Letter from M. Emmanuel Macron to the French people. Retrieved from https://www.elysee.fr/en/emmanuel-macron/2019/01/13/letter-to-the-french-people-from-emmanuel-macron

Moritz, J.M. (2015). Does Jesus Save the Neanderthals? Theological Perspectives on the Evolutionary Origins and Boundaries of Human Nature. *Dialog, 54*(1): 51-60. https://dx.doi.org/10.1111/dial.12154

Nooteboom, B. (2002). *Trust: Forms, Foundations, Functions, Failures and Figures.* Cheltenham, United Kingdom: Edward Elgar.

Omtzigt, P. (2021). *Een nieuw sociaal contract.* Amsterdam, The Netherlands: Uitgeverij Prometheus.

Peterson, G.R. (1999). The Evolution of Consciousness and the Theology of Nature. *Zygon, 34*(2), 283-306. https://dx.doi.org/10.1111/0591-2385.00213

Rodrik, D. (2015). *Economics Rules: Why Economics Works, When It Fails, and How To Tell The Difference.* Oxford, England: Oxford University Press.

Sacks, J. (2007). *The Home We Build Together: Recreating Society.* London, United Kingdom: Continuum. Sacks, J. (2009b). *Future Tense: Jews, Judaism, and Israel in the Twenty-First Century.* New York, NY: Schocken Books.

Sacks, J. (2010). *Covenant & Conversation, Exodus: The Book of Redemption.* Jerusalem, Israel: Maggid Books.

Sacks, J. (2011). *The Dignity of Difference: How to Avoid the Clash of Civilizations* (Rev. ed.). London, United Kingdom: Continuum.

Sacks, J. (2013b). *The Jonathan Sacks Haggada: Collected Essays on Pesaḥ.* Jerusalem, Israel: Maggid Books.

Sacks, J. (2015c). *Not in God's Name: Confronting Religious Violence.* London, United Kingdom: Hodder & Stoughton.

Sacks, J. (2016b). *Essays on Ethics: A Weekly Reading of the Jewish Bible.* Jerusalem, Israel: Maggid Books.

Segers, G.J. (2016). *Hoop voor een verdeeld land.* Amsterdam, The Netherlands: Uitgeverij Balans.

Stevenson, H., & Dryzek, J.S. (2014). *Democratizing Global Climate Governance.* Cambridge, United Kingdom: Cambridge University Press.

Tawney, R.H. (1926, 1998). *Religion and the Rise of Capitalism.* New Brunswick, NJ: Transaction Publishers.

7.   Transversal Reasoning on Change of Identity

Abstract

The aim of this chapter is to continue transversal reasoning (TR) with a conversation between Sacks and Bowles on change of identity, and between Sacks and Ariely on the governance of change of identity. The reason for TR is to explore its relevance for a social response to radical uncertainty in the context of climate change. The relevance of the conversation between Sacks and Bowles on change of identity is that it highlights the need for time, expressed as a journey of two stages. The first stage of the journey is based on who we are, the identity underlying the actions that caused climate change. The second stage of the journey orients us to a new and liberating identity, a new 'we'. It is about who humans and non-humans want to be with one another. Hope does not accentuate the outcome of a response to climate change, but the process towards the outcome. TR shows that other-regarding motivation, an essential ingredient for a social response, can be crowded out by monetary incentives. TR also shows that there is not yet an institution that can stimulate wise combinations of self-interest and other-regarding motivation in order to develop prudent policies. TR between Sacks and Ariely highlights a public Sabbath, a 'workplace of hope', as a possible key public institution to coordinate a social response to radical uncertainty in the context of climate change for all involved, not just religious people. A workplace of hope can also deepen existing meetings and summits by providing rituals to embrace radical uncertainty in the context of climate change.

Keywords: Transversal reasoning, Jonathan Sacks, Samuel Bowles, Dan Ariely, change of identity, crowding out, public Sabbath

7.1   Introduction

This chapter continues TR with a conversation on change of identity, one of the critical assumptions of Sacks' understanding of hope. In TR Sacks'

Hasselaar, J.J., *Climate Change, Radical Uncertainty and Hope: Theology and Economics in Conversation.* Amsterdam: Amsterdam University Press, 2023
DOI 10.5117/9789048558476_CH07

concept of change of identity will be brought into conversation with the concept of social preference 2, derived from the work of the economist Samuel
Bowles. This is followed by TR on the governance of change of identity in
a conversation between Sacks and Dan Ariely. We start by presenting the
concept of social preference 2 constructed out of the work of Bowles.

7.2   Bowles on social preference 2

In this section I focus on the concept of social preference 2, constructed
out of Bowles' book *The Moral Economy*. Social preference 2 refers to the
central role of the social context in the shaping of people's preferences.
Social preference 2 is distinguished from social preference 1, a concern,
positive or negative, for others (section 6.2). Bowles argues that people
do not act in a vacuum. The social context plays a central role in people's
preferences and therefore their actions. He considers preferences the "reasons
for behaviour". For Bowles, preferences include a heterogeneous melange
of "tastes (food likes and dislikes, for example), habits, emotions (such as
shame or anger) and other visceral reactions (such as fear), the manner
in which individuals construe situations (or, more narrowly, the way they
frame a decision), commitments (like promises), socially enforced norms,
psychological propensities (for aggression, extroversion, and the like), and
one's affective relationships with others" (Bowles, 2004, p. 99).

Bowles (2016, p. 85) distinguishes two ways in which the social context
influences what people prefer.

(1) *situation-dependent preferences*. Situation dependence arises because
people' actions are motivated by a heterogeneous repertoire of preferences,
for example spiteful, payoff-maximizing or generous. Which preference is
primed depends on the incentive, a reversible signal about the principal (for
example an employer) or the situation that affects the costs and benefits
associated with an action. A new situation, for example the withdrawal of
an incentive, changes which preference motivates a person's behaviour.

(2) *endogenous preferences*. These are processes that "typically include
the effects of interactions over long periods with large numbers of others,
such as the processes that occur in schooling, religious instruction, and
other forms of socialization not readily captured in experiments" (Bowles,
2016, p. 117).

Social preference 2 is of importance in decision-making, because it creates
an extra governance mechanism, for example for marketing, and can also
serve to internalize externalities like climate change.

Although people's preferences can change (social preference 2), Bowles argues that the driving force to include the well-being of others in one's preferences (social preference 1), can be crowded out by monetary incentives (rewards and penalties).[1] The aim of Bowles' book *The Moral Economy* is to contribute to a synergy between self-interest and other-regarding motives in order to develop prudent policies. Bowles calls such a synergy a crowding-in effect. The reason that Bowles pays attention to crowding in is because there are a growing number of experiments showing that monetary incentives can crowd out ethical and other-regarding motives. In Bowles' book a central example of such a crowding-out experiment is a field study in 10 day-care centres in the city of Haifa (Israel), taken from Gneezy and Rustichini's article 'A Fine is a Price' (2000). At six centres a fine was imposed on parents who were late picking up their children at the end of the day. Instead of picking up their children earlier, the parents responded to the fine by doubling the fraction of time they arrived late. The fine had become a price. After 12 weeks the fine was revoked, but the parents' enhanced tardiness persisted.

Generally speaking, Bowles argues that the kinds of incentives and constraints that people face in a liberal democratic and market-based society sometimes lead to a kind of crowding in of positive other-regarding motives rather than the crowding out more commonly seen in experiments. (Bowles, 2016, p. 150) According to him, these societies favour the evolution of trust among strangers. In finding more ways to stimulate a crowding-in effect, Bowles goes back two millennia. He gives us a glimpse of the civic culture of ancient Greece in order to find the rudiments of a paradigm that provides a synergy between self-interest and other-regarding motives. The Athenian citizens' assembly in 325 BCE designed a mechanism to set up a colony and naval station in the Adriatic. This project required thousands of people and 29 ships. Neither the people nor the ships were at the moment under public orders. All people and ships had to be recruited from private ownership. The assembly encouraged civic action by appealing to both material interest and moral motivation. They accomplished the project by framing the material interest and moral motivation so that the two work synergistically rather than at cross-purposes in order to set up the required colony and naval station.

Bowles explains why things might have turned out differently in the day-care centres in Haifa, if they had followed the example of the ancient Athenian assembly. He imagines Athenians travelling to Haifa in a time machine and being asked to help design the day care centres' policy for

---

1   It might be possible that other-regarding behaviour can also crowd out self-interest. However, this relation is not investigated by Bowles in his *The Moral Economy* (2016).

dealing with late parents. The Athenians then would have proposed thanking parents for arriving on time to pick up their children, because this reduces the anxiety that the children sometimes feel and allows the staff to leave in a timely manner to be with their own families. All parents with a perfect record unblemished by lateness for the next three months would be awarded with 500 Israeli shekel (NIS), given at the annual parents and staff holiday party, with an option to contribute their award to the school's Teacher of the Year celebration. However, this might not be all that the Athenians would propose, in Bowles' view. Parents who arrive more than ten minutes late, would pay a fine of NIS 1,000, with the payment of the fine also taking place publicly at the holiday party. The payment would also support the Teacher of the Year celebration. The message of the Athenians would have ended with the recognition that it is, of course, sometimes impossible, for reasons beyond parents' control, to arrive on time. If this occurs, the parents may explain the circumstances before a committee of parents and staff. If the lateness was unavoidable or if the fine would cause extreme hardship, the lateness will be publicly reported but no fine will be imposed. Bowles wonders if this Athenian version of the experiment would have reversed the crowding out that occurred in the absence of moral framing. (Bowles, 2016, p. 190)

On questions of feasible public policy and the governance of organizations Bowles argues for including something like a "wise combination of positive incentives and punishments with moral lessons, such as the mix of motivations appealed to by the decree of the Athenian assembly" (Bowles, 2016, p. 221). The need for such combinations is clear, for Bowles, because issues like climate change, asymmetric information, personal security and governing the knowledge-based economy cannot be adequately covered by contracts, based on self-interest, that do not contain everything that matters to parties in the exchange. (Bowles, 2016, p. 222) However, he states that an approach favouring wise combinations of self-interest and other-regarding motives, such as appealed to by the Athenian assembly, does not yet exist. He wonders whether such an approach adequate for addressing contemporary issues like climate change can be developed. "But we have little choice but to try. The Legislator's mandate is a place to start" (Bowles, 2016, p. 223). By the Legislator's mandate, Bowles is referring to the Athenian assembly.

7.3   TR between Sacks and Bowles on change of identity

This section develops TR between Sacks and Bowles on change of identity. In 7.3.1 the question is whether and how Sacks' ideas on change of identity interact with the concept of social preference 2 derived from Bowles. In section 7.3.2 we investigate the relevance of this conversation for a social response to radical uncertainty in the context of climate change.

7.3.1 On change of identity

Our question here is whether and how Bowles' concept of social preference 2 interacts with Sacks' concept of change of identity.

Bowles argues that the social context plays a central role in what people value and therefore how people act. I have called this social preference 2. This social preference 2 coincides with Sacks' line of thought, although Sacks uses a different term to characterize the embeddedness of human action. Sacks uses the term 'identity'. Identity is about who people are. For Sacks, this identity has individual and collective origins. On the one hand, identity is shaped by the decisions and actions of an individual. On the other hand, identity is shaped by the social context of the individual. Sacks' interpretation of the Exodus highlights two types of identity, expressed in the Hebrew words (1) *am*, and (2) *edah*. In the first case, people are defined by an identity based on a shared past, for example the slavery in Egypt. It is about the question: Who are you, individually and collectively? In the second case the identity is defined by a liberating vision. The question is here: Who do you want to be as an individual and collective?

Bowles does not use the term identity.[2] However, he does address the social formation of preferences. He considers the formation of preferences in two ways, situation-dependent preferences and endogenous preferences. The first refers to a reversible signal or situation that affects the costs and benefits associated with an action. The second is a long process of formation, for example as occurs in schooling. Sacks' concept of identity is most closely related to Bowles' endogenous preferences. According to Sacks, if there is an overarching theme in the Hebrew Bible, including the Exodus, it is that if people want to remain free, they themselves have to change the identities by which they live. In Sacks' view, identities can only change when people take small steps in a long process of individual

---

2   What is more, until recently identity, who people are, was largely missed by economics. However, in 1995 thinking about identity began with a letter of Rachel Kranton to future Nobel Prize-winner George Akerlof in which she objected to his recent paper. She wrote that Akerlof had ignored identity and that this concept was also critically missing from economics more generally. It was the beginning of a long collaboration on Identity Economics. "The incorporation of identity and norms then yields a theory of decision making where social context matters" (Akerlof and Kranton 2010, p. 6).

and societal transformation. (Sacks, 2005, p. 77) This is closely related to what Bowles calls 'endogenous preferences', which he considers a form of socialization over long periods with large numbers of others. However, Bowles does not connect socialization with a notion of liberation, as Sacks does.

In section 6.3.1 we have seen that positive other-regarding motives (social preference 1) are required to open up one's identity in order to include (the interests of) others. However, Bowles has shown with the Haifa experiment that monetary incentives (rewards and penalties), based on self-interest, can crowd out other-regarding motives. Therefore, Bowles advocates for an approach that can stimulate wise combinations of self-interest and other-regarding motives in order to develop prudent policies. Sacks and Bowles converge on the need for such an approach. In the search for such an approach, they also both turn to a classic at the roots of Western society for inspiration. At the same time, they diverge on the tradition of the classic. Bowles turns to the tradition of ancient Greece (Aristotle), in particular to the Athenian assembly two millennia ago.[3] Sacks turns to the Jewish tradition (Moses) of Torah, in particular to the Exodus, with the Sabbath as a key institution in the transformation process.

To conclude, in the interaction Sacks and Bowles converge on the embeddedness of human action. The focus of Bowles is on the embeddedness in the social context, while Sacks' focus is on the embeddedness in individual and collective identity. Sacks highlights a liberating transformation of identity, closely related to Bowles' endogenous preferences. People are not defined by their past identity. Bowles shows that positive other-regarding motivation can be crowded out by monetary incentives. Bowles and Sacks converge in arguing for an approach that can stimulate wise combinations of self-interest and other-regarding motives in order to develop prudent policies. They both turn to a classic at the roots of Western society for inspiration. However, they diverge on the tradition of the classic.

7.3.2 On climate change

What relevance does the conversation between Sacks and Bowles on change of identity have for a social response to radical uncertainty in the context of climate change?

---

3 An increasing number of economists are turning to the tradition of ancient Greece to deepen and extend conventional economic assumptions. See for example Nooteboom (2002), McCloskey (2006) and Klamer (2007).

The interaction between Sacks and Bowles' analysis highlights that radical uncertainty in the context of climate change cannot be embraced without a change of individual and collective identity underlying individual and collective actions in society and the economy. In other words, the interaction points to a transformative response to climate change. In Sacks' view this transformative response consists of two stages. The first stage is based on an identity underlying the actions that caused climate change. The focus of a response is here directly on the shared problem of climate change, for example CO_2 reduction[4] or limiting global temperature increase well below 2 degrees Celsius (Paris Agreement). However, if people limit themselves to this stage, they do not fully claim the potential of a transformative response to radical uncertainty in the context of climate change. Sacks' second stage orients us to an identity which is no longer based on a shared past, who people are, but on who people want to be. The second stage points to a new and common 'we' that includes the ones yet excluded, here among others the climate, people in areas affected by climate change, climate-refugees, young people and yellow vests. In other words, in the radically uncertain future something new and better is waiting to be fulfilled. TR makes it clear that for a transformation to be durable, people have to change the images they live by, by themselves. This takes time. TR orients us to the crucial role of education in forming new identities. Special attention should be given to educating the next generation in building new relationships with oneself and the other.

In economics, David Colander and Roland Kupers have proposed that the social cost-benefit analysis (SCBA) should be extended with a theory about endogenous norms or tastes. For them, climate policy should focus on the question of how tastes evolve, change and can be influenced, so that people can develop a more climate-friendly taste. (2014, p. 191) Bowles considers taste a preference. Therefore, the approach of Colander and Kupers seems to be closely related to what Bowles has called 'situation-dependent preferences'. Nevertheless, TR goes one step further and argues that SCBA should not only be extended with a theory about preferences. Sacks' notion of identity and Bowles' notion of 'endogenous preferences' advocate extending SCBA to deeper levels and related questions of meaning, like who are we as individuals and collective, and who do we want to become in relation to ourselves and one another?

---

4   In this study CO_2 is used as shorthand for greenhouse gases (GHGs) that include carbon dioxide (CO_2), nitrous oxide (N_2O), and halocarbons (a group of gases including chlorofluoro-carbon (CFC).

The conversation with Bowles shows also that ethical and other-regarding motivation can be crowded out by monetary incentives. Bowles refers explicitly to the case of climate-change policy when discussing crowding out. The possibility of crowding out other-regarding motivation in the context of climate change shows that essential motivations for dealing with radical uncertainty in the context of climate change can be discouraged. According to Bowles there is not yet an approach that stimulates crowding-in effects when it comes to climate policy. Bowles acknowledges that he does not know whether such an approach can be developed. In the search for an approach that stimulates a crowding-in effect, Bowles turns to the tradition of ancient Greece (Aristotle), in particular to the Athenian assembly. Sacks draws inspiration from the Torah, in particular the Exodus, with a public Sabbath as a key institution in the transformation process.

To conclude, the relevance of TR between Sacks and Bowles on change of identity is that it orients us to a transformative response to climate change. In such a response radical uncertainty in the context of climate change cannot be embraced without a change of identity. Such a response consists of two stages. In the first stage the response is based on an identity underlying the actions that caused climate change. It is based on who we are. The second stage is based on who we want to be. The interaction argues for extending the SCBA to questions of meaning. However, other-regarding motivation, required to change the identities, can be crowded out. Therefore, the interaction highlights the question whether an approach can be developed that stimulates crowding-in effects.

In the remaining sections, the focus of TR is on investigating the Sabbath as an approach that seeks a wise combination of self-interest and other-regarding motives. The reason for continuing with the Sabbath instead of Bowles' suggestion of the Athenian assembly is because this TR is based on Sacks' understanding of hope. This brings us to an interaction between Sacks and Ariely.

7.4   The economist Dan Ariely on Sabbath

In this section I focus on the concept of the Sabbath derived from Dan Ariely's book *The (Honest) Truth about Dishonesty: How We Lie to Everyone – Especially Ourselves* (2012). In 2011 Tomas Sedlacek still argued in his bestseller *Economics of Good and Evil* (2011) that the Sabbath has disappeared from today's economic theory (2011, p. 89). However, in 2012 Ariely pleaded for a return of the Sabbath as a coordination mechanism in economics. Before continuing TR, the economic contribution of Ariely will be explored.

The aftermath of the fall of Enron, an American energy company, in 2001 aroused Ariely's interest in dishonesty as a component of the human nature, and resulted in his book *The (Honest) Truth About Dishonesty* (2012). In this book, Ariely argues that one way to think about dishonesty is to suppose that everyone involved in the fall of Enron was deeply corrupt. However, he started to think that there might have been a different type of dishonesty at work, a wishful blindness that causes one to fail to see the signs of dishonesty all along. "I started wondering if the problem of dishonesty goes deeper than just a few bad apples and if this kind of wishful blindness takes place in other companies as well" (Ariely, 2012, p. 2). The many scandals of companies after 2001 have clearly answered that question, but in his book Ariely goes further. He investigates whether everyone could behave dishonestly at work and at home. Ariely presents various experiments on dishonesty. However, in the last chapter he asks what we should do about dishonesty. He refers to the financial crisis of 2007-09, and states that with this crisis:

> The temple of rationality has been shaken, and with our improved un-
> derstanding of irrationality we should be able to rethink and reinvent
> new kinds of structures that will ultimately help us avoid such crisis in
> the future. If we don't do this, it will have been a wasted crisis. (Ariely,
> 2012, p. 247)

Ariely considers human follies part of the human condition. In his view, this demands an extension of conventional economic assumption and related cost-benefit analysis (Ariely, 2012, p. 4). Ariely concludes his book with formulating that the next task is to figure out more effective and practical ways to combat dishonesty. It is here that he turns to the Sabbath.

Ariely points rightly to the fact that there are already many mechanisms or rituals that support the governance of the human condition, ranging from the Catholic confession (Christianity) to Prayaschitta (Hinduism), and from Ramadan (Islam) to the Sabbath (Judaism). He states that religious traditions provide rituals that can help people and society to counteract potentially destructive tendencies, including the tendency to be dishonest. Ariely has started carrying out some basic experiments, for example to determine whether memory and awareness of the Bible and Ten Command-ments might have an effect on how people behave. The result suggests that people's willingness to cheat could be diminished by reminders like the Bible and the Ten Commandments. Although using the Bible and the Ten

Commandments as honesty-building mechanisms seems to be effective, Ariely and his team decided to think of more general, practical and secular ways to reduce cheating, namely the code of honour that many universities use. One of the reasons for this shift was that for him the introduction of religious documents into society as a means to reduce cheating would violate the separation of church and state. (Ariely, 2012, p. 41)

7.5 TR between Sacks and Ariely on governance of change of identity

This section develops the TR between Sacks and Ariely on the governance of change of identity. In 7.5.1 the question is whether and how Sacks' institution of the Sabbath interacts with Ariely's institution of the Sabbath. In section 7.5.2 we will explore the relevance this conversation has for a social response to radical uncertainty in the context of climate change.

7.5.1 On governance

Sacks and Ariely converge in a view of the human condition that leads them to make space in their analyses for human imperfection (Sacks) or human follies (Ariely). At the same time, Sacks and Ariely diverge in their focus on the component of human nature. In his book Ariely focuses on dishonesty, but in a broader sense his book is about rationality and irrationality. Dishonesty is not explicitly a theme in Sacks' work. In chapter 4 we have seen that radical uncertainty is a theme for Sacks. At the same time Sacks would recognize many sides of human nature.

Sacks and Ariely also converge in the view that creatively developing ancient religious traditions, for Sacks in particular Judaism, can enrich and deepen contemporary times and questions. As a consequence, religious traditions are for them not simply prescribed ways of doing what earlier generations did. The opposite is true, I would say. In Sacks' view (section 4.5), each generation must add their interpretations to the texts of Torah in order to keep it a relevant and incisive guidance for the good life in every time and context. Sacks and Ariely converge in particular on the role of the Sabbath in governing elements of human nature in general, not just religious people. Because of their focus on different components of human nature, they highlight different dimensions of the Sabbath. For Ariely with his focus on dishonesty, the Sabbath is particularly important because of its dimension of resetting, in the sense of (1) moral reminder, (2) overcoming the 'what the hell' effect, and (3) turning a new page. For Sacks, there are several, never exhausted, dimensions of Sabbath. Let me recall four dimensions (section 4.8.3). First, Sabbath is seen as a *Utopia Now,* presenting a way of life that people may barely glimpse in the present. Second, Sabbath is a *neutral space* that values the dignity of difference. Third, Sabbath practices and, by doing so, protects and strengthens relations of *chessed.* Fourth, Sabbath is an *embodied truth* expressed for example in music, eating together and art.

Let me recall TR between Sacks and Bowles in which we discussed the search for an institution that stimulates the crowding-in effect of self-interest and other-regarding motivation (section 7.3.1). One dimension of the Sabbath given by Sacks is promising when it comes to this search, namely the Sabbath as tutorial of *chessed. Chessed* is the driving force that expressly aims to include the well-being of the other as well as one's own self-interests. By doing so, it seeks to stimulate a crowding-in effect.

Now for what may be a difficult diverging line between Sacks and Ariely. Sacks' understanding of hope presents the Sabbath as a key public institution in changing the individual and collective identities of all involved, religious and non-religious people. By doing so, he goes beyond a simple dualism of secular and religious. Ariely, however, proposes to reinvent Sabbath in a nonreligious way. What does Ariely mean by that? He does not answer this question regarding the Sabbath. If it is the same argument he uses in the context of the Bible and the Ten Commandments as honesty-building mechanisms, then it is because of (1) practical reasons and (2) reasons of a separation between church and state. If so, then Ariely seems to argue that religious coordination mechanisms do not belong in society at large (including business and politics), because they are not secular. Here Ariely walks into the trap of too simple a dualism between the secular and the religious. A separation between church and state is not about evicting religion from society *per se.* Ariely seems to confuse a desirable religious (or better said, denominational) neutrality of the state with something like a secular state. A separation between church and state means a legally guaranteed space for religious freedom (including secular beliefs) and plurality.

In my view, the Sabbath cannot be stripped in a secular way without losing much of its strength. Maybe it is possible when it comes to (dis) honesty, but certainly not when it comes to radical uncertainty. It is, for example, impossible to leave out the horizon of hope that gives meaning to the whole. This is not to say that the Sabbath should remain a religious institution only. Because the Sabbath addresses categorical dimensions of human nature, it is necessary to untie it from an in-group connotation, meant for a certain group of religious people and/or for the private domain.

The real question seems to be how to reinvent the Sabbath in such a way that it keeps its strength and gets a public and inclusive function. In the following, to accentuate the role of the Sabbath as public institution for all involved I replace the term 'Sabbath', which can be associated with Judaism, by the term 'workplace of hope'. One can wonder whether describing the Sabbath as a 'workplace of hope' is a *contradictio in terminis*, because the Sabbath literally means 'to stop' daily life, including working. However, the Sabbath is not simply a moment to stop daily work and become refreshed, but a moment to stop daily work and to practice a hopeful transformation.

To conclude, Sacks and Ariely converge on the public role of the Sabbath for coordinating human behaviour in general. They differ, however, in their focus on a particular aspect of human behaviour. The focus of Ariely is on dishonesty, Sacks' focus is on radical uncertainty. As a consequence, they highlight different dimensions of the Sabbath. Sacks and Ariely diverge also on what it means to reinvent the Sabbath as a public institution. In looking for a nonreligious Sabbath, Ariley seem to walk into the trap of too simple a dualism between the secular and the religious. The real question is: How to reinvent the Sabbath in such a way that it keeps its strength and gets a public and inclusive function? In order to accentuate the public role of the Sabbath, not just for religious people, but for all involved, it is here renamed 'workplace of hope'.

7.5.2   On climate change

What relevance does the conversation between Sacks and Ariely on the governance of change of identity have for a social response to radical uncertainty in the context of climate change?

The relevance of the conversation is that it highlights the Sabbath, here called 'workplace of hope', as a regular public institution that governs a transformative response to embrace radical uncertainty in the context of climate change. This workplace goes beyond a simple dualism between secular and religious, as it is a ritual to stimulate a change of identity by all involved. In section 6.5.2 we have seen that Frank Biermann stresses the need for more imagination and courage in order to improve the architecture of the governance of the earth system, including climate change. Biermann's own work is on strengthening (top-down) intergovernmental decision-making. However, TR focuses our attention on improving the governance from bottom-up by designing a workplace of hope with the following four dimensions:

(1) A workplace of hope, Utopia Now, is a regular moment during a transformative response to climate change that celebrates the new 'we' that people are aiming at in the present. In this celebrating moment people are reminded that they are no longer defined by climate change, but by the new reality that they are aiming at.

(2) A workplace of hope is a neutral space in the public domain, which orients people to something larger than their present identity. The Sabbath values the dignity of difference among the participants, because it is only the experience of sharing a common world with others who look at it from different perspectives that can make people aware of their own identity and open them up to the possibility of developing a new and common identity. Therefore different or even conflicting identities are valued. Hulme argues for such a place by stating that:

> ... while science as a social enterprise might aspire to reconcile competing facts through recursive inquiry, experimentation and validation, conflicting stories about climate change cannot be reconciled so easily. Different narratives gain their potency by being rooted in specific beliefs, values, moral commitments, myths and imaginaries that themselves emerge from different social, cultural and political movements, from different ways of seeing and being in the world. These stories need listening to, interrogating, deliberating and debating using the various forms of democracy and social interaction that exist within different social formations. (Hulme, 2019)

The workplace of hope can be seen as a form of democracy and social interaction, as Hulme describes in the quotation above. The workplace is not primarily a dispute about who is right, but provides a disciplined act of communicating (making views intelligible to others who do not share them), and listening (entering the world of another, role reversal). Gradually, the ones involved might learn how reality looks from the perspective of the other and how to include all interests involved.

(3) A workplace of hope stimulates relations of *chessed* that seek to include the well-being of the other, especially those yet excluded, as well as one's own self-interests. Climate change initiatives are never immune to setbacks like a disappointing summit in Copenhagen or the United States withdrawing from the Paris Agreement: there is much scope for despair, opportunistic behaviour, feelings of fear, futility or scepticism. A workplace of hope recognizes all of this, but does not surrender to it and stimulates taking small steps forward together.

(4) A workplace of hope is embodied truth that stimulates the development of meaningful relations between subjects, not only via reflection and practical steps forward, but also via the power of music, poetry, prayer, art and imagination. As such it can also become a site of resistance. Its mode of meaning-making is not confined to reflection and practical steps forward: the Sabbath can also draw upon the power of music, poetry, prayer and art. For instance, the playing of music possesses the ability to imagine a different reality other than the present one, and by doing so can start to make that reality real. One could take, for example, U2's 'In the Name of Love', originally about developing a new 'we' in the context of racial discrimination, and rewrite it in the context of climate change.

In section 7.3.2 we cited Bowles' explicit reference to climate change policy in connection with his point that positive other-regarding motivation, essential for developing a new 'we', can be crowded out by motivations of self-interest. Therefore a proper response to radical uncertainty in the context of climate change demands an approach that stimulates a wise combination of self-interest and other-regarding motives. Bowles wonders whether such an approach adequate for addressing contemporary issues like climate change can be developed. The Sabbath as a workplace of hope on several levels (micro and macro), based on the four dimensions given above, seems to have the potential for an approach designed to seek wise combinations of self-interest and other-regarding motives.

There are already numerous meetings and summits dealing with climate change. A next step can be to deepen meetings and summits with the practice of a workplace of hope in order to make them rituals to embrace radical uncertainty in the context of climate change.

I finish this section with a sketch of the very first attempt at a real-life workplace of hope, using the four dimensions above. The workplace described here is the initiative of the InspirationTable held in the Netherlands prior to the United Nations Climate Change Conference in Paris (Hasselaar, 2016).

(1) The InspirationTable as *Utopia Now*. The InspirationTable was held in the dunes near the North Sea beach of The Hague. There, with an eye to the rising sea level, work is underway to increase the height of the dikes by using new concepts like "working together with nature".

(2) The InspirationTable as a *neutral space*. The table was organized by churches in the Netherlands. The table was a neutral space in the public domain, facilitating an honest conversation about motives, dilemmas and interests in the context of climate change. The table brought together students and high-profile representatives from business, religion (Judaism,

Islam, Christianity), politics, NGOs, science and media. Among those representatives were the Dutch Climate Envoy and senior representatives of Rabobank, KPN, CNG Net[5], Royal Dutch Shell, Tata Steel, Dunea, Hivos, TEAR and Natuur & Milieu. Everybody was invited on their own and equal terms. The diversity among the participants was considered a resource to create value, rather than a source of clash.

(3) Building relations of *chessed*. The InspirationTable was a small-scale event that aimed to create an atmosphere of trust and interaction. The Table started with an 'iconoclastic fury' to stimulate face-to-face encounters instead of getting mired down in (enemy) images peoples have of each other.

(4) InspirationTable as *embodied truth*. The InspirationTable brought in the power of music and the sharing of food.

The interaction between Sacks and Ariely on the governance of change of identity orients us to designing a workplace of hope to strengthen the governance of climate change in the face of radical uncertainty. I close this chapter by referring to two recent initiatives of governments in dealing with climate change which seem to be closely related to the developed workplaces of hope.

(1) In 2018 the Dutch government initiated five so-called 'climate ta-bles', involving approximately 100 stakeholders, to try to reach a climate agreement. These tables are important sector platforms for discussions and negotiations and cover five sectors: Electricity, Built Environment, Industry, Agriculture & Land Use, and Mobility.[6] The central goal of the agreement is to reach a broad consensus on ways to reduce CO_2 emissions cost-efficiently. Thereafter the agreement will be implemented. How do these 'climate tables' relate to the workplaces of hope? Here I mention two similarities. First, the two seem to be rather similar, because in both cases the parties meet one another around a table. Second, both accentuate a more bottom-up approach with the participation of stakeholders instead of a top-down initiative by the government only. There are also at least two differences. First, the climate tables are not part of an ongoing process in which they regularly play a key role as the workplaces of hope do. The tables serve only as a forum to develop proposals that can be selected by the government and then be implemented. Second, the focus of the climate tables is not on a change of identity to develop a new 'we', but primarily

---

5   Since 2016 CNG Net is part of the company PitPoint clean fuels.
6   See the Climate Agreement: https://www.klimaatakkoord.nl/documenten/publica-ties/2019/06/28/national-climate-agreement-the-netherlands

on reducing CO_2 cost-efficiently. In a sense, one can say that the tables are part of multi-stakeholder SCBA, more oriented to implementing objective knowledge than to developing intersubjective knowledge in a process.

(2) In launching the French national debate in 2019, President Macron declared:

> You will be able to participate in debates near where you live or air your views on the Internet and put forward your proposals and ideas. In metropolitan France, overseas France or abroad as a French person living there. In villages, towns, districts, at the initiative of mayors, [other] elected officials, leaders of voluntary organizations, and ordinary citizens. In parliamentary, regional and departmental assemblies. (2019)

Macron and his government have selected four themes for this debate, which are seen as covering many of the nation's major challenges: (1) taxation and public spending, (2) the organization of the state and public services, (3) the ecological transition, and (4) democracy and citizenship. The outcome of this debate will "... allow us to build a new contract for the nation, to give structure to the action of the government and Parliament, and also France's positions at European and international levels" (Macron, 2019). How does this debate relate to the workplaces of hope? Here I mention two similarities. First, both highlight a bottom-up approach with the participation of all those involved, instead of a top-down initiative by the government only. Second, both conversations take as their point of departure the issue of identity, i.e. they aim at developing a new 'we'. There are also at least two differences. First, the national debate is not part of an ongoing process in which it regularly plays a key role as the workplaces of hope do. Second, in the national debate there still seems to be a central role for the government, which can be found, for example, in the expression "allow us to build a new contract *for* [emphasis added] the nation". In the workplaces of hope there is a central role for the people. This might be better expressed in "to build *with* the nation a new contract".

The relevance of TR on the governance of change of identity is thus that it orients us to the potential of the Sabbath as a workplace of hope in a transformative response to climate change. This workplace can deepen existing meetings and summits in order to make them rituals to embrace radical uncertainty in the context of climate change. One example of a real-life initiative has been given and the workplace of hope is set alongside two recent and related initiatives taken by governments.

7.6 Conclusion

In this final part of TR I have developed a conversation on change of identity between Sacks and the economists Bowles and Ariely in order to create a fuller understanding of a social response to radical uncertainty in the context of climate change.

TR between Sacks and Bowles shows that radical uncertainty in the context of climate change cannot be embraced without a transformation of individual and collective identity (Sacks) or preferences (Bowles) underlying individual and collective actions. The conversation also highlights the need to allow time for a response to climate change. The reason for this is that for a transformation to be durable, people have to change their identity or preferences by themselves. TR also shows that social preference 1, essential for the transformation, can be crowded out by self-regarding motives. TR makes it clear that there is not yet an approach that stimulates crowding-in effects when it comes to climate policy. In the search for an approach that stimulates a crowding-in effect, TR turns to a conversation between Sacks and Ariely on the governance of change of identity. The relevance of this part of TR is that it points to the potential of a public Sabbath as a workplace of hope, a key institution in a transformative response to climate change. A real-life sketch of a workplace of hope is given.

Bibliography

Akerlof, G.A., & Kranton, R.E. (2010). *Identity Economics: How Our Identities Shape Our Work, Wages, and Well-Being*. Princeton, NJ: Princeton University Press.

Ariely, D. (2012). *The (Honest) Truth About Dishonesty: How We Lie to Everyone–Especially Ourselves*. New York, NY: Harper.

Bowles, S. (2004). *Microeconomics: Behavior, Institutions, and Evolution*. Princeton, NJ: Princeton University Press.

Bowles, S. (2016). *The Moral Economy: Why Good Incentives Are No Substitute for Good Citizens*. New Haven, CT: Yale University Press.

Colander, D., & Kupers, R. (2014). *Complexity and the Art of Public Policy: Solving Society's Problems from the Bottom up*. Princeton, NJ: Princeton University Press.

Gneezy, U., & Rustichini, A. (2000). A Fine is a Price. *Journal of Legal Studies, 29*(1), 1-18.

Hasselaar, J.J. (Ed.). (2016). *We have a dream: InspiratieTafel Klimaatverandering: An Ongoing Conversation*. Amersfoort: The Old Catholic Church of the Netherlands.

Hulme, M. (2019, May 2). *Climate change narratives: beyond the facts of science.* Retrieved from https://mikehulme.org/climate-change-narratives-beyond-the-facts-of-science/

Klamer, A. (2007). *Speaking of Economics: How to Get in the Conversation.* Abingdon, United Kingdom: Routledge.

Macron, M.E. (2019, January 13). Letter from M. Emmanuel Macron to the French people. Retrieved from https://www.elysee.fr/en/emmanuel-macron/2019/01/13/letter-to-the-french-people-from-emmanuel-macron

McCloskey, D.N. (2006). *The Bourgeois Virtues: Ethics for an Age of Commerce.* Chicago, IL: The University of Chicago Press.

Nooteboom, B. (2002). *Trust: Forms, Foundations, Functions, Failures and Figures.* Cheltenham, United Kingdom: Edward Elgar.

Sacks, J. (2005). *To Heal a Fractured World: The Ethics of Responsibility.* New York, NY: Schocken Books.

Sedlacek, T. (2011). *Economics of Good and Evil, The Quest for Economic Meaning from Gilgamesh to Wall Street.* Oxford, United Kingdom: Oxford University Press.

8. Transversal Reasoning on Narrative

Abstract

This chapter continues transversal reasoning (TR) with a conversation between Sacks and John Kay & Mervyn King on narrative. The reason for TR is to explore its relevance for a social response to radical uncertainty in the context of climate change. TR between Sacks and Kay & King orients us to narrative reasoning as a distinct way of knowing to address radical uncertainty in climate change. In TR, Sacks' interpretation of the narrative of the Exodus provides a hopeful answer to the question of Kay and King: What is going on? In TR a narrative of hope is then developed in a lecture to be held at a climate summit. The chapter brings to an end the TR that started in chapter 5.

Keywords: Transversal reasoning, Jonathan Sacks, John Kay, Mervyn King, radical uncertainty, narrative

8.1 Introduction

This chapter brings to an end TR that started in chapter 5. The focus in this chapter is on narrative as part of Jonathan Sacks' understanding of hope. In TR Jonathan Sacks' narrative will be brought into conversation with the concept of narrative in the book *Radical Uncertainty* (2020) by John Kay & Mervyn King. Before beginning TR, we start by presenting the concept of narrative in the book of Kay and King.

8.2 The economists John Kay & Mervyn King on narrative

In this section I focus on the concept of narrative in John Kay and Mervyn King's book *Radical Uncertainty* (2020). The essence of this book, illustrated with many anecdotes, is about how to think about decision-making in a radically uncertain world, and how to cope with it. Kay and King argue

Hasselaar, J.J., *Climate Change, Radical Uncertainty and Hope: Theology and Economics in Conversation*. Amsterdam: Amsterdam University Press, 2023
DOI 10.5117/9789048558476_CH08

that people not only live in a world of risk, but also in a world of radical uncertainty. They choose to replace the distinction between risk and uncertainty deployed by Frank Knight and John Maynard Keynes "with a distinction between resolvable and radical uncertainty" (Kay and King, 2020, p. 14). Resolvable uncertainty is uncertainty which can be removed by looking something up or which can be represented by a known probability distribution of outcomes. "With radical uncertainty, however, there is no similar means of resolving the uncertainty – we simply don't know" (Kay and King, 2020, p. 14). In the world of radical uncertainty, "knowledge of the underlying process is imperfect, the processes themselves are constantly changing, and the ways in which they operate depend not just on what people do, but on what people think" (Kay and King, 2020, p. 44). Kay and King associate radical uncertainty with dimensions like ambiguity and ill-defined problems. They highlight that the ramifications of radical uncertainty go well beyond financial markets. Radical uncertainty is part of the essence of life, including individual, collective, economic and political decision-making.

As indicated, Kay and King reject the claim of conventional or neoclassical economics that radical uncertainty can be reduced to risk. In their view, "behind these efforts to escape radical uncertainty is the belief that there is a scientific truth...waiting to be discovered as new information gradually becomes available" (Kay and King, 2020, p. 100). Kay and King argue against such an understanding of scientific truth. In their view, the assumptions of conventional economics regarding human behaviour are useful as part of small-world approaches to constructing models that throw light on a problem. However, these models provide only partial insights into human behaviour in large worlds. (Kay and King, 2020, p. 376) When radical uncertainty is involved, it is not possible to define probabilities which can be estimated. The question that appears then is 'how to deal with decision-making under uncertainty', because decision-making for the future remains necessary.

When radical uncertainty is involved, Kay and King propose to stand back and ask the question: What is going on here? (Kay and King, 2020, p. 21) It seems obvious to start any decision-making with the question 'What is going on?'. But Kay and King argue that this is not that obvious. Asking this question is not per se to discover materiality of what is going on. For them, the relevance of asking this question lies in the possibility of becoming, in interaction with others, (more) aware of the prior opinions one uses to approach a certain situation. They argue that prior opinions can be an obstacle to good decision-making. Therefore, they highlight the importance of listening, seeking advice and inviting challenging opinions before drawing to a conclusion. "Intelligent views about actions, and the range of possible actions, are expressed at the end, not the beginning of the process of ascertaining 'what is going on here" (Kay and King, 2020, p. 179).

Kay and King argue that narrative reasoning is the most powerful way to organize our imperfect knowledge. (Kay and King, 2020, p. 410) They recall that narrative reasoning has been around for thousands of years to deal with radical uncertainty. "For too long, the type of intelligence that is necessary to cope with a world of radical uncertainty has been underestimated and undernourished (Kay and King, 2020, p. 176). Narratives allow us to understand 'what is going on here' in multiple, complementary ways. The power of a good narrative rests on its capacity to help us to make sense of a complex and confusing world. Such a narrative allows us to form a coherent and credible answer to the question 'What is going on here?'. (Kay and King, 2020, p. 218)

For Kay and King, the role of an economist is to help politicians, public servants, business people and families to think about their economic and social issues. They do so, not by providing a universal theory, but by selecting relevant narratives, problem- and context-specific, in order to illuminate the particular problem. These narratives can consist of stories and numbers, because, as already indicated in section 4.11, mathematical models can also be seen as narratives in the sense of a template to understand reality. The selection of narratives requires skill and judgement in order to advise people in reaching the decision they have to make. The selection of a narrative or framing of the situation

> ... begins by identifying critical factors and assembling relevant data. It involves applying experience of how these factors have interacted in the past, and making an assessment of how they might interact in the future. The process of decision-making requires an understanding of the broader context within which a specific problem must be tackled, and most judgements will need to be communicated to others and will require the assistance of others in their implementation. (Kay and King, 2020, p. 398)

Kay and King refer to the role that religion has played in being the source of an overarching narrative in most societies. They argue that for many adherents it still provides a moral code and a sense of direction. In societies where religion has declined, the space it left was filled for many first by Marxism, and more recently by market fundamentalism and environmentalism. (Kay and King, 2020, p. 220)

Recently, other economists have also commented on the role of the narrative in economics. Kay and King refer for example to the work of Shiller, who argues in his *Narrative Economics* (2019) that swings in sentiment are important in understanding why large and disruptive changes in economic behaviour happen. Shiller considers narratives a departure from optimising behaviour, and therefore irrational and emotional, a weakness in rational human behaviour. However, Kay and King argue "... the importance of narratives stems not from a weakness in human behaviour but from the nature of decision-making in a world of radical uncertainty" (Kay and King, 2020, p. 315). In other words, Kay and King consider narratives an indispensable way of interacting with reality. This kind of interaction is distinct from the reasoning in conventional economics, but not irrational. "A narrative is needed to answer the question 'What is going on here?'" (Kay and King, 2020, p. 315).

The above description of Kay and King provides ingredients for TR between them and Sacks on narrative.

8.3   TR between Sacks and Kay & King on narrative

This section develops TR between Sacks and Kay & King. The overall topic is narrative. In 8.3.1 the question is whether and how Sacks' understanding of narrative interacts with Kay and King's concept of narrative. Section 8.3.2 is about the relevance of this conversation for a social response to radical uncertainty in the context of climate change.

8.3.1   On narrative

Sacks and Kay & King converge in considering narrative reasoning a distinct way of knowing, a different epistemology from objective knowledge. For Sacks, Torah, expressed in narrative reasoning, is a way of knowing distinct from *ḥokmah*, objective knowledge as employed in natural and social sciences (Sacks, 2016a, p. xxxix). More specifically, Kay and King consider narrative reasoning additional to the neoclassical rationality of optimizing behaviour. Sacks and Kay & King converge also in valuing both epistemologies by stating that the two approaches uncover different dimensions of reality and need each other to gain a fuller understanding of reality. In the work of Kay & King, the focus of narrative reasoning is on covering the dimension of radical uncertainty. For Sacks, the scope of narrative reasoning is broader. In his view, narrative reasoning is indispensable for covering and better understanding several dimensions of the human condition, including radical uncertainty and, for example, the gift of freedom.

In terms of Kay and King's approach to radical uncertainty, the narrative of the Exodus provides a way to deal with the question 'What is going on here'. On the surface it seems to be a factual description of what is going on. It is God who liberates the Israelites by means of ten plagues from slavery in Egypt. However, such a reading misses the complete meaning of the narrative. For Sacks, the complete meaning of what is going on becomes visible in the counter narrative beneath the surface. This counter narrative highlights a journey in which people gradually learn to change the identity–the images of themselves, others and the world–they live by. In the first part of the journey, the people have hardly any understanding of what is going on, because their identity is still defined by their past. Therefore in the narrative, their identity of being enslaved is challenged by an external cause. In the second part of the journey, the people gradually change that identity by themselves. The new identity is based on a shared vision of the future that creates space for all involved. This change of identity takes time, because it is impossible to suddenly change the images people live by. (Sacks, 2010, p. 330)

This interpretation of the Exodus is not a naive invitation to a better world. The danger of losing the way and having hope overtaken by fear, opportunism, and status quo is ever present. Two institutions, Sacks points out, serve to counter such threats, the covenant and the Sabbath. In section 4.8.2 I argued that the covenant is an exchange of promises that values the plurality among people. Section 4.8.3 indicated that most crucial in the transformation is the public Sabbath, a regular workplace in which people, often with conflicting identities, build on trust and learn to take responsibility for a shared future.

Sacks and Kay & King diverge on the role of religion regarding narratives. Kay and King pay little attention to the role of religion in their book. They state that religion has been source of an overarching narrative in most societies, and that, even after the decline of religion in Western societies, it still can play this role for many of its adherents. For Sacks, religious narratives as found within Judaism are not limited to religious adherents. In his view, the central narrative in this study, the Exodus, thematizes a particular interpretation of radical uncertainty, namely a hopeful one, accessible to both religious and non-religious people. Kay and King don't refer extensively to particular interpretations of radical uncertainty, although they do state that uncertainty does not always represent a threat or despair. It can also

be a source of life worth living and joy. (Kay & King, 2020, p. 428) In Sacks'
view, it is a misunderstanding that a religious narrative like the Exodus,
and its interpretation of radical uncertainty, is limited to Judaism. For him
Judaism brings a particular understanding of the good life, namely one of
hope, to the universal human conversation. (Sacks, 2009b, p. 8) The Exodus
has inspired Christians, but in section 4.10 we have also seen that several
scientists propose a retelling of the Exodus with a focus on climate change.
Through its multiple retellings the Exodus story has become engrained in
many societies.

To conclude, the relevance of TR between Sacks and Kay & King is that
it familiarizes us with narrative reasoning as a distinct way of knowing
that is of particular value when addressing radical uncertainty. Sacks'
interpretation of the narrative of the Exodus provides a multilayered, nuanced and hopeful answer to the question of Kay and King: What is going
on? Sacks' interpretation of the Exodus orients us to a journey in which
people gradually become aware of, and learn to change, their prior opinions
if these opinions are an obstacle to good decision-making. Nevertheless,
Sacks and Kay & King diverge on the role played by religious narratives. Kay
& King consider narratives thematized in religious traditions as limited to
the adherents of that tradition, while Sacks contends that the narratives
found in Judaism are not limited to Jews. For Sacks, the Exodus brings a
particular understanding of the good life, namely a hopeful one, to the
universal conversation.

8.3.2   On climate change

What relevance does a conversation between Sacks and Kay & King on
narrative have for a social response to radical uncertainty in the context
of climate change?

TR between Sacks and Kay & King orients us to the possibility of narrative
reasoning, in particular a narrative of hope, to interpret radical uncertainty
in the context of climate change. Narrative reasoning is a different kind of
reasoning from the more systematic one on which I have so far constructed
this study. Nevertheless, I wish to do more than merely take note of narrative
reasoning. Although I realize that this demands a (sudden) change of style,
in the following I develop a narrative of hope. TR has shown that hope is
best expressed in a narrative. An ingredient of such a narrative is that one
has to give oneself, because questions should be answered, such as what
is going on in this situation for me and how am I part of it. The following
is an effort to compose such a narrative of hope in the context of radical

uncertainty associated with climate change. The narrative can be read as a lecture intended for a climate summit.[1]

COVID-19

With the outbreak of COVID-19 it became quiet in my street. Before, pupils and students had created traffic blocks under my window as part of their climate change strikes. Airplanes from and to nearby Amsterdam Schiphol Airport flew over every 5 minutes. But suddenly, schools and universities were closed. Pupils and students were locked down in the houses of their parents or student houses. Schiphol's runway for flights became an aircraft parking lot. A tiny little virus, officially called SARS-CoV-2 and commonly called corona or COVID-19, did what strikes and agreements had not yet done, namely brought about a sharp reduction in CO_2 emissions[2].

Two pandemics

In the first wave of corona, Robert Shiller, winner of the Nobel Prize in economic sciences in 2013, wrote in The Guardian (1 April, 2020) that we should not talk about one pandemic, but two. The first pandemic is that of the coronavirus. The second pandemic is the fear of what corona will bring. The two pandemics are not simultaneous, but they are related. The fear of the virus can fan the flames of the fear of economic and social losses. The prognosis of the International Monetary Fund (IMF) showed how badly economies in the Eurozone suffered under the coronavirus in 2020. The outlook of January 2021 indicated that Germany's economy shrank in 2020 by 5.4%, France's by 9.0% and Italy's by 9.2%. At an 11.1% decline, Spain was hardest hit. These abstract numbers represent the economic losses of businesses, shops, hairdressers, theatres, cinemas, bars, and restaurants that had to shut down in villages and cities. People lived in fear of losing their jobs and income. Just as we referred to the Great Depression of the 1930s, we now talked about the Great Lockdown of 2020. In 2021 the Eurozone economy was projected to grow by 4.2 %. At the same time, the coronavirus crisis made us realise that society, the economy, and the future are not feasible and predictable, but rather are vulnerable and radically uncertain. Economists pointed out the radical or fundamental uncertainty connected

---

1   This section 8.3.2 consists at some length, 4 pages, of a narrative, a retelling of the Exodus in the context of climate change.
2   In this study CO_2 is used as shorthand for greenhouse gases (GHGs) that include carbon dioxide (CO_2), nitrous oxide (N_2O), and halocarbons (a group of gases including chlorofluoro-carbon (CFC).

with prognoses. There was, and maybe still is, uncertainty about renewed waves and new variants of the virus, and but also about the effectiveness of policies, changes in human behaviour and the availability of vaccines. Besides economic losses, one can also refer to the many social losses by elderly people in isolation, by people who have not been able to meet family and friends, and by younger people who have missed out on school and university or getting together with friends. Now there is the added uncertainty about how the war in Ukraine will develop, with possible consequences all over the world.

Exodus

It's easy to forget that the outbreak of the coronavirus coincided with Pesach and the Easter period. Pesach and Easter invite us to enter into conversation with the ancient story of the Exodus. The younger generation may not be familiar with this classic rooted in Islam, Judaism and Christianity. This might be good news, because it allows this generation to read the story afresh as a hopeful story for our times. Generations before us have also used this story to create perspective in dark times. It was, for example, Dr. Martin Luther King who said, and I quote, "Let us not wallow in the valley of despair. So I say to you, my friends, that even though we must face the difficulties of today and tomorrow, I still have a dream" (King, 2003, p. 219). In formulating his dream, King was inspired by words from the classic story of the Exodus.

At first, the story might seem to be about a god who frees the slaves from Egypt using 10 plagues. In short, it seems to be about an almighty god who works for us people. How we would love to have a god like that in times of coronavirus; a leader who liberates us from all our burdens and losses. Jonathan Sacks, British intellectual and former Chief Rabbi in the United Kingdom, claimed that this is a shallow interpretation of the Exodus story. In his commentary on the book of Exodus he shows that it contains a hidden narrative. There's the shared suffering of the slaves in Egypt. They are people of fate. They are forced to serve the Pharaoh, son of sun god Ra, and are worth even less than the stones of the Pyramids they are forced to build. Moses is called to lead the slaves on a journey, into a radically uncertain future. There is the promise that it is possible to build a society in which everyone is son or daughter of God. This society is founded on the building blocks of faith, hope and love. Sacks emphasises that faith isn't about accepting a set of (religious) creeds, but about trust in a path of love and solidarity beyond one's own group. A society in which people aren't a means to an end, but are seen in all ways as valuable, regardless of achievements or who they are. That makes the story of Exodus a story about people of faith, people who won't let themselves be defined by shared suffering, but by who they want to be, living not only with, but also for each other. In this way a new society can be born in the crisis, one in which new and creative connections are made and human beings become more human. Jonathan Sacks passed away on 7 November 2020. May his memory be a blessing to us all.

Journey
During COVID-19 experts argued that future decision-making should not focus narrowly on corona-related issues. They dreamed of a 'new normal' or a 'post-corona era' that includes a response to climate change. The outlook of the IMF mentioned earlier stressed the need for investments in a green infrastructure coupled with rising carbon prices, which would help with economic recovery from the corona crisis in the near term while putting the global economy on a path of net zero emissions by 2050 and holding temperature increases to safe levels. But now, after COVID-19, we know better. In 2020, CO_2 emissions dropped temporarily due to responses to the COVID-19 pandemic. Since then, however, CO_2 emissions have exceeded pre-pandemic levels.

The politics of hope derived from Exodus, however, is not a naive invitation to a better post-corona era, a Promised Land. It doesn't see hopeful change as a pill or an injection, a quick fix that can easily be realised. It sees hope as a journey in which people gradually learn how to include the ones yet excluded, here among others the climate, people in areas affected by climate change, climate-refugees, young people and yellow vests. The journey of hope is not a straight line or a smooth path. It is a journey through the desert with many setbacks, feelings of fear and doubt, opportunistic behaviour, dead ends and the longing for a misremembered past built on coal and other fossil fuels. The journey is long, because the images we live by are part of the problem. We, with our images, are part of the problem. Can we also become part of the solution?

The Exodus encourages us to create a learning society. Especially in the first part of the learning process we will encounter many conflicts. Some parties with vested interests want to try to keep everything business as usual. Other parties with great ambitions for a sustainable future come to grief when confronted with the hard facts of reality. Yet others feel as if their voices are not heard at all. But, in the second part of the learning process the realization begins to dawn that we need one another in the long term. The desert is a place of birth of a whole new kind of relationship between human beings, and between humans and nonhumans. In this second part of the journey, people with seemingly conflicting interests can come together in a land of promise. They make a promise to one another in a covenant, based on principles of who we want to become as persons and a society. In this land of the promise we don't have to agree with one another in the present. We will and do disagree, sometimes fiercely, for example about how to deal with climate change and the time needed for a transition. But, when it comes to our hopes for our children, the greater purpose, we are probably not all that different. What is more, hope values the dignity of difference, because only by facing different points of view, can we become aware of the images we live by. This awareness is the opening to something that is more than the sum of its parts. Take for example Unilever and the World Wildlife Fund: in a different context from climate change, these parties with seemingly conflicting interests together founded the independent Marine Stewardship Council (MSC), a label enabling consumers to choose seafood products from environmentally well managed fisheries.

Sabbath re-invented

When we look around, we already see countless acts of people responding to the call to take responsibility for the future. However, let us not be naïve. In the present there are many conflicting interests and dead ends; and corona shows us that tiredness, self-interest, opportunism and indifference can easily replace acts of hope and solidarity. Therefore it would be helpful, if not necessary, to have something that fosters hope, trust, and solidarity while being on the way.

Let's go back, one more time, to the old classic of the Exodus. This story gives a surprising answer to the question of whether there is something to guide us during the time of transition. It refers to the Sabbath as a key institution. I hear you wondering: the Sabbath, that religious institution? Well, partly. The Exodus does not refer to the Sabbath as a religious institution for believers, but as a public institution for all involved—believers, non-believers and everyone in between. This public Sabbath can serve as a regular workplace of hope in times of climate change. Therefore, it is time to design the Sabbath in four ways to become a workplace of hope for all.

First, it is time to design the Sabbath as a neutral space that considers differences as a source of renewal and innovation, rather than the source of polarisation and stagnation it often is today.

Second, it is time to design the Sabbath as a space that builds trust by listening and postponing our judgements instead of debate.

Third, it is time to design the Sabbath as a regular Utopia Now. An occasion that reminds us that the present situation determines no longer who we are, as we celebrate where we are heading.

Fourth, it is time to design the Sabbath as a space of hope expressed in joy, sharing food and drink, music and art, instead of using only objective knowledge and statistics.

A politics of hope challenges us to create workplaces of hope in the heart of our society, not in a new-normal future, but in the present, here and now. Hope is just beyond where we are. The only thing we have to do is to respond to its call. To say it in the words of Amanda Gorman's poem:

For there is always light,
if only we're brave enough to see it
If only we're brave enough to be it

Thank you

Now that the lecture is over, it is time to sum up this section. TR between Sacks and Kay & King points us to narrative reasoning as a distinct way of knowing as we address radical uncertainty. I have taken this seriously by trying to compose a narrative of hope in the context of climate change, with the corona crisis as my point of departure. With this narrative TR has come to an end.

8.4   Conclusion

In this chapter I have developed TR between Sacks and the economists Kay & King on narrative in order to create a fuller understanding of a social response to radical uncertainty in the context of climate change. TR between Sacks and Kay & King familiarizes us with narrative reasoning as a distinct way of knowing as we address radical uncertainty in climate change. Sacks' interpretation of the narrative of the Exodus provides a hopeful answer to the question of Kay and King: What is going on? Sacks' understanding of narrative orients us to a journey in which people gradually become aware of, and learn to change, their prior opinions if these opinions are an obstacle to good decision-making. Sacks and Kay & King diverge on the role of religion in relation to narratives. For Kay & King, narratives thematized in religious traditions are limited to the adherents of that tradition. In Sacks' view, narratives found in Judaism are not limited to Jews. For Sacks, the Exodus brings a particular understanding of the good life, namely a hopeful one, to the universal conversation. A narrative of hope was then developed in a lecture to be held at a climate summit. This chapter brings to an end TR that started in chapter 5. The next chapter will conclude this study.

Bibliography

Gorman, A. (2021). *The Hill We Climb: An Inaugural Poem for the Country.* New York, NY: Viking Books for Young Readers.

International Monetary Fund. (January 2021). *World Economic Outlook Update.* Retrieved from https://www.imf.org/en/Publications/WEO/Issues/2021/01/26/2021-world-economic-outlook-update

Kay, J. & King, M. (2020). *Radical Uncertainty: Decision-making for an unknowable future.* London, United Kingdom: The Bridge Street Press.

King, M.L. (2003). I Have a Dream. In J.M. Washington (Ed.), *A Testament of Hope: The Essential Writings and Speeches of Martin Luther King, Jr.* (pp. 217-220). New York, NY: HarperCollins Publishers.

Sacks, J. (2009b). *Future Tense: Jews, Judaism, and Israel in the Twenty-First Century.* New York, NY: Schocken Books.

Sacks, J. (2010). *Covenant & Conversation, Exodus: The Book of Redemption.* Jerusalem, Israel: Maggid Books.

Sacks, J. (2016a). *The Koren Sukkot Maḥzor.* Jerusalem, Israel: Koren Publishers.

Shiller, R.J. (2020, 1 April). Now the world faces two pandemics–one medical, one financial. *The Guardian.* Retrieved from https://www.theguardian.com/business/2020/apr/01/now-the-world-faces-two-pandemics-one-medical-one-financial-coronavirus

9. Conclusions

Abstract
This chapter concludes the study with a summary of the main conclusions
of transversal reasoning (TR) between Jonathan Sacks and the economists
Bart Nooteboom, Samuel Bowles, Dan Ariely and John Kay & Mervyn King.
The relevance of TR is that it presents and deepens alternative critical
assumptions for the ones underlying conventional economic modelling, in
particular the social cost-benefit analysis (SCBA), in order to develop more
properly a social response to radical uncertainty in the context of climate
change. The study shows that Wentzel van Huyssteen's postfoundational
approach allows a rather successful conversation between theology and
economics. To conclude the postfoundational approach, the chapter answers
the question of what both disciplines can learn from TR employed here.
Finally, limitations and recommendations for further research are presented.

Keywords: Transversal reasoning, Jonathan Sacks, Bart Nooteboom,
Samuel Bowles, Dan Ariely, John Kay, Mervyn King, Wentzel van Huyssteen, radical uncertainty

9.1 Introduction

This study explores the meaning of the neglected notion of hope for a social
response to radical uncertainty in the context of climate change. The *impetus*
for this exploration came from a suggestion made by Zygmunt Bauman. His
remark has brought me into uncharted territory, namely a conversation
between theology and economics, which has hardly been undertaken in
recent times.

But the necessity for this conversation emerged out of the debate within
economics on radical uncertainty in the context of climate change. Radical
uncertainty, uncertainty inherent in the human condition (derived from
Hannah Arendt), is not adequately addressed by the critical assumptions
underlying conventional economic modelling, in particular the social

Hasselaar, J.J., *Climate Change, Radical Uncertainty and Hope: Theology and Economics in
Conversation.* Amsterdam: Amsterdam University Press, 2023
DOI 10.5117/9789048558476_CH09

cost-benefit analysis (SCBA), including its Ramsey rule, used to develop a social response to climate change. The Stern/Nordhaus-controversy provides an illustration of controversies about parameters and judgement in SCBA that have been central to responses to climate change for many years. Following Rodrik's approach to economics, I point out that an economic model is only useful when it captures the most relevant aspects of reality. Therefore, it is not just perfectly legitimate, but also necessary in this study, to question the critical assumptions underlying SCBA: (1) objective knowledge, (2) the interests of one dynasty expressed in terms of a 'representative individual' and (3) fixed preferences. Alternative critical assumptions are required in order to address more properly radical uncertainty related to climate change. I have argued that Sacks' understanding of hope, derived from the ancient narrative of the Exodus, lends itself to several alternative critical assumptions for addressing radical uncertainty: *emunah* (a particular type of trust), *chessed* (a particular type of love), change of identity and two supporting institutions, namely covenant and public Sabbath. Sacks' understanding of hope demands not simply copying truths of generations before us. Hope needs to be born in every time and generation again by interpreting and living sensitively and creatively the critical assumptions underlying hope in the given context, here radical uncertainty in the context of climate change.

Economics brought me to theological questions and the concept of hope in the work of Jonathan Sacks—and to a renewed way of doing theology as an account of the good life. In order to complete the circle, and allow a fuller understanding of a social response to radical uncertainty in the context of climate change, I bring Sacks' understanding of hope into conversation with five economists: Bart Nooteboom, Samuel Bowles, Dan Ariely and John Kay & Mervyn King. This can be seen as a pilot conversation between theology and economics, a kind of intellectual pop-up salon. It led to the following research question:

> *What is the relevance of a conversation between the theologian Jonathan Sacks and the economists Bart Nooteboom, Samuel Bowles, Dan Ariely and John Kay & Mervin King for a social response to radical uncertainty in the context of climate change?*

The research question is broken down into three sub-questions. The sub-questions will be answered in next section. The central question is answered by summarizing the main conclusions in section 9.3. Section 9.4 shows what the disciplines involved can learn from the applied TR. Limitations and directions for further research can be found in section 9.5.

9.2 Answering the sub-questions

This section answers the three sub-questions.

9.2.1 Conversation between theology and economy

The first sub-question is about the possibility to construct a conversation between theology and economics.

In chapter 3 I constructed a framework, using van Huyssteen's post-foundational approach to rationality, to make a conversation between theology and economics possible. This postfoundational approach has four key characteristics: (1) recognizing the embeddedness of rationality in human culture, (2) interpreting a shared reality as common ground in all forms of inquiry, (3) critically investigating one's own embeddedness by the participant of an interdisciplinary interaction, (4) considering problem solving the most central and defining activity of all research traditions. The key to a postfoundational interdisciplinary interaction is expressed in the notion of transversal reasoning (TR), which is a conversation between different disciplines on a shared problem. The postfoundational approach was originally created for an interaction between theology and natural science. In this study I have shown that van Huyssteen's approach allows a conversation between theology and economics. A more general reason for this is that a postfoundational notion of rationality is not limited to the debate of religion (including theology) and natural sciences. Van Huyssteen's approach is a description of human rationality as itself constantly under construction in engaging with reality. A more particular reason is that I have honoured the three guidelines for a possibly successful postfoundational conversation, namely (1) a focus on specific theologians and economists instead of the rather a-contextual terms 'theology and economics'; (2) these theologians and economists engage in specific kinds of theology and economics with postfoundational characteristics; and (3) the interaction is on a clearly defined and shared problem.

9.2.2 Sacks' understanding of hope

The second sub-question is about the meaning and possible societal impact of Jonathan Sacks' understanding of hope.

In chapter 4 I created a systematic overview of Sacks' approach of *Torah* and *ḥokmah,* based on an extensive study of the literature, in order to answer this question. *Torah veḥokmah* refers to an ongoing conversation between two complementary domains of knowing, Torah (theology or philosophy) and secular wisdom (natural and social sciences). Sacks' understanding of hope is primarily rooted in Torah, especially in the narrative of the Exodus. As indicated, it lends itself to several critical assumptions for a social response to radical uncertainty: *emunah, chessed,* change of identity and the related institutions of covenant and public Sabbath.

The Exodus as a narrative of hope provides a particular perspective on reality, accessible to all. Therefore the Exodus has not only been the subject of an ongoing conversation within Judaism. It has also inspired Christians. And the story of the Exodus does not end in Christianity. The story has been told and retold over and over again in societies, for example by African-Americans in their struggle for civil rights. Recently, several scientists have proposed, directly and indirectly, a retelling of the Exodus in the context of climate change.

9.2.3 Applying TR

The third sub-question is: How can a conversation between Jonathan Sacks and the economists Bart Nooteboom, Samuel Bowles, Dan Ariely and John Kay & Mervin King be constructed in such a way that it can lead to the creation of a fuller understanding of a social response to radical uncertainty in the context of climate change?

In chapters 5 through 8 I constructed a conversation in turns between the critical assumptions and narrative mode of Sacks' understanding of hope and a related concept in the work of Nooteboom, Bowles, Ariely or Kay & King. Each turn of TR consists of two parts. The first part deals with the question whether the critical assumption or narrative mode and the concept of the economist concerned interact. And if so, to what extent are there similarities and differences. Do Sacks' assumptions or mode and the economist supplement or deepen one another? Can we find obvious areas of disagreement and do we find specific issues that need to be discussed further? The second part of TR deals with the relevance of the conversation in part 1 for a social response to radical uncertainty in the context of climate change.

To summarize, in this section I have answered the sub-questions. In next section I will answer the research question of this study.

9.3   Main conclusions

In this section the central research question is answered by summarizing the main conclusions of the second part of TR in chapters 5 through 8. First I will draw conclusions related to TR based on (1) *emunah*, (2) *chessed*, (3) change of identity, and (4) narrative. Thereafter I will bundle conclusions on covenant and public Sabbath to make the practical implications of this study more visible.

9.3.1   Conclusions on *emunah*

The relevance of the conversation between Sacks and Nooteboom on *emunah* is that it familiarizes us with a form of knowledge that can be described as relational knowledge. It is a third form of knowledge, besides objective and subjective knowledge. Relational knowledge allows us to embrace radical uncertainty in the context of climate change. In discourses on climate change, elements of this kind of knowledge can already be found in Van der Sluijs' plea for post-normal science. The driving force of *emunah* is *chessed*.

9.3.2   Conclusions on *chessed*

The relevance of the conversation between Sacks and Bowles on *chessed* is that it highlights the importance of *chessed* and social preference 1, besides self-interest, when it comes to a social response to radical uncertainty in the context of climate change. People inspired by *chessed* seek to build new relationships in which the other and oneself are considered subject rather than only object. In the midst of radical uncertainty, new relationships are built, especially with those who are yet excluded, for example the climate, people in areas affected by climate change, climate-refugees, young people and yellow vests. Important to note here is that the excluded 'other' should not be seen in abstract terms, but should be known by name and seen as having a value in him- or herself.

Chessed orients us especially to creating relations between people with different or even conflicting identities, for example a director of an environmental NGO and the CEO of an oil company. Identity refers to the images people live by—images of themselves, others and the world. *Chessed* stimulates opposition in order to transform the identities people live by. Diversity is seen as a source of renewal and creativity instead of a source of polarization and paralysis as it often seems to be today.

Chessed also contains the possibility to explore nonhuman reality as a subject rather than only object. Some identities may have been useful in the past, for example 'water as enemy', but that does not mean that they are still useful when it comes to a social response to radical uncertainty in the context climate change. An example of a new relationship with nature can be expressed in concepts like 'working together with water'. Although one can argue that such a concept still retains an instrumental approach to nonhumans. The idea of extending *chessed* to nonhuman beings might be better expressed in studies in a new field defined by Frans de Waal as evolutionary cognition, which tries to treat every species on its own terms. TR shows that taking responsibility in the context of climate change is not necessarily a painful matter of self-sacrifice, nor feeling guilty about your ecological footprint. The consequence of building relations of *chessed* with one another is in essence joy. The bottom-up approach of *chessed* coincides with recent climate analyses that concentrate on deliberative democracy, the role of non-state actors like citizens, cities and business.

It is especially Bowles who orients us to the (potential) role of negative other-regarding motivations, like parochial altruism, hate and envy, in the midst of radical uncertainty in climate change. This raises the question of how to govern relations of *chessed* in the midst of radical uncertainty. I come back to this in section 9.3.5.

9.3.3   Conclusions on change of identity

The relevance of the conversation between Sacks and Bowles on change of identity is that it highlights the need for time, expressed in a journey of two stages, when it comes to a transformative response to radical uncertainty in the context of climate change. The first stage of the journey is based on who we are, the identity underlying the actions that caused climate change. The focus of a response is here directly on the shared problem of climate change, for example reducing CO_2[1]. The second stage of the journey orients us to a new and liberating identity, a new 'we'. It is about who humans and nonhumans want to be with one another. Hope does not accentuate the outcome of such a transformative response to climate change, but the process towards the outcome. The reason for this is that, due to radical uncertainty, the outcome cannot be known in advance. What TR does emphasize is the

---

1   In this study CO_2 is used as shorthand for greenhouse gases (GHGs) that include carbon dioxide (CO_2), nitrous oxide (N_2O), and halocarbons (a group of gases including chlorofluoro-carbon (CFC).

crucial need for time in this transformative response. A transformation is only durable when the people involved change their identities by their own choice. This takes time. TR pays special attention to the education of young people in building new relationships with oneself and the other, including nature.

In TR Bowles introduces the notion of crowding out: monetary incentives can crowd out other-regarding motivation, which shows that an essential ingredient for a social response can be discouraged. Bowles advocates an approach that can stimulate wise combinations of self-interest and other-regarding motivation in order to develop prudent policies. However, according to Bowles there is not yet an institution that stimulates crowding-in effects when it comes to climate policy. Bowles gives us a glimpse of the tradition of ancient Greece in order to find such an institution, namely the Athenian assembly of two millennia ago. Sacks' understanding of hope highlights a public Sabbath as key institution for a transformative response to radical uncertainty in the context of climate change. I return to this in section 9.3.5.

9.3.4 Conclusions on narrative

TR between Sacks and Kay & King orients us to the possibility of narrative reasoning. A transformative response to radical uncertainty in climate change is best expressed in a narrative of hope. To take this insight seriously, an attempt has been made to construct a narrative of hope, expressed in a fictive lecture to be held at a climate summit.

Let me pause this summing up of conclusions. The conclusions above are not a naive invitation to a better world. TR explicitly shows that a transformative response to climate change is not a pill or an injection, a quick fix that can easily be realised. TR sees the shaping of fundamental and lasting transformations in identity as a journey that takes time. While on the way, we will encounter many conflicting interests, dead ends, false turns and acts of parochial altruism, self-interest and opportunism. The question is therefore whether there is something that can guide us during a transformative response to radical uncertainty in the context of climate change. Is there something that fosters hope and *chessed*? Is there something that supports us to enter a journey, the meaning and outcome of which we may barely glimpse. TR gives a surprising answer to that question and refers to the institutions of covenant and especially public Sabbath to protect and stimulate relations of *chessed*.

9.3.5　Conclusions on covenant and public Sabbath

Probably the most important part of TR is that it orients us to institutions that cultivate relations of *chessed* and add up to a very practical way to embrace radical uncertainty in the context of climate change. In this section I first draw conclusions on the covenant, then I will focus on the public Sabbath.

The relevance of the conversation between Sacks and Nooteboom on the level of governance of *chessed* is that it highlights an institution, the covenant. The covenant formalizes relations that seek to honour oneself and the other as subject when it comes to radical uncertainty in the context of climate change. In discourses on climate change, Bierman stresses the need for more imagination in the governance of the earth system, including climate change. One way to bring about such an improved architecture of governance is to reform or strengthen (top-down) intergovernmental decision-making, as Bierman proposes. Another way, highlighted in TR, is to strengthen a bottom-up approach as comes to expression in a covenant. A covenant is a (bottom-up) agreement between two or more people, better said subjects, who voluntarily and each on their own terms exchange promises to take responsibility for a shared future. A covenant does not mean that everybody agrees with one another. In a covenant people can in fact sharply disagree with one another, for example a director of an environmental NGO and the CEO of an oil company. What is more, the covenant seems to have the potential to include nonhumans as well, although it is still hard to imagine what this will look like. TR accentuates that not only collaboration is important in a covenant, but that competition and hierarchy based on the principles of the covenant are as well, in order to ensure that the many interests run parallel in the midst of radical uncertainty. In TR a real-life example of a covenant of hope is given.

The relevance of the conversation between Sacks and Ariely on the level of governance of change of identity is that it highlights the public Sabbath. The public Sabbath is a key public institution with the potential to coordinate a social response to radical uncertainty in the context of climate change for all involved, not just religious people. A transformative response to climate change is hard to complete. Therefore, it is crucial to have a coordination mechanism, a public Sabbath. In order to accentuate the public and inclusive role of the Sabbath, it is here renamed 'workplace of hope'. It may feel counterintuitive to describe the Sabbath as a workplace, because it literally means 'to stop' daily life. However, Sabbath is not simply a pause that refreshes. It is the pause that transforms the identity people live by—the images they have of themselves, the other and nature. Such a workplace consists of four dimensions. First, the workplace is a regular moment that celebrates the new 'we' that people are aiming at, in the present. Second, a workplace of hope is a neutral space in the public domain, which values differences among the participants involved. Third, the workplace practices and, by doing so, protects and strengthens, relations of *chessed* that seek to create space for all involved. Fourth, the workplace stimulates the development of meaningful relations between people not only via reflection and practical steps forward, but also via music, poetry, eating together and art. These dimensions of the workplace of hope can deepen existing meetings and summits in order to make them rituals to embrace radical uncertainty in the context of climate change. TR presents the InspirationTable as a possible real-life sketch of a workplace of hope.

A summary of the main conclusions provides an answer to the research question. In this study I have argued that the critical assumptions underlying the economic model of SCBA run into serious limitations when it comes to radical uncertainty in the context of climate change. What insights does this study, based on critical assumptions underlying hope, present in relation to SCBA?

First, the study presents an additional form of knowledge, relational knowledge. In SCBA economists like Stern and Nordhaus, 'professional experts', try to optimize objectively a social response to climate change up to about 200 years ahead, supported by techniques to substitute for a lack of objective knowledge. Relational knowledge highlights a transformative response by all involved, including 'day-by-day experts', in which they gradually learn together, in a cyclical interaction of celebration, reflection and practice, how to internalize the externality of climate change.

Second, the study orients us to a different way to cover the interests of the members of one dynasty. In order to keep the analysis simple, SCBA assumes these interests in terms of a 'representative individual'. However, TR makes it clear that such a simplification omits a crucial aspect of what makes us human, especially when it comes to radical uncertainty in climate change. TR highlights the crucial role of plurality among participants. It does not view plurality as a problematic source of conflict, but as a crucial source to open up the identity of those involved in order to create a new 'we'. In addition, in SCBA a social response is distinguished from private decision making. This study shows a necessary interaction between the individual and societal level.

Third, SCBA assumes that people's preferences are given. This study makes it clear that, due to radical uncertainty, people can only gradually learn what they prefer.

Fourth, the study extends the notion of the social planner, often seen as a top-down (global) government, to include governance from bottom up, in particular a covenant and workplace of hope. TR stresses that a bottom-up approach is not opposed to the other forms of governance, but can be supported by and help to flesh out approaches of government and market.

Finally, TR extends the kind of questions commonly raised by SCBA in climate policy: How much reduction of CO_2 emissions is required? How fast should a reduction take place? How should the reductions be distributed? What may be the costs of a reduction? (section 2.3). TR adds underlying questions of meaning: Who are we as individuals and collective? In what or whom do we put our trust? What is it that we hope for? Who do we want to become in relation to ourselves and one another?

By providing the conclusions and insights presented in this section 9.3, TR between Sacks and Nooteboom, Bowles, Ariely and Kay & King has shown that working together provides a fuller understanding of the shared problem and a better practical response. Therefore TR in this study has rather successfully explored alternative critical assumptions to address radical uncertainty in relation to climate change. TR provides necessary insights to enable politicians, public servants, business people, religious leaders and in particular ordinary people to act under conditions of radical uncertainty in the context of climate change.

9.4   What disciplines can learn from TR

After sharing the resources of interdisciplinarity in TR, a postfoundational approach points back to the boundaries of one's own discipline (section 3.4). What can both disciplines learn from TR employed in this study?

9.4.1   Theology

What can theology as a discipline learn from TR? Here I present three points that emerge from the present study.

First, I have shown that van Huyssteen's postfoundational approach can be used in order to develop an equal interaction between theology and economics. In TR it became visible that there is a deep historical conflict in the legacy of the research traditions of theology and economics. However, it has also shown that there is no need for that conflict to be their destiny. Working together on shared problems creates the opportunity to renew the relationship between theology and economics.

Second, in his work Sacks seeks God in people who in themselves seem to point to something or someone beyond themselves. In TR *chessed* challenges the imagination to seek God not only in people and relations between them, but also in the ways nonhuman beings relate to each other, and to human beings. A perspective of hope based on *chessed* sees the whole of reality—human beings, animals, trees, climate—as a relational system. All are dependent on one another.

Third, the study challenges theology to explore a variety of forms of governance available within religious tradition(s) in order to support individuals and society at large in dealing with the human condition, with all its imperfection, dishonesty, radical uncertainty and crowding out-effects.

9.4.2 Economics

What can economics as a discipline learn from the interaction with theology?

First, that there is an interaction possible between economics and theology. In recent decades economics has been enriched by cross-overs with psychology (behavioural economics) and with sociology (identity economics). TR has shown that the applied interaction between economics and theology is neither artificial nor ideologically constructed. It emerged out of the debate within economics on uncertainty in the context of climate change. In that sense, economics has brought me to theological questions.

Second, Sacks' understanding of hope can supplement the critical assumptions and insitutions of conventional economics, at least when it comes to radical uncertainty. At the same time, TR shows that that elements of Sacks' understanding of hope are already present within economics, as indicated in the pilot conversation with Bart Nooteboom, Samuel Bowles, Dan Ariely and John Kay & Mervin King.

Third, economics can learn from TR that a mix of the general forms of governance—hierarchy, competition and relational contracting—is needed to deal with radical uncertainty. Several economists are not only rediscovering the theme of radical uncertainty, but are doing so from either a more or less Keynesian or Hayekian perspective, respectively government (hierarchy) or market (competition). TR orients us to a mix of governance to deal with uncertainty.

9.5 Limitations and further research

Limitations. The interaction between theology and economics presented here has at least three limitations.

First, the entry point of the present study is theology. In the study I have brought theology in conversation with economics. One may argue that less thorough attention is paid to (radical uncertainty regarding) climate change in other sciences. The main reason for this limitation is that I have a background in theology and economics, but not in other sciences. Therefore I have limited myself in particular to theology and economics.

Second, the reason to opt for Sacks is because of his treatment of radical uncertainty with a concept of hope and his postfoundational approach to theology. As a consequence, I do not relate Sacks extensively to his background (orthodox) Judaism.

Third, I was raised and educated in a Western, Christian and academic context. This embeddedness has influenced, and therefore also limited, the choices I have made and the insights I have gained in this study.

Further research. On a theoretical level, Sacks' understanding of hope is open to further interaction. It can be extended with other assumptions present in the Exodus, for example *mishpat*, justice done by the law, and *tzedakah*, which refers to social justice (Sacks, 2000, p. 125; 2005, pp. 32-33). In this research I touched upon the relationship between Jonathan Sacks and Christianity. However, an explicit elaboration on this relationship was beyond the scope of this study. Further research can investigate how Sacks' understanding of hope relates to the work of thinkers and theologians like Fromm, Bloch, Gutiérrez, Moltmann, Northcott and Deane-Drummond. A study can also explore how Sacks' understanding of hope relates to seemingly similar approaches in other cultures, like the process of indaba, rooted in Zulu culture, and highlighted by Archbishop Makgoba as a promising concept to overcome polarization in church and society on contemporary issues (Nesbitt, 2017). Further research can also extend TR with other economists such as Akerlof and Kranton with their *Identity Economics* (2010), Daniel Kahneman with his *Thinking, Fast and Slow* (2011), and Raghuram Rajan with his *The Third Pillar* (2019). The question can also be raised as to what kind of leadership is required in the several stages of a transformative response to climate change. Such a question can be explored by analysing the role of leadership in the Exodus, but also by considering the book *The Practice of Adaptive Leadership* (2009) by Heifetz, Grashow and Linsky.

On a practical level, there is also room for further research. A key characteristic of Sacks' understanding of hope is that it neither can be calculated in advance, nor be fully developed without living it. This study remained a bit abstract, because it contributed to a mainly theoretical discussion. But it is only in doing that we learn what it means to develop a hopeful response to radical uncertainty in climate change. The proof of the pudding is in the eating. In this study a public Sabbath emerged as key public institution in a transformative response to climate change. To speed up a social response to climate change, reinventing a public Sabbath, conceptualised as a workplace of hope, should be an important priority for further research and policy. Much work has to be done to design it as a convincing workplace for all involved and to measure its influence. A first step would be constructing a hope design studio to provide the conditions needed to develop such a workplace.

Last but not least, in this study TR focussed on the shared problem of radical uncertainty in the context of climate change. Climate change is just one of issues addressed by the Sustainable Development Goals (SDG's). TR can also be developed in the context of other SDGs that include radical uncertainty.

Bibliography

Nesbitt, P.D. (2017). *Indaba! A Way of Listening, Engaging, and Understanding across the Anglican Communion*. New York, NY: Church Publishing.

Sacks, J. (2000). *A Letter in the Scroll: Understanding Our Jewish Identity and Exploring the Legacy of the World's Oldest Religion*. New York, NY: Free Press.

Sacks, J. (2005). *To Heal a Fractured World: The Ethics of Responsibility*. New York, NY: Schocken Books.

Bibliography

Akerlof, G.A., & Kranton, R.E. (2010). *Identity Economics: How Our Identities Shape Our Work, Wages, and Well-Being*. Princeton, NJ: Princeton University Press.

Akerlof, G.A., & Shiller, R.J. (2009). *Animal Spirits: How Human Psychology Drives the Economy, and Why It Matters for Global Capitalism*. Princeton, NJ: Princeton University Press.

Arendt, H. (1958, 1998). *The Human Condition* (2nd. ed.). Chicago, IL: The University of Chicago Press.

Ariely, D. (2012). *The (Honest) Truth About Dishonesty: How We Lie to Everyone–Especially Ourselves*. New York, NY: Harper.

Biermann, F. (2014). *World Politics in the Anthropocene*. Cambridge, MA: The MIT Press.

Borgman, E. (2017). *Leven van wat komt: Een katholiek uitzicht op de samenleving*. Utrecht, The Netherlands: Meinema.

Borgman, E. (2020). *Alle dingen nieuw: Een theologische visie voor de 21ste eeuw: Inleiding en Invocatio*. Utrecht, The Netherlands: KokBoekencentrum Uitgevers.

Bovenberg, A.L. (2016). *Economieonderwijs in balans: kiezen en samenwerken*. Tilburg, The Netherlands: Tilburg University.

Bowles, S. (2004). *Microeconomics: Behavior, Institutions, and Evolution*. Princeton, NJ: Princeton University Press.

Bowles, S., & Gintis, H. (2011). A *Cooperative Species: Human Reciprocity and Its Evolution*. Princeton, NJ: Princeton University Press.

Bowles, S. (2016). *The Moral Economy: Why Good Incentives Are No Substitute for Good Citizens*. New Haven, CT: Yale University Press.

Brennan, G., & Waterman, A. (2008). Christian theology and economics: convergence and clashes. In I. Harper & S. Gregg (Eds.), *Christian Theology and Market Economics* (pp. 77-93).

Cheltenham, United Kingdom and Northampton, MA: Edward Elgar Publishing.

Bruckner, P. (2013). *The Fanaticism of the Apocalypse: Save the Earth, Punish Human Beings*. Cambridge, United Kingdom: Polity Press.

Buber, M. (1923, 2013). *I and Thou*. London, United Kingdom: Bloomsbury.

Bunnin, N., & Yu, J. (2004). *The Blackwell Dictionary of Western Philosophy*. Malden, MA: Blackwell publishing. http://dx.doi.org/10.1002/9780470996379

Calhoun, C. (2002). *Dictionary of the Social Sciences*. New York, NY: Oxford University Press. http://dx.doi.org/10.1093/acref/9780195123715.001.0001

Carasik, M. (Ed.). (2005). *The Commentators' Bible: The JPS Miqra'ot Gedolot: Exodus*. Philadelphia, PA: The Jewish Publication Society.

Chandler, D., & R. Munday (2016). *A Dictionary of Media and Communication* (2nd. ed.). Oxford, United Kingdom: Oxford University Press. http://dx.doi.org/10.1093/acref/9780199568758.001.0001

Colander, D., & Kupers, R. (2014). *Complexity and the Art of Public Policy: Solving Society's Problems from the Bottom up.* Princeton, NJ: Princeton University Press.

Conradie, E.M., & Koster, H.P. (Eds.). (2020). *T&T Clark Handbook of Christian Theology and Climate Change.* London, United Kingdom: T&T Clark.

Crossley, N. (1996). *Intersubjectivity: The Fabric of Social Becoming.* London, United Kingdom: SAGE Publications.

Deane-Drummond, C. (2008). *Eco-theology.* London, United Kingdom: Darton, Longman and Todd.

De Grauwe, P. (2012). *Lectures on Behavioral Economics.* Princeton, NJ: Princeton University Press.

de Waal, F.B.M. (2016). *Are We Smart Enough to Know How Smart Animals Are?* New York, NY: W. W. Norton & Company.

Deltacommissie. (2008). *Working together with water: A living land builds for its future.* Retrieved from http://www.deltacommissie.com/doc/deltareport_full.pdf

Eagleton, T. (2015). *Hope without Optimism.* Charlottesville: University of Virginia Press.

Espagne, E., Nadaud, F., Fabert, B.P., Pottier, A., & Dumas, P. (2012). *Disentangling the Stern/Nordhaus Controversy: Beyond the Discounting Clash.* Milan, Italy: FEEM Working Paper (61.2012). http://dx.doi.org/10.2139/ssrn.2160751

Evans, C.A. (2014). Exodus in the New Testament: Patterns of Revelation and Redemption. In T. B. Dozeman, C.A. Evans. & J.N. Lohr (Eds.), *The book of Exodus: Composition, reception, and interpretation* (pp. 440-464). Leiden, The Netherlands: Brill.

Gneezy, U., & Rustichini, A. (2000). A Fine is a Price. *Journal of Legal Studies, 29*(1), 1-18.

Gollier, C. (2018). *Ethical Asset Valuation and the Good Society.* New York, NY: Columbia University Press.

Gorman, A. (2021). *The Hill We Climb: An Inaugural Poem for the Country.* New York, NY: Viking Books for Young Readers.

Gutiérrez, G. (2003). *We Drink from Our Own Wells: The Spiritual Journey of a People.* Maryknoll, NY, Orbis Books.

Hajer, M. (2011). *The energetic society: In search of a governance philosophy for a clean economy.* The Hague, The Netherlands: pbl Netherlands Environmental Assessment Agency.

Halík, T. (2016). *I Want You to Be: On the God of Love.* Notre Dame, IN: University of Notre Dame Press.

Halík, T. (2019). *Niet zonder hoop: Religieuze crisis als kans.* Utrecht, The Netherlands: KokBoekencentrum Uitgevers.

Hamilton, C. (2015). *Requiem for a Species: Why We Resist the Truth about Climate Change.* London, United Kingdom: Routledge.

Harari, Y.N. (2017). *Homo Deus: A Brief History of Tomorrow.* London, United Kingdom: Vintage.

Harris, M.J., Rynhold, D., & Wright, T. (Eds.). (2013). *Radical Responsibility: Celebrating the Thought of Chief Rabbi Lord Jonathan Sacks.* New Milford, CT: Maggid Books.

Hasselaar, J.J. (Ed.). (2016). *We have a dream: InspiratieTafel Klimaatverandering: An Ongoing Conversation.* Amersfoort: The Old Catholic Church of the Netherlands.

Hasselaar, J.J. (2020a). Hope in the Context of Climate Change: Jonathan Sacks' Interpretation of the Exodus and Radical Uncertainty. *International Journal of Public Theology* 14, pp. 224–240.

Hasselaar, J.J. (2020b). Hope to Embrace Radical Uncertainty in Climate Change. In E. Van Stichel, T. Eggensperger, M. Kalsky, & U. Engel (eds.), *Fullness of Life and Justice for All* (pp. 51-68). Adelaide, Australia: ATF Theology. https://doi.org/10.2307/j.ctv16t6ms2.8

Hasselaar, J.J., & IJmker, E.C. (eds.). (2021). *Water in Times of Climate Change: A Values-driven Dialogue.* Amsterdam, The Netherlands: Amsterdam University Press.

Hasselaar, J.J. (2022a). Jonathan Sacks. In M. Poorthuis, & W. Veen (eds.), *De moderne theologen: Perspectieven op de 21ste eeuw* (pp. 290-297). Amsterdam, The Netherlands: Boom uitgevers.

Hasselaar, J.J., Pattberg, P. & Smit, P.B. (2022b). Sowing Hope in a Polarized Agricultural Debate. In H. Zorgdrager & P. Vos (Eds.), *The Calling of the Church in Times of Polarization. Volume 46: Studies in Reformed Theology* (pp. 155-176). Leiden, The Netherlands: Brill.

Hauri, A., Tavoni, M., & Van der Zwaan, B.C.C. (2012). Modeling Uncertainty and the Economics of Climate Change: Recommendations for Robust Energy Policy. *Environmental Modeling and Assessment, 17,* 1-5. https://link.springer.com/article/10.1007/s10666-011-9271-5

Hayden, P. (Ed.). (2014). *Hannah Arendt: Key Concepts.* Oxon, United Kingdom: Routledge.

Hayek, F.A. (1945). The Use of Knowledge in Society. *The American Economic Review, 35*(4), 519-530. Retrieved from http://www.aeaweb.org/journals/aer

Hayek, F.A. (1989). The Pretence of Knowledge. *The American Economic Review, 79*(6), 3-7. Retrieved from http://www.nobelprize.org/nobel_prizes/economicsciences/laureates/1974/hayeklecture.html

Hayhoe, K. & Hayhoe, W.D. (2020). A response to Heather Eaton. In E.M. Conradie & H.P. Koster (Eds.), *T&T Clark Handbook of Christian Theology and Climate Change* (pp. 27-30). London, United Kingdom: T&T Clark.

Heal, G., & Kriström, B. (2002). Uncertainty and Climate Change. *Environmental and Resource Economics, 22*, 3-39. http://dx.doi.org/10.2139/ssrn.302399

Heal, G., & Millner, A. (2013). *Uncertainty and Decision in Climate Change Economics.* Cambridge, MA: National Bureau of Economic Research Working Paper (18929).

Hoogen, T. van den (2011). *A Taste of God: On Spirituality and Reframing Foundational Theology.* Münster, Germany: LIT Verlag.

Horowitz, M.C. (Ed.). (2005). *New Dictionary of the History of Ideas.* Vol. 4. Detroit, MI: Charles Scribner's Sons.

Hulme, M. (2009). *Why We Disagree About Climate Change: Understanding Controversy, Inaction and Opportunity.* Cambridge, United Kingdom: Cambridge University Press.

Hulme, M. (2019, May 2). *Climate change narratives: beyond the facts of science.* Retrieved from https://mikehulme.org/climate-change-narratives-beyond-the-facts-of-science/

International Monetary Fund. (January 2021). *World Economic Outlook Update.* Retrieved from https://www.imf.org/en/Publications/WEO/Issues/2021/01/26/2021-world-economic-outlook-update

IPCC. (2014). *Climate change 2014: Mitigation of Climate Change. Contribution of Working Group III to the Fifth Assessment Report of the Intergovernmental Panel on Climate Change.* Cambridge, United Kingdom and New York, NY: Cambridge University Press.

IPCC. (2022a). *Climate Change 2022: Impacts, Adaptation and Vulnerability. Contribution of Working Group II to the Sixth Assessment Report of the Intergovernmental Panel on Climate Change.* United Kingdom and New York, NY: Cambridge University Press.

IPCC. (2022b). *Climate Change 2022: Mitigation of Climate Change. Contribution of Working Group III to the Sixth Assessment Report of the Intergovernmental Panel on Climate Change.* United Kingdom and New York, NY: Cambridge University Press.[1]

Kate, L. ten, & Poorthuis, M. (Eds.). (2017). *25 Eeuwen theologie: Teksten/toelichtingen.* Amsterdam, The Netherlands: Boom uitgevers.

Kay, J. (1993). *Foundations of Corporate Success: How Business Strategies Add Value.* Oxford, United Kingdom: Oxford University Press.

Kay, J. & King, M. (2020). *Radical Uncertainty: Decision-making for an unknowable future.* London, United Kingdom: The Bridge Street Press.

---

[1] These three IPCC-references differ in style from that proposed by the IPCC. This is due to the APA citation style guidelines used here.

Keesmaat, S.C. (1999). *Paul and His Story: (Re)Interpreting the Exodus Tradition.* Sheffield, United Kingdom: Sheffield Academic Press.

Keynes, J.M. (2008). *The General Theory of Employment, Interest and Money* (later edition). Middletown, RI: BN Publishing.

Kim, S.C.H. (2011). *Theology in the Public Sphere: Public Theology as a Catalyst for Open Debate.* London, United Kingdom: SCM Press.

King, M.L. (2003). I Have a Dream. In J.M. Washington (Ed.), *A Testament of Hope: The Essential Writings and Speeches of Martin Luther King, Jr.* (pp. 217-220). New York, NY: HarperCollins Publishers.

King, M. (2017). *The End of Alchemy: Money, Banking and the Future of the Global Economy.* London, United Kingdom: Abacus.

Klamer, A. (1989). A Conversation with Amartya Sen. *Journal of Economic Perspectives, 3*(1), 135-150. http://dx.doi.org/10.1257/jep.3.1.135

Klamer, A. (2007). *Speaking of Economics: How to Get in the Conversation.* Abingdon, United Kingdom: Routledge.

Köhn, J. (2017). *Uncertainty in Economics: A New Approach.* Cham, Switserland: Springer.

Kooten, C.G. van (2013). *Climate Change, Climate Science and Economics: Prospects for an Alternative Energy Future.* Dordrecht, The Netherlands: Springer.

Koppl, R., & Luther, W.J. (2012). Hayek, Keynes, and Modern Macroeconomics. *The Review of Austrian Economics, 25*(3), 223-241. http://dx.doi.org/10.2139/ssrn.1580145

Latour, B. (2004). *Politics of Nature. How to Bring the Sciences into Democracy.* Cambridge, MA: Harvard University Press.

Lemoine, D.M., & Traeger, C.P. (2012). *Tipping Points and Ambiguity in the Economics of Climate Change.* Cambridge, MA: National Bureau of Economic Research Working Paper (18230).

Lemoine, D.M. (2020). The Climate Risk Premium. How Uncertainty Affects the Social Cost of Carbon. *Journal of the Association of Environmental and Resource Economists, 8*(1): 27-57. https://www.journals.uchicago.edu/doi/10.1086/710667

Lewis, P. (2008). Uncertainty, power and trust. *The Review of Austrian Economics, 21*, 183-198. http://dx.doi.org/10.1007/s11138-007-0038-9

Li, Z., Müller, J., Wakker, P.P., & Wang, T.V. (2017). The Rich Domain of Ambiguity Explored. *Management Science*, published online in Articles in Advance 17 Aug 2017. https://dx.doi.org/10.1287/mnsc.2017.2777

Lovin, R.W., & Mauldin, J. (Eds.). (2017). *Theology as Interdisciplinary Inquiry: Learning with and from the Natural and Human Sciences.* Grand Rapids, MI: Wm. B. Eerdmans Publishing.

Macron, M.E. (2019, January 13). Letter from M. Emmanuel Macron to the French people. Retrieved from https://www.elysee.fr/en/emmanuel-macron/2019/01/13/letter-to-the-french-people-from-emmanuel-macron

Makgoba, T. (2009). Politics and the Church—Acting Incarnationally: Reflections of an Archbishop. *Journal of Anglican Studies, 7*(1), 87-91. http://dx.doi.org/10.1017/S1740355309000175

McCloskey, D.N. (2006). *The Bourgeois Virtues: Ethics for an Age of Commerce.* Chicago, IL: The University of Chicago Press.

Millner, A., Dietz, S. & G. Heal (2010). *Ambiguity and Climate Policy.* Cambridge, MA: National Bureau of Economic Research Working Paper (16050).

Moltmann, J. (2015). *The Living God and the Fullness of Life.* Geneva, Switzerland: World Council of Churches.

Morgan, T. (2015). *Roman Faith and Christian Faith: Pistis and Fides in the Early Roman Empire and Early Churches.* Oxford, United Kingdom: Oxford University Press.

Moritz, J.M. (2015). Does Jesus Save the Neanderthals? Theological Perspectives on the Evolutionary Origins and Boundaries of Human Nature. *Dialog, 54*(1): 51-60. https://dx.doi.org/10.1111/dial.12154

Nesbitt, P.D. (2017). *Indaba! A Way of Listening, Engaging, and Understanding across the Anglican Communion.* New York, NY: Church Publishing.

Nolan, A. (2010). *Hope in an Age of Despair.* New York, NY: Orbis Books.

Nordhaus, W. (2008). *A Question of Balance: Weighing the Options on Global Warming Policies.* New Haven, CT: Yale University Press.

Nordhaus, T., & Shellenberger, M. (2004). *The Long Death of Environmentalism.* Retrieved from http://www.thebreakthrough.org/images/Death_of_Environmentalism.pdf

Nordhaus, T., & Shellenberger, M. (2007). *Break Through: From the Death of Environmentalism to the Politics of Possibility.* New York, NY: Houghton Mifflin Company.

Nooteboom, B. (2002). *Trust: Forms, Foundations, Functions, Failures and Figures.* Cheltenham, United Kingdom: Edward Elgar.

Nooteboom, B. (2012). *Beyond Humanism: The Flourishing of Life, Self and Other.* Basingstoke, United Kingdom: Palgrave Macmillan.

Nooteboom, B. (2017). *Vertrouwen: Opening voor een veranderende wereld.* Utrecht, The Netherlands: Uitgeverij Klement.

Omtzigt, P. (2021). *Een nieuw sociaal contract.* Amsterdam, The Netherlands: Uitgeverij Prometheus.

Pearson, C. (2010). Editorial: Special Issue–Climate Change and the Common Good. *International Journal of Public Theology, 4.* Leiden, The Netherlands: Brill, 269-270. Retrieved from http://www.brill.com/international-journal-public-theology

Perman, R., Ma, Y., Common, M., Maddison, D., & McGilvray, J. (1996, 2011). *Natural Resource and Environmental Economics* (4th. Ed.). Harlow, United Kingdom: Pearson Education Limited.

Peterson, G.R. (1999). The Evolution of Consciousness and the Theology of Nature. *Zygon, 34*(2), 283-306. https://dx.doi.org/10.1111/0591-2385.00213

Poorthuis, J.H.M. (1992). *Het gelaat van de Messias: Messiaanse Talmoedlezingen van Emmanuel Levinas*. Zoetermeer, The Netherlands: Boekencentrum.

Quiggin, J. (2008). Uncertainty and Climate Change Policy. *Economic Analysis & Policy, 38*, 203-210. Retrieved from http://www.journals.elsevier.com/economic-analysis-and-policy

Reeves, J. (2013). Problems for Postfoundationalists: Evaluating J. Wentzel van Huyssteen's Interdisciplinary Theory of Rationality. *The Journal of Religion, 93*(2), 131-150. http://dx.doi.org/10.1086/669209

Reeves, J. (2019). *Against Methodology in Science and Religion: Recent Debates on Rationality and Theology*. Abingdon, United Kingdom: Routledge.

Rodrik, D. (2015). *Economics Rules: Why Economics Works, When It Fails, and How To Tell The Difference*. Oxford, England: Oxford University Press.

Roos, M. W. M. (2015). *The Macroeconomics of Radical Uncertainty*. Essen, Germany: Ruhr Economic Papers (592). http://dx.doi.org/10.2139/ssrn.2721683

Rootselaar, F. van. (2014, 15 February). De mens kan niet wereldwijd denken. *Trouw*. Retrieved from https://www.trouw.nl/nieuws/de-mens-kan-niet-wereldwijd-denken~b1d47b61/

Sacks, J. (1997). *The Politics of Hope*. London, United Kingdom: Jonathan Cape.

Sacks, J. (2000). *A Letter in the Scroll: Understanding Our Jewish Identity and Exploring the Legacy of the World's Oldest Religion*. New York, NY: Free Press.

Sacks, J. (2005). *To Heal a Fractured World: The Ethics of Responsibility*. New York, NY: Schocken Books.

Sacks, J. (2007). *The Home We Build Together: Recreating Society*. London, United Kingdom: Continuum.

Sacks, J. (2009a). *Covenant & Conversation, Genesis: The Book of Beginnings*. Jerusalem, Israel: Maggid Books.

Sacks, J. (2009b). *Future Tense: Jews, Judaism, and Israel in the Twenty-First Century*. New York, NY: Schocken Books.

Sacks, J. (2010). *Covenant & Conversation, Exodus: The Book of Redemption*. Jerusalem, Israel: Maggid Books.

Sacks, J. (2011). *The Dignity of Difference: How to Avoid the Clash of Civilizations* (Rev. ed.). London, United Kingdom: Continuum.

Sacks, J. (2012). *The Great Partnership: God, Science and the Search for Meaning*. London, United Kingdom: Hodder & Stoughton.

Sacks, J. (2013a). *A Judaism Engaged with the World*. Retrieved from http://www.rabbisacks.org/a-judaism-engaged-with-the-world/

Sacks, J. (2013b). *The Jonathan Sacks Haggada: Collected Essays on Pesaḥ*. Jerusalem, Israel: Maggid Books.

Sacks, J. (2015a). *Covenant & Conversation, Leviticus: The Book of Holiness*. Jerusalem, Israel: Maggid Books.

Sacks, J. (2015b). *Lessons in Leadership: A Weekly Reading of the Jewish Bible.* Jerusalem, Israel: Maggid Books.

Sacks, J. (2015c). *Not in God's Name: Confronting Religious Violence.* London, United Kingdom: Hodder & Stoughton.

Sacks, J. (2016a). *The Koren Sukkot Maḥzor.* Jerusalem, Israel: Koren Publishers.

Sacks, J. (2016b). *Essays on Ethics: A Weekly Reading of the Jewish Bible.* Jerusalem, Israel: Maggid Books.

Sacks, J. (2021). *Morality: Restoring the Common Good in Divided Times.* London, United Kingdom: Hodder & Stoughton.

Sapienza, P., Toldra-Simats, A., & Zingales, L. (2013). Understanding Trust. *The Economic Journal, 123,* 1313-1332. http://dx.doi.org/10.1111/ecoj.12036

Schillebeeckx, E. (1983). *God among Us: The Gospel Proclaimed.* New York, NY: Crossroad.

Schoen, E.L. (2000). Review: The Shaping of Rationality: Toward Interdisciplinarity in Theology and Science by J. Wentzel van Huyssteen. *International Journal for Philosophy of Religion, 48*(2), 121-123. http://dx.doi.org/10.1023/A:1004080214599

Sedlacek, T. (2011). *Economics of Good and Evil, The Quest for Economic Meaning from Gilgamesh to Wall Street.* Oxford, United Kingdom: Oxford University Press.

Segers, G.J. (2016). *Hoop voor een verdeeld land.* Amsterdam, The Netherlands: Uitgeverij Balans.

Shiller, R.J. (2020, 1 April). Now the world faces two pandemics—one medical, one financial. *The Guardian.* Retrieved from https://www.theguardian.com/business/2020/apr/01/now-the-world-faces-two-pandemics-one-medical-one-financial-coronavirus

Sluijs, J.P. van der (2012). Uncertainty and Dissent in Climate Risk Assessment: A Post Normal Perspective. *Nature of Culture, 7*(2), 174-195. http://dx.doi.org/10.3167/nc.2012.070204

Spadaro, S. (2013, September 30). *A Big Heart Open to God: An Interview with Pope Francis.* Retrieved from https://www.americamagazine.org/faith/2013/09/30/big-heart-open-god-interview-pope-francis

Skidelsky, R. (2020). *What's Wrong with Economics? A Primer for the Perplexed.* New Haven, CT: Yale University Press.

Skrimshire, S. (2014). Eschatology. In M. S. Northcott & P. M. Scott (Eds.), *Systematic Theology and Climate Change: Ecumenical Perspectives* (pp. 157-174). London: United Kingdom: Routledge.

Stackhouse, M. L. (2007). *Globalization and Grace: Volume 4: Globalization and Grace (Theology for the 21st Century).* New York, NY: Continuum.

Stern, N. (2006). *The Economics of Climate Change: The Stern Review.* Cambridge, United Kingdom: Cambridge University Press.

Stevenson, H., & Dryzek, J.S. (2014). *Democratizing Global Climate Governance.* Cambridge, United Kingdom: Cambridge University Press.

Tanner, K. (2005). *Economy of Grace.* Minneapolis, MN: Augsburg Fortress.

Tawney, R.H. (1926, 1998). *Religion and the Rise of Capitalism.* New Brunswick, NJ: Transaction Publishers.

The Roman Catholic Bishops of the Netherlands, (1999 November 1). *Living with One and the Same Hope: On the Meaning of the Meeting with Judaism for Catholics.* Retrieved from https://www.dagvanhetjodendom.nl/wp-content/uploads/2013/02/1999-bishopsnl-same-hope.pdf

Tirosh-Samuelson H., & Hughes A.W. (Eds.). (2013). *Jonathan Sacks: Universalizing Particularity.* Leiden, The Netherlands: Brill.

Tracy, D. (1981). *The Analogical Imagination: Christian Theology and the Culture of Pluralism.* New York, NY: Crossroads.

Trautmann, S. & Kuilen G. van de. (2015). Ambiguity Attitudes. In G. Keren & G. Wu (Eds.), *The Wiley Blackwell Handbook of Judgement and Decision Making* (pp. 89-116). Oxford, United Kingdom: Blackwell.

United Nations, General Assembly. (2015, 25 September). *Transforming Our World: The 2030 Agenda for Sustainable Development.* Retrieved from https://sdgs.un.org/2030agenda

United Nations, Framework Convention on Climate Change. (2016, 29 January). *Report of the Conference of the Parties on Its Twenty-First Session, held in Paris from 30 November to 13 December 2015.* Retrieved from https://unfccc.int/resource/docs/2015/cop21/eng/10a01.pdf

van Huyssteen, J.W. (1993). Theology and science: The quest for a new apologetics. *HTS Teologiese Studies / Theological Studies, 49*(3), 425-444. http://dx.doi.org/10.4102/hts.v49i3.2501

van Huyssteen, J.W. (1999). *The Shaping of Rationality: Toward Interdisciplinarity in Theology and Science.* Grand Rapids, MI: Wm. B. Eerdmans Publishing.

van Huyssteen, J.W. (2006). *Alone in the World: Human Uniqueness in Science and Theology (Gifford Lectures).* Grand Rapids, MI: Wm. B. Eerdmans Publishing.

van Huyssteen, J.W. (2014). Postfoundationalism in Theology: The Structure of Theological Solutions. *Ephemerides Theologicae Lovanienses, 90*(2), 209-299. http://dx.doi.org/10.2143/ETL.90.2.3032676

Visscher, M. (2014, 13 December). Ecomodernisten: de nadruk op veerkracht. *Vrij Nederland,* 42-47. Retrieved from http://www.vn.nl/

Volf, M. & Croasmun, M. (2019). *For the Life of the World: Theology That Makes a Difference.* Grand Rapids, MI: Brazos Press.

Wakker, P.P. (2011). Jaffray's ideas on ambiguity. *Theory and Decision, 71*(1), 11–22. http://dx.doi.org/10.1007/s11238-010-9209-4

Wijngaards, A.E.H.M. (2012). *Worldly Theology: On Connecting Public Theology and Economics* (Doctoral dissertation). Retrieved from http://mobile.repository.ubn. ru.nl/bitstream/handle/2066/93624/93624.pdf?sequence=1

Williams, R. (2012). *Faith in the Public Square*. London, England: Bloomsbury.

Printed and bound by CPI Group (UK) Ltd, Croydon, CR0 4YY

23/04/2025

14661017-0001